MANAGING PEOPLE

EFFECTIVE SUPERVISORY
MANAGEMENT SERIES

MANAGING PEOPLE

ROGER BENNETT

**KOGAN
PAGE**

First published in 1989 by
Kogan Page Ltd,
120 Pentonville Rd, London N1 9JN
in association with the National Extension College,
18 Brooklands Avenue, Cambridge CB2 2HN (0223 316644), and
the Institute of Supervisory Management,
22 Bore Street, Lichfield, Staffordshire WS13 6LP (0543 251346).

Printed and bound in Great Britain by
Richard Clay Ltd, Bungay, Suffolk.

British Library Cataloguing in Publication Data
Bennett, Roger
   Managing people.
   1. Great Britain. Business firms. Personal management
   I. Title   II. Series
   658.3'00941

ISBN 1 85091 800 7

Contents

Preface

The three volumes in this series are about practical management skills, particularly those interpersonal supervisory skills which enable managers to communicate effectively, influence others, lead, plan, coordinate and control. Organisations increasingly recognise the links that (undoubtedly) exist between management training — notably in the field of interpersonal skills (counselling, team briefing, performance appraisal, interviewing, handling grievances, personal assertiveness, etc) — and efficient performance at the place of work. Several recent initiatives, including the Training Commission sponsored 'Handy Report' and the McCormick–Constable Report of the British Institute of Management, have confirmed this trend.

Industry today requires managers who are formally trained and competent in practical administrative technique. These important studies have drawn attention to the pressing need for new approaches to management education, especially the need to anchor management courses against occupationally relevant administrative competencies immediately applicable in any organisation regardless of type of ownership or physical size; not against abstract theories and applications suited mainly to the requirements of very large commercial firms.

The pace of technical and organisational change is today so rapid that few young managers can expect not to experience many job changes, employing organisations and employment environments during their working lives. Managers must now be able quickly and easily to transfer the skills and knowledge they acquire in one job to other, perhaps quite different fields. This requires systematic and analytical approaches to management training, with management being regarded as a 'profession' in the conventional sense. Thus, managers should value their abilities and qualifications in their *own* right and not just for their usefulness in obtaining jobs. Managers must attempt seriously to maintain professional standards when completing tasks, taking a genuine pride in the quality of their work: efficient and socially responsible management needs to be viewed as an end in itself and not simply a means for earning a living.

In preparing the books I have tried to blend theory with practice and to provide an abundance of practical advice. The texts focus on current 'state of the art' management methods, particularly those involving information technology and the crucially important government advisory bodies (ACAS for example) and Codes of Practice which affect managerial issues. Throughout, I assume that organisations wish to be 'good employers' showing genuine concern for the environment, for employment protection, community development and equal opportunities. My aim is to provide you with a *working* rather than theoretical knowledge of relevant contemporary legislation, techniques and concepts. After reading these books you will, I hope, be able to undertake a variety of useful practical management tasks — counsel, make a presentation, chair a meeting, write a job description, negotiate, appraise the performances of subordinates, and so on.

The three volumes cover all the Institute of Bankers' *Nature of Management* and *Supervisory Skills* syllabuses, plus the entire programmes of the National Examinations Board for Supervisory Studies and the Institute of Supervisory Management. Demand for teaching materials for shorter interpersonal management skills courses constantly expands, and the books will, I suggest, be especially useful for management short courses (including residential management training programmes) that emphasise practical management techniques. The effects of the Handy/McCormick-Constable initiatives will soon be felt in the provision of management skills courses in universities, polytechnics and other higher education colleges, and I look forward to these books contributing to these exciting new schemes. Undergraduates on BA in Business Studies degrees, engineering students pursuing B Eng and M Eng programmes (which now incorporate compulsory courses in management), students enrolled for the CNAA Diploma in Management Studies, or the BTEC Certificate in Management Studies, and students of the major professional accountancy and other business studies bodies who need to pass an examination in management in order to qualify in their respective fields will benefit from using the books.

The texts consist essentially of a skills building programme designed to spring-board a newly appointed or junior manager — concerned primarily with supervisory and executive management duties — to a level of competence at which he or she can assume a more senior and responsible role. This requires the analysis of the managerial situations (especially interactive situations) which junior and middle managers regularly encounter, and the development of an inventory of knowledge and techniques directly applicable to modern supervisory management work. Accordingly, great emphasis is placed on the management of change, the employment implications of change (stress, control of grievances, need for human resource planning, etc), and hence on the need to influence people in order to gain commitment on difficult issues. Individuals new to management have to learn how to persuade, to lead, motivate, organise others and take high-quality decisions. They must refine their communications abilities (including the capacities to listen and counsel sensitively) and develop the arts of advocacy, negotiation, and oral and written presentation. Nearly all managers must supervise subordinates' activities; so the development of interpersonal skills is relevant for all kinds of managerial work.

My thanks are due to Tim Burton of the National Extension College for quickly and efficiently managing the development of the project, Ellen Brawn, who read the entire manuscript and is responsible for all the checklists, reviews, summaries and activities that it now contains, David Hall of the Institute of Supervisory Management for his comments on earlier drafts, Pauline Goodwin and Penelope Woolf of Kogan Page for expediting production of the text, and to Valerie Evans who typed the manuscript. I gratefully acknowledge the permission granted by the editors of *Modern Management*, the *Training Officer* and *Export* for the use of material previously published in those journals in article form. Parts of chapters 1 and

4 are based on material prepared for my text *Organisation and Management* published by Pitman in June 1988. I thank Pitman Publishing for their kind permission to adapt this material. Thanks are also due to the Equal Opportunities Commission for permission to reproduce parts of its Code of Practice on employment matters.

Roger Bennett
September 1988

1

Recruitment, Selection and Induction

Objectives

At the end of this chapter, you will be able to:

- identify and explain the implications of current employment legislation, in particular as it relates to contracts of employment and discrimination
- recognise good practice in the recruitment, selection and induction process
- prepare job specifications, job descriptions and person specifications as an aid to the recruitment and selection of staff.

Before devising a procedure for selecting and inducting new staff you should first consider the *type* of staff your department requires. Do you need full time or part time employees? Will the appointments be temporary, permanent, or subject to probation? Currently, the jobs of part time staff become legally 'protected' (ie incumbents may claim unfair dismissal or redundancy payments through industrial tribunals if they are sacked) after two years if the employees work 16 hours or more per week, or after five years of continuous employment if they work more than eight hours weekly. Full time workers are protected (and hence able to claim unfair dismissal, redundancy payments, etc) if their contracts are for more than two years, or for shorter periods but renewed one after another beyond two years. If you hire a temporary replacement for a woman on maternity leave and you make it clear (preferably in writing) that the appointment will cease on the absent woman's return to work, then Courts will automatically deem the dismissal of the replacement to be fair.

Activity

Take a quick look at the staff in your department and divide them into the following categories:

	Temporary	Permanent
Full time		
Part time		

Can you identify a clear trend? As you read on you will see the implications of recruitment policy.

Use of casual non-protected labour enables you to vary the size of your labour force without legal repercussions and normally without adverse industrial relations effects — trade unions and staff associations are typically not prepared to represent casual and/or part time workers, perceiving them as a threat to full time jobs, and the ease with which casual labour can be hired and fired means you can quickly discard unsatisfactory employees. Moreover, part time workers are much cheaper than full time staff (there is no superannuation, no promotion, no annual pay rise and no sick pay other than the statutory minimum). Non-unionised casual workers have no statutory union rights (time off for union work, the right to appoint safety representatives, the right to be consulted about intended redundancies, etc) and will not be involved in works committees and other potentially troublesome consultation procedures.

Nevertheless, the deliberate employment of casual workers in preference to full timers on permanent appointments can rarely be recommended. Casually employed staff often lack commitment to their work, have (usually) received less training than full time colleagues, and frequently resent being employed part time and/or on short term contracts. Also, numerous frictions can arise from the employment of casual workers alongside permanent employees. Casual staff resent having to do the same work as full time colleagues for lower pay and without equivalent conditions of service. Permanent workers, on the other hand, may regard casual employees as inferior and a danger to their security of employment, particularly where the overwhelming majority of casual workers are women and/or belong to an ethnic minority group. There are few opportunities for job enrichment in such circumstances; morale is usually low and rates of absenteeism and staff turnover are high. Even though casual workers are not normally unionised, industrial disputes still occur and because they are not resolved through agreed management/union procedures they are likely to be highly disruptive in the longer term. Grievances persist indefinitely in casual labour systems, transmitted from one generation of casual workers to the next without any possibility of resolution.

Self-check

List the arguments for and against casual workers in preference to permanent, full time appointments. Try to use your own experience as well as the information in the text.

Answer
Arguments for may include greater flexibility to cope with changes in staffing requirements, easier to dismiss unsatisfactory workers, cheaper, fewer statutory rights.

Arguments against may include lack of loyalty to the firm, low morale, no incentive to work hard, high absenteeism and labour turnover, lack of job security, hostility from full time staff.

You should participate enthusiastically in recruitment and selection procedures. Carelessness here can cause waste for the firm and harm to individuals (wrongly) selected for posts and having to dismiss unsuitable people shortly after they are hired causes a bad atmosphere throughout the firm. Frequent staff changes disrupt the department's work and the costs of induction and training increase. Consciously plan your departmental human resource requirements — anticipate resignations (ask staff to give as much notice as possible before they leave) and ensure that somebody is always available to cover for anyone who resigns suddenly.

Advise the personnel department of your anticipated recruitment needs and of any known potential sources of labour supply (local colleges that have provided good recruits in the past, government training schemes, etc) but never requisition new staff haphazardly. Do you *really* need a replacement for a vacant post? Can you rearrange work to make that job unnecessary? Note that some vacancies are easier to fill than others, so that changes in departmental staff responsibilities following a resignation might ease the burden of recruitment, especially where specialist skills are involved.

Activity

Do you participate in the recruitment and selection of staff to your department?

If the answer is yes, list the tasks you have undertaken and outline the procedures followed.

If the answer is no, identify who is involved in the process and reasons why you have not played an active role.

Recruitment procedures and the degree of staff involvement will vary from firm to firm. In many organisations, only the most senior staff are invited to participate in the process, while some prefer to involve as many as possible of the staff who will work with the new recruit.

Recruitment

Recruitment is usually the responsibility of the personnel department, which you notify whenever one of your workers resigns or approaches the age of retirement or when you feel that the volume of work in the department justifies the employment of extra staff. If a requisition for the replacement of a resigning employee is refused, make sure the refusal is in writing and reply with a written request for advice on how you should adjust departmental working methods to deal with the resulting staff shortage.

Normally you will be expected to draft or revise a job specification for the vacant post, including precise details on the skills, experience and qualifications it requires, starting date and particulars of any special conditions (eg shift work) attached to the position. The personnel department then drafts and places a job advertisement in suitable media. In drafting the job specification be as detailed as you can but make sure you do not incorporate any irrelevant skills, experience or qualifications requirements since these might discriminate unfairly against certain groups. Comprehensive job specifications lead to accurate job advertisements and hence to fewer unsuitable applicants replying to advertisements and less time wasted in sifting through applications.

An increasingly frustrating problem for departmental managers (who often need to obtain replacement staff quickly) is the practice of some employers of asserting that they are 'equal opportunity' employers while actually having no commitment to equal opportunities at all. Such organisations prepare long equal opportunity statements promising not to discriminate when recruiting staff, insist that job advertisements be placed (at enormous expense) in many magazines and newspapers (some of which are not remotely relevant to the advertised post) and that a large number of candidates be interviewed by a large panel drawn from diverse parts of the organisation, even though the person who will actually be offered the job has already been selected. Unsuspecting candidates travel from all over the country to attend interviews and much administrative time and managerial effort is wasted.

Equal opportunities recruitment is obviously desirable, but must be undertaken seriously and with the full commitment of the recruiting managers involved. The concept of equal opportunities is trivialised if bogus rituals are performed after an appointment has effectively been determined. Such artificiality encourages personnel and line executives to ignore (in practice if not in public) equal opportunity issues and leads to cynicism and disillusion among the existing staff.

Self-check

What is the purpose of a job specification?

Answer
It identifies the skills, experience and qualifications required and gives any special features about the post. It forms the basis for the advertisement so the clearer the job specification, the fewer unsuitable candidates should apply.

Activity

Draft a job specification for your own post.
   It might be useful to design a format for job specifications. Not only would this standardise the layout but also act as a blueprint for information needed.

Legal considerations

You are not allowed when recruiting staff to discriminate unfairly against members of a particular sex or racial group and special provisions apply to rehabilitated criminals and disabled persons. However, there are no laws to prevent a firm refusing to employ a known trade union member (though it is illegal under the Employment Protection Acts to dismiss an employee for union membership once that person has been appointed) or from discriminating against applicants on the grounds of their sexual orientation.

Organisations with more than 20 employees must, under the Disabled Persons (Employment) Acts of 1944 and 1958, ensure that at least 3 per cent of their labour forces consist of disabled people. The legislation also demands that the disabled be given preference for certain jobs, eg lift or car park attendants. However, the 3 per cent quota need not be met if the employment of disabled people would cause safety hazards or if the firm can prove either that disabled employees could not do the work or that insufficient numbers of disabled people have applied for jobs. Breach of these Acts is a criminal (rather than a civil) offence, though in practice very few firms consciously seek to break the law in these respects. Limited companies employing more than 250 workers are legally obliged to include in their annual directors' report a statement outlining what the company has done during the previous year to recruit, train and promote disabled persons. Also, the Manpower Services Commission has issued a Code of Practice asking employers to recognise the special needs of disabled people (special access, conveniently situated tools and working materials, work locations which avoid use of stairs, etc) and requesting employers' sympathy for workers who require time off for treatment, rearrangement of working methods, special training and so on.

Under the Rehabilitation of Offenders Act 1974 a 'rehabilitated' person does not have to disclose to a recruiting firm the fact that he or she has a criminal record, provided the applicants' conviction has been 'spent', and it is unlawful for an employer to deny someone a job solely on the grounds that the applicant has a spent conviction. If an applicant is asked to declare on an application form whether he or she has a criminal record or is questioned about this during an interview, the applicant is entitled to deny ever having been convicted of the spent offence. A conviction becomes 'spent' following the elapsing of a certain time period, although some convictions can never be spent (notably life sentences and other sentences of imprisonment for more than 30 months). The time period involved varies according to the gravity of the offence. Thus, a prison sentence of up to six months becomes spent after three years; while sentences of between 6 and 30 months are spent after five years; a probation order is spent one year after it expires and so on.

There are exemptions to the legislation and candidates for certain jobs do have to reveal past convictions. The jobs involved are: lawyers, chartered accountants, medical practitioners, nurses, dentists, vets, prison officers, firearms dealers, social and health workers and any form of work with children under the age of 18. If a job applicant (or one of your existing subordinates) has a spent conviction that you know about, you must not reveal this information to anyone else since you could then be sued for defamation and/or the aggrieved person could make a formal complaint to the police, who might then prosecute you under the 1974 Act.

You may feel that this law is unfair on the grounds that you believe it necessary to ensure that everyone you hire is trustworthy and reliable. Remember, however, that a person's criminal record might have arisen many years previously and involve only a minor offence. Moreover, criminal records are held only by those who were caught and punished at the time. It is hardly proper that such individuals be punished again through not being able to get a job.

Blacklists of individuals are not illegal under British law. Thus, it is not unlawful to deny a totally law abiding citizen a job simply because his or her name appears on an employer's blacklist. Trade union activists and others frequently involved in industrial disputes are particularly vulnerable to blacklisting. The only remedy available to them is to sue for libel, which is extremely expensive, technically difficult in law and usually impossible because blacklisted individuals typically do not know that their names appear on blacklists circulated to prospective employers. The Data Protection Act does not help because it applies only to *mechanised* records and the major blacklisting organisations have already transferred all their records to manual card index systems not covered by the Act.

Self-check

What is the quota of disabled persons required under the Disabled Persons (Employment) Acts? Does your firm comply with this quota?

What is meant by a spent conviction under the Rehabilitation of Offenders Act? Identify five jobs where this legislation would not apply.

Answers

The quota is 3 per cent. Unfortunately the number of firms who actually comply with the law is small.

A candidate is not obliged to admit to a criminal record provided that a specified time has elapsed since the prison sentence, the length of time depending on the gravity of the offence.

Jobs where this legislation does not apply include any form of work with minors, social work, prison officers, lawyers, medical practitioners, nurses etc.

It is unlawful to discriminate on racial or sex grounds when recruiting employees. It is equally unlawful to discriminate against men or women, or against married (but not single) persons. An 'ethnic minority' is defined as a group distinguished from others by a sufficient combination of shared customs, beliefs, traditions and characteristics derived from a common or presumed common past, even if the distinctions are not biologically determined.[1] Thus, Jews and Sikhs have both been accepted as distinct 'ethnic' groups by the English Courts under the Race Relations Act.

Indirect as well as direct sex or race discrimination is unlawful. Not only must the firm not treat one sex or ethnic minority less favourably when recruiting ('direct' discrimination) — say by specifying that only males or whites will be employed, but also the employer must not impose any requirement or condition which adversely affects the prospects of a member of a particular race or sex when applying for a job. However, there are many exemptions (eg genuine occupational qualifications) to the Act and the law relating to its implementation is complicated. In practice, it is difficult to prove that discrimination actually occurred. Moreover, compensation awarded by industrial tribunals to aggrieved persons is derisory, even if blatant discrimination took place (awards of about £100 are not uncommon). In the case of indirect discrimination no compensation can be awarded if the recruiting firm can demonstrate that it did not *intend* to discriminate.

Both the Commission for Racial Equality (CRE) and the Equal Opportunities Commission (EOC) issue detailed advice on recruitment matters in their Codes of Practice, and you should always follow these guidelines. Thus, you ought not to impose unreasonable age limits for recruitment to posts where age is immaterial (such limits are unfair to women who are often unavailable for work during early careers on account of child bearing and rearing responsibilities). Check job specifications to ensure that resulting job advertisements do not imply that applications from a certain sex or ethnic group will not be welcome and make certain you are not demanding unreasonably high qualifications that only one sex or racial category is likely to possess.

If you genuinely intend appointing an outside person to a

vacant post then ask yourself whether the newspapers and magazines in which the job advertisement will appear might not be seen by suitably qualified minority individuals or by one of the sexes and if this is the case suggest to the personnel department an appropriate alternative. Be prepared to accept recognised overseas qualifications as equivalent to those obtained in the UK, and openly indicate to the personnel officer your willingness to take recruits of both sexes and any ethnic origin. Word of mouth recruitment is efficient, but could lead to discrimination. Accordingly, the CRE Code suggests (sec 1.10(a)) that workers should not be recruited via personal recommendations of existing employees where the workforce concerned is wholly or predominantly white, black or Asian.

Most people would agree that employment, training and promotion opportunities should be available to everyone regardless of race, sex, religion, or physical disability that does not affect job performance. Unfortunately however certain minorities, women and the physically handicapped are enormously under-represented in many companies. The least a firm can do is try to avoid discrimination. It should monitor the representation of minority groups in its workforce and collect statistics on how many members of various minorities apply for jobs. Data is also needed on the proportions of women and ethnic minority candidates shortlisted for various categories of post, on how many are appointed, their participation in training schemes, how many are promoted and when and why they resign.

Self-check

Distinguish between direct and indirect discrimination.

Answer
Direct discrimination is where a firm specifies who should apply for the post either by sex, or colour, or ethnic origin.

Indirect discrimination is much more difficult to prove since it concerns conditions or requirements imposed which would exclude some people from applying. Such conditions might relate to age limit, qualifications, work experience.

Selection methods

'Selection', as opposed to 'recruitment', means the assessment of candidates and the choice of the candidate most suitable for the job. The first consideration is whether there exist internal candidates for the vacant post. Much time and expense can be saved through internal promotions or transfers and a policy of internal promotion enhances the morale of currently employed staff. Many organisations advertise vacancies both internally and externally, using internal candidates as a standard against which outsiders are compared, so that an internal candidate is offered the position provided no outstandingly superior external candidate appears.

Well designed application forms are essential to the selection process. Moreover, the information they contain offers a basis for personnel records and thus for human resource planning, including the preparation of skills inventories and redeployment programmes. The case for incorporating a wide range of questions into an application form, covering many aspects of the applicant's life, is therefore strong, since the information can be used for developing the successful candidate's future career. Unfortunately, the distinction between questions useful for assessing a person's general employment potential and those which unjustifiably pry into confidential personal affairs is often vague. Questions relating to (say) race or religion would normally be inappropriate, but should (for example) questions be asked about the number and ages of the applicants' children, or whether the applicant is married or about his or her general medical condition? Young married women often complain they are denied appointments because of employers' fears they will leave employment to have children and women who have young children already might be refused employment (despite this being illegal under the Sex Discrimination Act) on the assumption they will frequently be absent from work looking after them.

Selection procedures seek to match the requirements of jobs with the attributes of candidates. The more detailed the job description the easier it is to identify the best applicants, so job descriptions should clearly specify the personal characteristics needed for each job's successful completion as well as providing a comprehensive breakdown of the tasks involved. All necessary competencies (eg the ability to operate equipment, interpret technical data, write reports, mix easily with other people, withstand stress etc) should be listed. Job content can be established through work study or through your own interpretation of the duties involved. In the latter case, however, ensure you do not impose unrealistic targets so impossibly high that any selected candidate is bound to fail.

Next, draw up a 'person specification' to define the background, education, training, personality and other characteristics of the person best suited to fill the vacancy. In other words, draft a pen portrait of the *ideal* candidate to provide you with a list of qualities to look for when preparing a short list. The person you describe may not exist, but will act as a standard against which applicants can be compared. Schemes for categorising the various qualities needed to perform certain types of work have existed for many years, the best known being the Fraser plan[2] and the Rodger 'Seven Point' system.[3]

The Fraser plan

This has five headings for assessment, as listed below.

Impact on other people

Some work involves regular contact with others. Salespeople, receptionists, supervisors, teachers, etc need external appearance, manners and communications skills that are not so important for socially isolated jobs (eg long-distance lorry driving). Jobs requiring social interaction need agreeable people who mix easily. Such jobs are unsuitable for hostile, aggressive individuals.

Qualifications and experience

These refer to the minimum skill and educational levels necessary for a job, evidenced by formal qualifications (certificates and diplomas) and documented work experience.

Innate abilities

A job might require the ability to think quickly, assimilate large quantities of information, exercise mental agility and interpret complicated issues.

Motivation

Repetitive, production line work is not intellectually stimulating; financial reward is probably the major motivating factor here. Other jobs present opportunities for creativity and self development, and thus would be appropriate for people with drive, enthusiasm, self-direction and personal ambition.

Emotional adjustment

Employees who cannot easily withstand stress should not attempt harrowing or emotionally arduous work. Some jobs can be very distressing. Dealing with irate customers, coping with belligerent operatives or unsympathetic colleagues is necessarily stressful. Working environments themselves can create stress; excessive noise or temperatures are particularly harmful.

The Rodger plan

The Rodger plan is similar, assessing candidates in each of the following areas.

Physical make-up

Health and fitness, appearance, dress, speech and manner.

Attainments

General education and training, academic and professional qualifications.

General intelligence

Intellectual capacity, critical and interpretive abilities.

Specific aptitudes

Particular endowments including manual dexterity, mathematical or literary competence.

Interests

Involvement in leisure activities that might assist employees in their work, eg strength building sports for manual workers or artistic pursuits for designers and others concerned with creative tasks.

Disposition

Maturity, reliability, ability to cope with tense situations, capacity to keep calm in turbulent circumstances, ability to influence and direct others.

Personal circumstances

Domestic or other relevant personal situations potentially affecting capacity to perform a job, eg shift-work or work involving prolonged absences from home would not be suitable for people in certain family circumstances.

You can conveniently adapt either of these schemes to meet your particular circumstances. Write out a list of the things you will be looking for in respect of a particular job within each category (headings may be added, altered or deleted according to the type of work). For example, you might require a person with good eyesight but not physical strength, a certain educational certificate, experience in a specific industry doing a particular job, experience of supervising staff, emotional stability, the willingness to work shifts, etc. Prepare a checklist of these and other relevant factors, and ask yourself how (indeed whether) they can be measured.

Divide your requirements under each heading into 'essential' and 'desirable' sections. Check carefully to ensure that all your 'essential' column entries are really necessary, bearing in mind legal and equal opportunities considerations. Hand this specification to the personnel department and ask for completed application forms to be scanned for those applicants meeting the specified requirements. If there are insufficient applicants possessing all the necessary qualities, ask personnel to draw out all applicants who have (say) 80 per cent of the desired attributes. Then, if there are still not enough candidates, 60 per cent, then 50 per cent. Thereafter it is probably not worthwhile pursuing the search for suitably qualified individuals at the salary offered and using existing advertising media. You need to rethink the entire situation.

Alternatively, the personnel department might send you all completed applications received but divided into three categories: 'clearly suitable' for interview, 'possibly' suitable, and 'clearly unsuitable', leaving the final choice of shortlist to you. In

---

Self-check

What is the difference between a job description and a person specification?

Answer
A job description gives a detailed breakdown of the tasks the successful candidate will have to carry out, including areas of responsibility, number of subordinates.

A person specification represents a personality sketch of the ideal person to fill the post and acts as a blueprint against which each candidate can be objectively assessed. While the ideal candidate may not exist, the specification acts as a guide.

---

this case you need to look through all the completed applications, though paying most attention to those in the 'clearly suitable' bundle. Difficulties arise in the allocation to these categories of people of widely varying background, experience and paper qualifications. An older woman (say) may possess certificates and diplomas with titles quite different to those obtained by a younger person. She may have been absent from the labour force for several years while raising children and then may have worked in an industry unlike your own. How are you to compare her application with that of, for example, a young man who joined one of your immediate competitors straight from college a couple of years ago? There are no straightforward solutions to this difficult problem, but there are some common factors to look for in an application form. For example, has the applicant a good record of passing examinations first time or were several attempts required? Are there observable gaps in particular subject areas (mathematics or English for example)? Did the candidate drop out of particular courses? The fact that any of these are true does not necessarily mean the candidate is unsuitable, only that the issue should be further explored during the interview.

Examine the relevance of any particular set of qualifications to the advertised post and look for evidence of the candidate's interest in attending relevant courses. A willingness to update in one area usually indicates a willingness to acquire further knowledge in others.

How much responsibility did the applicant carry in his or her previous position? Can you identify a distinct pattern in the applicant's career, and if so how relevant is the vacant post to this career pattern? Did the applicant achieve promotion with previous employers and how long did he or she remain in each job?

Nearly all application forms ask candidates to provide the names and addresses of referees. I have to state that I believe this practice to be essentially useless. Candidates will only quote referees who they expect to give good recommendations and normally they will discuss this with the referee in advance. Often, the application form demands that the candidate's current employer be included in the list of referees, but the very fact that the individual is looking for another job implies an unsatisfactory relationship between that person and his or her existing firm and there need be no presumption that this results from any fault of the worker. Also, the individual might (reasonably) not want the current employer to know that he or she is seeking another job, for fear of appearing disloyal and/or prejudicing future promotion prospects with that employer. Note also that organisations do not give candidates the names and addresses of past employees whom applicants can contact to ask questions about a firm's suitability as an employer. Much time, effort and expense is wasted in the processes of requesting, writing, mailing and reading references.

If you feel that a reference from a past employer would be useful then, subject to the candidate's permission, try to obtain a reference by telephone, since in this way you will be able to assess the referee's sincerity more accurately — people are often franker when speaking than when writing — and referees are always aware that adverse written comments could fall into the applicant's hands and be construed as defamatory and subject to an action for libel. Remember too that within the candidate's current organisation (including a school or college) there will be many people whom the candidate may nominate as a referee and obviously the person most likely to submit a good reference will be chosen. References from schools or colleges will emphasise academic attainments, but note here that excellent students do not necessarily become excellent workers.

Activity

When a vacancy next arises in your department, prepare a job specification, job description and person specification for the post. For the person specification you may use the Fraser Plan, Rodger 'Seven Point' System or your own adaptation.

Be sure to check the accuracy of the information and ensure that the factors you have identified can be measured. Avoid the trap of including too many 'essential' entries or you may be unable to short-list a sufficient number of candidates.

Employment interviewing

You will almost certainly be required to conduct job interviews during the course of your work as a supervisor. Interviewing is an art that requires careful planning and control. Employment interviewing differs from disciplinary interviewing, grievance interviews, counselling and exit interviews, although all have the common element that they seek to *obtain information*. In a job interview, your purpose is to elicit useful information on the candidate's past history as it relates to the vacant post and to assess his or her ability to do the job properly. Also, candidates are normally invited to ask questions about the firm, the job and terms and conditions of employment.

The golden rule of employment interviewing is always to put candidates into a state of mind in which they willingly disclose the maximum amount of information. This state of mind is possible only if candidates are comfortable, at ease and do not feel intimidated. Uncomfortable, ill at ease candidates will not be as frank as those who are relaxed, confident and in full control of their responses. Hostile, overbearing interview environments with several interviewers aggressively firing complex questions at a candidate who is left groping for words will not encourage responses that are open and sincere. Candidates are prevented from presenting themselves properly and this will reduce the volume of data on which decisions can be based. Everyone feels nervous in tense situations, since fear is a natural innate reaction to external threat. It signals the need for caution

---

Activity

Cast your mind back to the last selection interview you attended either as interviewer or candidate. Respond yes or no to the following questions:
— did the interview start on time?
— was there more than one person on the interview panel?
— was the interview panel well organised?
— was the environment friendly and relaxing?
— were the questions clear and precise?
— were the questions relevant to the post?
— was the candidate given sufficient time to respond to questions?
— was time allowed at the end of each interview for the performance of each candidate to be assessed and evaluated?

A negative response to any of these questions indicates an area where the interview technique might be improved.

As you read on, you will see what constitutes good interview technique.

---

in hostile surroundings. Environments that do not frighten or intimidate enable interviewees to express themselves comprehensively and in uninhibited ways. Thus candidates should be interviewed promptly at the appointed time or, if delay is inevitable, apologies should be offered. Their reception should be friendly and constructive, with comfortable chairs and, if possible, no large table to create mental barriers between candidate and interviewers. If smoking is permitted, ashtrays should be available, if not, a sign to that effect should be prominently displayed. Interruptions from telephone calls, secretaries, etc disturb concentration and should not be allowed.

Most authorities (including the CRE and EOC) suggest that all employment interviews be conducted by more than one person. This is good advice, as a second opinion is always useful and acts as a check on bad interviewing habits. However, interview panels should always be as small as possible, subject to the proper representation of all seriously interested parties: overlarge panels create dramatic atmospheres more applicable to the theatre than employment interviews. Large panels (and any more than three is 'large') usually mean that supervisors and managers in that organisation do not have enough work to do and thus seek to fill out their time by sitting-in on job interviews for staff in other departments. Also, members of a large panel might ask candidates irrelevant and disconnected questions.

Begin an interview with friendly, supportive and sympathetic remarks, starting perhaps with innane comments about the weather, travel arrangements or similarly uncontroversial matters. Use the candidate's completed application form as your introduction to the main body of the interview, but do not ask questions that have already been answered on the form. Rather, seek supplementary information to probe the candidate's potential for effective performance in the advertised post. An interview is a matching exercise, comparing job requirements with a candidate's attributes. Checklists, with headings similar to the Fraser or Rodger schemes can usefully be devised to guide you through the interview and remind you of the attributes that you are seeking, but detailed notetaking is inadvisable because of its disturbing effects on the candidate's concentration. Always assess candidates *immediately* after their interviews and not at the end of a long interviewing session. Important points arising from the early interviews will by then have been forgotten and the last one or two people interviewed might thus be placed at an advantage.

Open ended questions such as 'What made you decide to do that?' or 'Why did you enjoy that type of work?' are usually more productive in obtaining information than direct queries. Generally worded questions invite the candidate to discuss feelings, opinions, and perceptions of events. Simple 'yes/no' questions will not draw out the candidate's views. Much of the skill of interviewing lies in listening — interviews should be discussions, not interrogations. Tell the candidate precisely what information is required, and give as much time as is necessary for a comprehensive answer. Never make critical or insensitive remarks during the interview.

Some managers behave most peculiarly when interviewing job applicants. They speak in pompous, unnatural accents, dress in suits (and men in ties) even though normally they dress casually or in white coats or overalls, and adopt formal and old fashioned modes of address to others — people they have known for years and with whom they are on first name terms are suddenly addressed as Mr or Mrs! Others seek to impress candidates with their own importance. They discuss their own work, they moralise and spend much of the interview expressing personal opinions on various issues, wasting time and contributing nothing to the quality of the interview.

Act naturally when interviewing — remember that the person you appoint has to work with you as you are, not as you transitorily appear during the interview. Avoid the aggressive question; it serves only to intimidate and prevent the free flow of information. Candidates naturally feel nervous during interviews. It is unfair for interviewers — who control the situation, are on their home territory and are not subject to stress — to harangue and harass distressed candidates. The deliberate creation of stressful environments, you might argue, is justified if the vacant job involves stress. But the ability to handle an aggressive interview proves only the candidate's ability to handle an aggressive interview; it does not necessarily reveal the capacity to cope with stress and aggression outside the artificially constructed interview situation.

Do not ask irrelevant questions, and avoid 'revealing' questions, ie those which disclose your attitudes and beliefs. An example would be the question 'I like watching football, don't you?' The candidate will probably respond in a manner calculated to impress, regardless of the opinion actually held.

Two other common interviewing mistakes are firstly, to compare candidates with oneself since, through holding over-inflated opinions about your own abilities you might, incorrectly, assume that the candidate most like yourself is best suited for the job and secondly, applying inappropriate selection criteria. The latter might involve men who interview women associating attractive physical appearance with work ability, appointing people the interviewer knows socially or, generally, assuming that one desirable characteristic in an applicant means the person is equally worthy in other respects. Well-spoken candidates for example are not necessarily industrious. Note how this phenomenon could work in the opposite direction, an interviewer may conclude (wrongly) that weakness in one area implies low calibre overall.

> **Activity**
> Refer back to your responses to the questions in the last activity. Based on what you have studied, what steps can be taken to improve your interview technique?

Selection tests

Few firms bother with selection testing, relying instead on candidates' formal educational qualifications and stated experience as evidence of their ability. However, tests can be useful where candidates possess no academic certificates and/or have no work experience or where large numbers of equally qualified applicants have to be considered and substantial interviews with each candidate are not physically possible. Many difficulties are involved in setting tests and correctly interpreting the results. Time and effort is required to devise a test and it might not actually measure the abilities it is intended to measure (intelligence tests, for instance, often measure learned responses rather than 'intelligence'). High or low marks obtained in a test do not necessarily indicate high or low ability to do a job properly, only the capacity to achieve certain marks under test conditions. Tests can give inconsistent results when repeated on people of known equivalent ability and can fail to discriminate between good and bad candidates (good quality applicants should consistently achieve high marks and vice versa).

The commonest type of test used in employment selection is the achievement test, which seeks to evaluate the candidate's level of competence in a particular skill (typing, shorthand, driving, machinery, etc). Such tests are intended to discover individuals who claim to possess a skill they do not actually have or who have grossly exaggerated their abilities. An achievement test is directly relevant to the work the successful candidate will do, but necessarily covers only a part of the successful candidate's eventual duties. A candidate who fails the test is assumed incapable of doing the entire job, which need not be true. For example, a secretary might fail to achieve a predetermined minimum shorthand speed under test conditions but this does not necessarily mean the candidate is an inadequate secretary overall. Tests are undertaken in specific test conditions. Success in a driving test for instance proves that the candidate did well over the test circuit, yet he or she may not otherwise be a good driver. Job applicants feel nervous during tests and this may cause them to do badly. It is a fact that people who have previously experienced a particular type of test do better on average than people attempting that type of test for the first time. Thus, candidates who have already taken and failed a similar test will have an advantage, yet these might be precisely the sort of candidates the test is intended to discover.

Interesting equal opportunities considerations are raised by the practice of employment selection testing since some ethnic and other minority groups consistently do badly in certain types of achievement test because they have not had access to educational and training programmes necessary to equip them with the basic skills expected of test candidates. The CRE Code of Practice (sec 1–13) recommends that tests be directly relevant to the job applied for, that tests should not contain irrelevant questions on matters which may be unfamiliar to racial minority applicants (eg general knowledge questions about subjects more likely to be familiar to indigenous applicants) and that poor standards of English be tolerated provided use of English at a high standard is not essential to the job. Also, scoring mechanisms should be regularly reviewed to ensure they are free of unjustifiable bias.

In general, high marks obtained in a test do not guarantee that the appointed candidate will succeed in the vacant post. High marks to not show why the candidate did well: low marks do not say why the candidate failed. Achievement tests, moreover, do not evaluate the whole person, only that part covered by test questions and candidates who do well in a test might wrongly assume they possess knowledge or ability which in fact they do not have. Never conclude that a subordinate is exceptionally competent just because he or she did well in a test.

Making the offer

Choose the successful candidate carefully. Do not allow pressure of work to force you into accepting unsuitable employees

Activity

Does your firm use any tests to supplement the selection interview? If so, what tests are used and when? How useful have you found such tests?

Many experts feel that the selection interview alone is not a scientific and objective basis on which to select the right person for the vacant post. There are a wide variety of tests available, including those for assessing aptitude, intelligence and personality. Today, many organisations use Recruitment Consultancy firms to run such tests for them, particularly for senior management posts.

— they will probably underperform and create many difficulties (need for extra training, counselling, perhaps even the need for a transfer to a different type of work) in the long run. Equally, do not appoint someone who is obviously overqualified and who will become bored and frustrated in the advertised position. Try to fit the applicant to the objective needs of the post. Do not automatically appoint the candidate most like the previous job occupant (who may not have done the job efficiently) or who is most like current employees. You *must* make and retain a written record of the *reasons* for your decision in case you are accused of unfair race or sex discrimination. Always assume that you will be challenged and that you will have to argue your case in an industrial tribunal, since the adoption of this frame of mind will help you make an objective decision.

Following an offer of employment a number of legal and other formalities must be completed. Under the Contracts of Employment Act 1972 (subsequently incorporated into the Employment Protection Act 1975) all employees are entitled to a written contract of employment within 13 weeks of starting work. An 'employee' in this sense means someone who is to work more than 16 hours a week, or who has already worked eight hours a week for at least five years. Under the Act, the following information must be included in the written statement.

● names and addresses of employer and employee
● job title

- date of commencement
- usual hours of work
- the rate of pay and how and when payment will be made
- terms and conditions regarding
  — Sick pay
  — Holiday pay
  — Pension schemes
- grievance and disciplinary procedures
- special conditions relating to membership of a particular trade union
- length of notice to be given by either side
- arrangements for working overtime.

Contracts of employment are important because they establish the existence of an obligation to pay wages in return for a predetermined amount of work. Breach of a contract of employment will on the one hand provide the firm with grounds for fair dismissal and on the other enable the worker to sue for unpaid wages. The contract is the basis of the firm's disciplinary procedures and is the ultimate determinant of the work an employee must do. Contracts invariably figure prominently in cases in industrial tribunals since they establish such matters as length of service, hours of work, average wages for compensation claims, and (importantly) whether continuity of employment exists. Note that a 'contract' is established the instant the successful candidate accepts your offer, verbally or in writing. The written statement which follows merely confirms the details of the arrangement — though it is permissible for the statement itself to refer the employee to other documents (booklets explaining superannuation schemes, grievance procedures, etc) where issues are examined in much greater depth. In this case however the documents referred to must by law be freely available to all employees.

Apart from the minimum information required by statute the written statement should in your own interests include as much supplementary detail as possible, especially on potentially contentious issues such as shift work obligations, compulsory overtime or the requirements that staff occasionally be searched on leaving the premises or be prepared to relocate to other parts of the country. Once the written statement is issued, the firm

---

Self-check

Which employees are entitled to a written contract of employment within 13 weeks of starting work?

Answer
Any employee who works more than 16 hours a week or who has already worked 8 hours a week for at least five years.
   Does your firm comply with this requirement?

---

cannot alter its terms and conditions without the permission of the individual worker. If it does so it is in breach of contract and the employee can claim to have been unfairly dismissed! Thus, you cannot impose new shift rosters, working hours, changes in benefits or access to appeals procedures unless the alterations are covered by the contract or if the worker agrees to them (in which case the firm must alter the contents of its written statement of terms and conditions within one month of the change). Workers' objections to changes are heard by industrial tribunals which assess whether the changes are 'reasonable' in view of all the circumstances of the 'dismissal'.

Apart from the period of notice specified in the contract, certain minimum periods are imposed by law. The Employment Protection Act 1975 demands that at least a week's notice be given to a worker with more than one month's but less than two years' service and one extra week's notice for each year of employment thereafter (so that, for instance, a worker with eight years' service is entitled to eight weeks' notice) up to a maximum of 12 weeks.

A harrowing problem that can arise when an appointment is being finalised concerns the medical examinations that many large firms, particularly those which operate superannuation schemes, require of their new employees. What happens if the individual fails the medical, especially if he or she has already given up another job? It is bad practice indeed to appoint and then dismiss someone following a failed medical examination conducted several months after the employee has started a new job. Who should conduct the examination; a company doctor, or the individual's own? Doctors' opinions regarding a person's fitness for employment can radically differ.

Activity

Obtain a standard contract of employment form or refer to your own contract. How easy is it to follow and understand? Are you familiar with your firm's superannuation scheme, grievance and disciplinary procedures? If not, where can you get further information and assistance?

Many people do not read their contracts of employment and therefore, are not aware of the terms and conditions of their employment. Nor do they know where to go for information. Would you be able to respond to questions from your staff?

Induction

Induction — the process of introducing recruits to an organisation and explaining their role within it — usually begins with a guided tour of the building. Induction is important because impressions gained by new employees during this period can influence their perceptions of the firm for many years to come. Also, good induction procedures help employees fit into strange and initially uncomfortable environments quickly and without fuss. Newcomers invariably join the firm wanting to succeed. They wish to do a good job, to be accepted by colleagues and generally to become part of the organisation. Induction procedures should help recruits achieve these objectives.

Recruits need to know where they should go for help if they experience problems. A new entrant should be told what to do if he or she:

- has a problem with money or understanding the wage system
- has a medical problem
- feels that working conditions are unsafe
- does not get on with other people in the department
- has difficulty with the work
- is bullied or harassed
- has a complaint
- does not receive adequate training.

The problems are lack of time for transmitting this information and the unsuitability of the environments in which inductions sometimes take place. No-one is capable of absorbing large amounts of (perhaps uninteresting) information in one go, so induction should be staggered. Try to make the recruit feel welcome. Do not repeat points already made at the interview or in the written job description circulated to candidates at the time of application; rather, expand on the information the newcomer already possesses. Explain the firm's organisation structure, the recruit's duties and responsibilities, training and promotion opportunities and so on. At some point you will have to explain expected performance and quality standards and the norms of behaviour and protocol already established within the organisation. Some companies issue staff handbooks to employees which detail general health and safety matters, security arrangements, performance appraisal practices, formal grievance procedures, union membership agreements etc. These manuals are particularly suitable for mundane and infrequently encountered problems such as sick pay, lost property, jury service, pension scheme benefits and so on but not for more urgent issues such as timekeeping, how to report absences, overtime requirements and (importantly) the whereabouts of fire exits, fire fighting equipment, first aid facilities and protective clothing. Small matters to do with how and where to make private telephone calls, no smoking areas, meal break times, hygiene requirements, luncheon vouchers, etc must also be explained.

Initial induction is best undertaken privately away from the workplace. Then, the recruit should be introduced to the people with whom he or she is to work (write their names down on a piece of paper and give it to the recruit — names are quickly forgotten on first meeting) and to the person to whom the recruit is responsible. This latter individual should be instructed to help the recruit in every way possible and to be a friend and adviser during the newcomer's first couple of weeks. The recruit should feel free to approach this person at any time in order to seek guidance on any problem. Arrange to see the recruit at the end of his or her first day and again at the end of the first week to discuss progress achieved during induction.

Activity

Does your firm have an induction programme for new recruits? If
so, examine the content of the programme, how long it lasts and
how useful new recruits find the exercise.

The nature and the duration of the programme will vary from
firm to firm. Large firms may arrange for all new recruits to be
brought together for a half-day, one day or even one week in the
Training Department. It is good practice, in all organisations, to
place a newcomer with an experienced member of staff, who can
give guidance on procedures etc and offer support.
The objective of any good induction programme is to help the
new recruit to settle into his/her new environment.

A good induction procedure causes the recruit to feel part of
and committed to the organisation and to be partly socialised
into its working methods, norms and interpersonal relations.
The newcomer should understand the internal communication
system and be able to find things out independently. Often, new
jobs are associated with new lifestyles, unfamiliar travel and
work routines, new relationships and possibly a change of home
and thus might create high levels of anxiety. Recruits can easily
feel bewildered and unwanted by the existing staff and much
sympathy is needed during this potentially harrowing experience. If a recruit quits after the first day or week, refuse to accept
the resignation. Explain to the newcomer that everyone has
difficulty in adapting to new circumstances and that truly
rational decisions can only be taken after a reasonable settling-
in period has elapsed. No-one should even think of resigning
until at least two weeks have elapsed after starting a new job.

The exit (termination) interview

Exit interviews are, in a sense, the direct opposite of employment interviews. You should invite (and positively encourage)
all resigning subordinates to attend an exit interview to discover
why they are leaving (real reasons may differ from those stated
in resignation letters) and hence be in a position to implement

measures to prevent others leaving for the same reason. Much can be learnt about the informal structure of an organisation during exit interviews. Some reasons for leaving are unavoidable: illness, career development, moving to another area, women who want to devote all their time to young children, etc. Other resignations can be averted. Examples of avoidable resignations include those caused by personality clashes (avoidable through lateral staff transfers), or by boredom and dissatisfaction resulting from poor job design, marginally inadequate pay or poor working conditions that could be improved.

Prepare for an exit interview by looking up the worker's job specification and employee records (absenteeism and sickness rates, etc) and ask the resigning worker's colleagues how they rate his or her work, and why *they* think he or she is leaving. Check this information against the reasons stated in the employee's resignation letter and note discrepancies. Express regret at the fact the worker has quit and explain at once that although you would like that person to remain, your primary purpose is to gather information that will enable you to correct anything improper that led to the resignation. Be friendly, thank the worker for attending the interview and be as relaxed and informal as you can. The mood of an exit interview is quite different to any other, if only because the worker has nothing to lose by stating opinions frankly. Encourage the employee to talk freely, to describe work experiences and how he or she sees the firm and personal work relationships with other people. The most troublesome problem encountered with resignations concerns clashes of personality between employees. In this type of case, offer to mediate the dispute — invite the worker to discuss the situation and suggest that a compromise short of resignation might be possible (transfer to another department or independent arbitration for example). Use open ended questions (eg 'What made you feel that way?') but do not allow yourself to be drawn into an argument; and never take sides — simply listen and observe.

Summary

This chapter will have shown you how important the recruitment, selection and induction process is to modern businesses.

There is *no one right way* but there are good practices for firms to follow.

Take a close look at the recruitment and selection procedures of your own firm, paying particular attention to the documents used and staff involved.

In light of what you have studied in this chapter, what changes and improvements would you recommend?

Notes

1 This was established by the House of Lords in the case of *Mandla v Lee* [1983] IRLR 209.
2 Fraser, J M, *A Handbook of Employment Interviewing*, MacDonald and Evans, London, 1954.
3 Rodger, A, *The Seven-Point Plan*, National Institute for Industrial Psychology, London, 1952.

2
Training

Objectives

At the end of this chapter you will be able to:

- identify the training needs within your department
- design effective training programmes for staff and devise suitable methods of evaluating the programmes
- select an appropriate training technique to meet the training objectives set.

Executive managers frequently assist in the on job training of subordinates, and sometimes have to devise complete training schemes. You need to be able to identify training needs, design on job training programmes, instruct trainees and evaluate the effectiveness of training methods. Training is necessarily intertwined with performance appraisal and promotion systems and involves a wide range of instructional activities. The purpose of training is to improve employees' performances in their current jobs and/or equip them for more demanding roles. It is expensive: special instructors may have to be employed, external courses must be financed, internal courses need resourcing with materials, personnel and physical facilities and there is no guarantee that trainees will actually benefit from participating in programmes. Trainees usually do not produce while undergoing training and there are lots of incidental expenses (hotel accommodation, travel, meal allowances, etc).

Putting aside questions of in-company staff morale, it might not make economic sense to spend enormous sums on training existing employees for higher level work if competent people can be cheaply recruited from outside. Equally pointless is the (not uncommon) practice of training far more employees in a certain type of work than there are vacancies in that area. This policy, while ensuring a ready supply of qualified internal applicants whenever needs for a particular skill arise, causes high labour turnover as workers become increasingly frustrated at not being able to perform the work for which they were trained. Indeed, 'overtraining' policies can backfire, resulting in shortages of trained internal applicants for higher level jobs.

Training seeks to improve and develop the knowledge, skills and/or attitudes of employees. Apart from the benefits accruing to the individual worker (greater versatility, extra skills, etc), many advantages accrue to the firm. Employees become more flexible, the productivity and quality of work should improve, job satisfaction might increase (with consequent reductions in absenteeism and staff turnover rates) and the business need not fear the consequences of new technology.

Activity

Does your firm have a training policy for staff and if so, what does it involve?

Examine your own attitude towards staff training. Do you consider it to be a waste of money or a worthwhile investment? Do you actively encourage all your staff, irrespective of their sex, age or ethnic origin, to attend training courses?

The maximum benefits to be derived from training can only be achieved if all parties involved have a positive attitude.

Identifying training needs

The increasing pace of technological change is perhaps the biggest single impetus for training programmes. In the first half of this century, skilled workers acquired their abilities through apprenticeships and college courses which equipped them with knowledge and skills sufficient for their entire working lives, while unskilled employees did jobs requiring little or no training. Today, however, few people can expect to do the same work in the same way for more than a few years, and the number of jobs available for totally untrained workers has declined. You should be able to identify training needs from:

- underperformance by subordinates, evidenced by low quality output, lack of initiative, bad decisions or general incompetence
- the acquisition of new and unfamiliar equipment or the introduction of new working methods
- perusal of subordinates' job specifications to identify gaps between what they are doing and what they should be doing
- analysis of the strengths and weaknesses of your department.

Further information should be available from the organisation's human resource plan (if it has one), which should incorporate forecasts for the supply and demand of various categories of labour. The plan will compare employees' current skills with those expected to be needed in the future and highlight deficiencies. Some firms prepare 'skills inventories' classifying employees according to their qualifications, technical knowledge, experience and special abilities. Such data needs to be comprehensive, detailed, held in a form that allows easy cross-referencing and regularly updated.

Self-check

How might you identify that a member of your staff requires training?

Answer
— Introduction of new equipment with which they are unfamiliar
— Poor performance in current post
— Preparation for a move to a new post requiring new skills
— Special training required to overcome a problem which is preventing the individual from fulfilling his/her potential.

You may have identified different reasons but the main thing to bear in mind is that training should not be seen as a punishment.

Discuss your subordinates' training requirements with them, otherwise, training deficiencies might be revealed through job analysis and/or work study exercises or from subordinates' own suggestions. Training should never be regarded as punishment for inadequate performance. If it is, the individuals concerned will resent being put on a programme, will refuse to learn and thus will not benefit from instruction. Project to subordinates a positive image of the training function. The need for training in new skills and the continuous refinement of existing competencies should be accepted as a natural feature of working life and you can set a good example here through personally attending training courses.

Activity

Draw up a list of each of your subordinates' current activities and alongside each name write a brief statement of the functions you expect that person to be undertaking in 12 months' time. Then list all the new equipment you anticipate the department will acquire over the next year and who will operate it. For each subordinate, ask yourself what would happen to the department's work were that person suddenly to leave the firm, how quickly you would be able to find a replacement and what training the new recruit would require. Recall examples of outstandingly bad performance that have occurred within the department over the last few months, and list their causes. Predict likely resignations, and specify the people best able to take over the work of employees who might resign.

Comment

You should by now have a clear indication of the department's present training needs and be in a position to plan a programme having regard for the long term career aspirations of each of your subordinates.

Define the knowledge (what the employee needs to know), skills (what he or she must be able to do) and attitudes (how the worker should perceive the job) necessary for satisfactory performance in various positions. Then detail all the training inputs needed to remedy current deficiencies. You now possess a 'training specification' from which a training plan may be devised. This plan should list all your training requirements and relate them to the company's stock of human resources. Trained personnel may be available in other departments, so that interdepartmental transfers could save the cost of training. Jobs need to be analysed in terms of expected standards of performance, levels of expertise required, the costs and other consequences of not using trained personnel and the feasibility of their being done by externally recruited staff who were trained elsewhere.

Note that in devising a training plan it is unlawful (under the Race Relations and Sex Discrimination Acts) for an employing organisation to discriminate in the ways it affords access to opportunities for training.[1] Thus it is generally unlawful to refuse to send a woman on a training course on the assumption that she will later give up her job to have children or that her career pattern will differ to that of a man in any other way. Paragraph 25(f) of the Equal Opportunities Commission's Code of Practice on the prevention of sex discrimination recommends that policies and practices regarding selection for training, day release or other staff development activities should be carefully and regularly examined for direct and indirect discrimination. Where imbalances in training between the sexes are found, their causes should be identified to ensure they are not discriminatory. In particular, age limits for access to training should be questioned, since many women will be older than male colleagues of equivalent rank on account of their child-bearing role.

Note however that it is not unlawful to arrange special training for persons of a particular sex or racial group provided it can be shown that within the previous 12 months only a small minority of that sex or racial group was performing a certain type of work. Indeed, the EOC Code of Practice suggests [para 42(a)] that firms actively consider training female employees for work which is 'traditionally the preserve of either sex'. The Commission for Racial Equality recommends in its Code of Practice [para 1.16(c)] that staff responsible for selecting employees for training should actually be *instructed* not to discriminate on racial grounds and urges that special training (including language training) be offered to members of ethnic minorities who 'lack particular expertise but show potential', especially for supervisory posts [para 1.45(e)]. If one of your subordinates complains of unfair discrimination in selection for training on the grounds of race or sex and you refuse to investigate the complaint then the refusal *itself* constitutes grounds for a case in the industrial tribunal! You must therefore be *seen* to investigate such a complaint carefully and the procedures used in the course of the enquiry must be accurately and comprehensively documented.

In drafting a training plan, difficulties arise in selecting appropriate programmes for particular individuals. A recruit may feel that he or she should be trained for management, whereas you might think that he or she be trained for manual work. You need, therefore, to establish a training hierarchy whereby each employee moves systematically from one course to another within a unified staff development, planned experience and promotion programme. The successful completion of a course should be viewed as a stepping stone to another and lead to new career opportunities. The plan might cover (say) the next 12 months and should specify training objectives and anticipated expenditures.

You will be most involved in on job rather than off job training. But you still need to be able to assess whether off job programmes are worthwhile. Define the results you expect from training — what the trainees should be able to do and by when. Do you want your staff to learn new skills quickly (and perhaps not as thoroughly as they could over a longer time), or do you want them to be trained gradually in anticipation of new working methods? Do you want your subordinates' *attitudes* to change along with their skills and knowledge?

Evaluation

Improved performance should result from all training activities. For manual workers the success of a training programme might be quantified in terms of better productivity, higher quality of output, less absenteeism, lower staff turnover, greater adaptability, fewer accidents and less need for close supervision. Unfortunately, improved performance in many jobs is difficult to express quantitatively in the short term and some skills acquired on courses undertaken today might not be used until the future.

Self-check

What are the benefits, for both the firm and the individual, of having a training and staff development programme?

Answers
The firm
— ensures that its workforce has the necessary skills for the current tasks in hand
— ensures that its workforce has the necessary skills to meet future needs
— helps to identify those with management potential thus helping to secure management succession
— well-motivated staff
— low staff turnover.

The individual
— improves job security
— improves promotion prospects
— gains financial rewards
— greater job satisfaction.

Your ideas may differ from those mentioned above but the main thing to remember is that training can bring benefits to all concerned.

Training can improve workers' morale, create better interpersonal relationships, instil in employees a sense of loyalty to the organisation and provide other intangible benefits. Note however that it is not sufficient merely to ask workers whether they feel more efficient in consequence of attending a course; hard objective evidence is also required. Courses which participants have particularly enjoyed (especially residential courses) may be popular not because of their intrinsic educational value but because of their holiday camp atmosphere, recreational facilities, friendships established among course members and so on. Always ask the question, 'What difference would it make if this training did not take place?' If the answer is 'not much', then you must critically reassess the value of your training activities.

Relate the outcomes from training to your initial objectives and your training plan. Isolate divergences, and explain why they occurred. Interview subordinates on completion of a course and ask them whether it was relevant to their work, whether it taught them things they did not previously know, whether it was too easy or too difficult, how well supported the programme was in terms of course materials, instructors, facilities, etc and how they think the knowledge gained will help their future careers. Keep a written record of the answers and repeat the interview after at least six months have elapsed since finishing the course. Does the employee feel the same about the course six (or twelve) months later as he or she felt the day it ended, and if not why not? Without doubt, the 'organisational climate' of a company that engages in regular training differs to that in a firm which does not, and this alone might justify training expenditures.

Self-check

Why is it important to evaluate training?

Answer
Training is costly in terms of both time and money. Therefore, it is essential that steps are taken to measure the effectiveness of any training programme. The employee must also perceive the programme as being useful or he or she may be reluctant to undertake any further training. Regular meetings should be held with the trainee to discuss the relevance of the programme and any amendments necessary.

Training methods

In general, the faster a trainee acquires knowledge the better, because lower costs are then incurred. To some extent however you 'get what you pay for' where training is concerned. If you expect a high level of performance after an employee has completed a course you need to devise the course more carefully than if little improvement in performance is required.

On job training at the workplace might involve verbal instruction, demonstration of how to use tools or equipment or simply the trainee observing someone doing a job to get the 'feel' of its characteristics. Trainees usually perceive on job instruction as immediately and directly relevant to their work, but problems arise in controlling the quality of training: good workers may be bad instructors and the workplace might not provide a suitable environment for the efficient transmission of skills. Workflows are interrupted during demonstrations and bad working habits can be passed on. Thus, training is sometimes undertaken off the job — either externally in a college or training centre or within the firm in a section of the premises specially reserved for such purposes. Trainees can then learn in a relaxed, non-threatening atmosphere, free from workplace pressures and distractions. Expert trainers may be employed full time, so that technically correct methods will be taught.

Off job training consciously seeks to provide a learning situation where people acquire skills quickly and are not seen making mistakes by departmental supervisors and other colleagues. Simplified equipment might be installed for training purposes and professional, systematic step-by-step instruction can be applied. Against these advantages are the higher costs of off job training, the artificial nature of the environment in which work is performed (possibly causing some trainees not to take the training seriously) and potential conflicts between the way a trainee is shown how to do things on the course and how the same operations are performed (differently) at the actual place of work. Full time trainers can lose touch with current working practices. Disputes between managers (especially workplace supervisors) and instructors about how work should be completed commonly occur. Also, workers may have difficulty in adjusting from the easy going, tolerant, atmosphere of an off job centre to the high pressure environment of (say) a production line or busy office.

External courses

Courses at local (or national) state colleges or private training centres may be of high quality, but are not necessarily of direct and immediate relevance to an employer's needs. Curricula and syllabuses are controlled by the college, not the firm. Staff are employed by the institution and might be unaware of a firm's

---

Self-check

What is the difference between on-the-job and off-the-job training?

Answer
On-the-job training takes place at the work station, with an experienced employee being asked to demonstrate how to operate a piece of equipment or do a particular job.

Off-the-job training takes place in a college or training centre and involves trained instructors.

---

particular training requirements. However, attendance at an external course does bring people into contact with participants from other firms and thus encourages a broader approach to issues and all the course planning and administration is done by the college.

Self-check

What is the main disadvantage with training courses run by external establishments? Can anything be done to overcome the problem?

Answer
Students frequently complain that the content of the course is not wholly relevant to their current post, or that their firm does a particular job in a completely different way to the one demonstrated. An expensive solution may be to ask the college to run a special course for employees from your firm and invite college staff to the workplace to observe methods of work, but you may then lose the benefit of gaining insight into how other firms operate.

External courses are used extensively for management training, especially for instruction in interpersonal skills (interviewing, delegation, grievance control, etc). Sometimes, they are employed as a device for easing an individual's transition into a management role, particularly when individuals are selected for management posts from the ranks of those whose work they will direct and control. Frequently, however, people have grave doubts about moving into management — they fear they will lose technical abilities diligently acquired over many years, and that they do not possess personalities appropriate for management. The transition from operative, clerk or secretary to manager can be traumatic: old skills are used less frequently, while new ones — leading a team, motivating others, counselling, initiating change, etc — become increasingly important. Managers must concentrate on general issues rather than technical detail, no matter how interesting the technical detail might be. Colleagues who were previously of equal rank become subordinates. Managerial work may turn out more complicated than was first expected, and newly promoted managers are often distressed to find they are excluded from unofficial information 'grapevines' as they begin to support rather than question higher authority.

Great anxiety can arise during this period. The individual has moved from the top of one hierarchy (as an operative) to the bottom of another (as a manager). There is need therefore for an induction scheme, or 'status passage'[2] to ease the transition between roles. External courses, particularly residential courses, are ideal for gradually and painlessly shifting the individual from one status to the next. Thus, selection for and attendance on a residential course acts as a catalyst in a person's career, marking the end of one set of relationships and attitudes and introducing another. Promoted individuals are given the opportunity to *redesignate* themselves as managers, to incorporate managerial images into their self-identities and to begin to *feel* like managers.

Techniques of training

Whichever training techniques are selected, training programmes cannot succeed unless trainees want to learn. Thus, trainees must recognise their deficiencies and see the training offered as a means for remedying them. People who stubbornly insist they have nothing to learn will not benefit from training.

Activity

Since moving into management, what new skills have you had to acquire?

What aspects of your management role have you found most difficult?

The biggest problem most people face is coping with the change of status. Suddenly you are expected to give orders, motivate others, organise workloads and be responsible for the smooth running of the section. For many it is a lonely position and the 'buck stops with you'.

Programmes should develop steadily, and not exceed the intellectual capacities of trainees. Each participant's progress on the course should be regularly monitored and trainees should themselves be able to assess how well they are doing. If you have to devise a programme, make the training methods as varied and interesting as possible and involve trainees in course planning as much as you can. Do not expect too much progress in too little time; failure to allocate sufficient time for absorption of instructional material can hinder learning in the longer run. Other basic principles of learning theory are that the trainee should:

- be presented with clearly defined targets
- enjoy the learning experience and thus become involved with and committed to the programme
- receive reinforcement of good performance, possibly through the allocation of higher grades
- be able to transfer abilities learnt in relation to one task to the completion of other similar tasks, eg a person who has learnt to word process using one software package will quickly be able to operate another.

A great many training techniques are available including the following. In choosing a particular method, you should consider the existing level of skill and the attitude of the trainee, the cost of the method (including the effects of workers being tied up with training rather than producing output), and its relevance to the needs of the job and to wider training objectives.

Coaching

This involves an experienced instructor transmitting knowledge on a person to person basis. Often it consists of a demonstration followed by the trainee imitating exactly what the instructor has done. The instruction is immediate, direct and the instructor is seen to be taking a personal interest in the trainee. Account may be taken of a trainee's special needs and the pace of instruction can be varied to suit the trainee's capacity to absorb information. Teaching is relatively informal. Participants progressively attain higher levels of skill. Simple tasks are demonstrated first, then more complicated tasks after the simple tasks have been mastered. The trainee is intimately involved in the learning process and the instructor is available to remedy mistakes on the spot as they occur.

A trainee can repeat difficult operations, ask questions and gradually gains confidence as the instruction proceeds. Against these benefits are the difficulties that firstly, a demonstration is wasted if the trainee fails to concentrate at crucial moments, so that the entire demonstration has to be repeated and secondly, an incompetent instructor will teach incorrect working methods. A parallel approach is for the trainee to learn things independently and then be questioned by an instructor. This exposes gaps in the trainee's knowledge but may damage his or her self-confidence. A congenial rapport between trainee and instructor should exist, therefore, before attempting this technique of instruction.

Formal lectures

A lecture is a verbal transmission of predetermined sets of facts and opinions within a controlled environment, usually without the active participation of trainees (other than simply listening and taking notes). The quality of a lecture depends largely on how much preparation the lecturer has undertaken, and on his or her skill in presenting information. Inarticulate lecturers are not effective. Equally, good lectures have little impact on students who are unwilling to learn. A lecture should emphasise *major* points, since only a few of the points made during a lecture (about 25 per cent at most) are remembered by the audience. Most people have difficulty in concentrating on a lecture for more than an hour.

The knowledge transmitted in a lecture can be reinforced and consolidated via handouts. Unfortunately, trainees who know that handouts will be distributed might not pay full attention and, although trainees always *intend* to study handout material, much remains unread.

Lectures remain the primary medium of instruction of very many training and educational programmes. They are cheap (a lecture can be given to a large audience) and generally recognised as a 'proper' teaching method. If you are asked to give a lecture, you must do three things: *prepare* the lecture, *plan* its presentation and *perform* its transmission. Preparation involves listing the desired outcomes from the lecture, selecting priorities (you cannot mention every aspect of a topic during a lecture) and itemising your points. Planning concerns selecting an appropriate time and venue (if you have a choice) and putting together your teaching materials (handouts, visual aids, etc). 'Performance' is about your means of delivery, how you lead the audience through the material, and other aspects of the presentation.

Discovery training

This requires trainees to investigate and discover the fundamental principles of their jobs and how they are best performed. Trainers take a back seat, merely overseeing the progress of the assignment. Trainees learn how to ask the right questions as well as find answers. The advantages are firstly, its relevance to the trainee's job, secondly, trainers' ability to assess trainees' investigative and analytical abilities as well as their technical competence and thirdly, that the results of the investigative training programmes are useful for improving efficiency at work. However, discovery training programmes can be expensive to prepare and difficult to administer and positive outcomes cannot be guaranteed.

To devise a discovery learning scheme, ask the trainee to define the characteristics of a task (or complete job) and what skills and knowledge he or she feels necessary for its satisfactory completion. Then have the trainee suggest sources of the information needed to conduct an analysis (colleagues, technical and organisational manuals, etc). You then impose a timetable and monitor progress.

In a sense, the allocation to a trainee of any individual assignment is an application of discovery learning. The trainee is given tasks to complete alone, and the outcomes are 'examined' by an instructor who comments on the quality of the work, and who allocates grades to indicate how well the trainee is progressing.

Skills analysis

A skilled and experienced worker is selected and his or her method of doing work broken down and analysed. This analysis forms a specification for the training of other workers, with detailed listings of all the tasks they must perform and the characteristics needed to perform them successfully. The details may be extremely precise, even to the description of hand, finger and foot movements.

Skills analysis is used in 'Training Within Industry' programmes initiated by the Department of Employment. These courses instruct supervisors in the technique of breaking jobs down into separate operations and analysing how each part should be accomplished. The result is a complete description of what a trainee needs to know. Each segregated job component is then taught separately. TWI is cheap, easy to understand and apply and is (still) widely used in industry. However, current working practices are transmitted from one generation to the next (even when outdated) and the training that results from these exercises may be superficial.

Related techniques are *task analysis*, which looks at the skills and behaviour patterns needed to undertake a job; and *faults analysis* which diagnoses the faults that typically occur when performing certain duties.

Job rotation

Planned experience programmes, whereby employees regularly change their jobs, enable employees to acquire an overall understanding of the organisation. This should equip trainees for higher level positions. Transfers are horizontal, and are usually intended to familiarise the trainee with a particular type of work rather than become expert in that field. Movements are preplanned and occur relatively frequently to stimulate interest and motivation. Job rotation broadens individual perspectives, encourages loyalty to the firm, and helps trainees empathise with the problems experienced in specific departments. Disadvantages include the following:

- The experience gained from just a short period in a department might not be really worthwhile. Casual observation of someone else's work might inculcate casual attitudes towards its importance
- Placings are usually predetermined through a staff development plan, which may not suit the needs of a particular individual. However, if preset plans are adjusted for certain people management may be tempted to allocate trainees randomly as ad hoc replacements for staff on sick or maternity leave, or as temporary stand-ins following unexpected resignations
- During short term postings, staff may be given mundane, low level duties the performance of which teaches them nothing.

Job rotation programmes must be carefully and regularly monitored. Responsible people should be put in charge of the trainee during his or her stay in each department and there should exist a checklist of experiences, knowledge to be acquired and duties to be undertaken against which trainees progress can be assessed. The trainee might be given specific assignments within each department and asked to prepare a report on his or her findings.

Programmed learning

This consists of the presentation of instructional material in small units (called 'frames') followed immediately by a list of questions that the trainee must answer correctly before progressing to more difficult work. The questions are an integral part of the scheme, and are usually designed in such a way that it is not possible to complete the programme without answering them. If an answer is incorrect the trainee is immediately referred back to the appropriate point in the instructional material (usually a study manual) for revision. Frames are carefully ordered into a logical progression of knowledge and levels of difficulty.

The advantages of programmed learning are that trainees can move at their own pace, become actively involved in the learning process and can do their training independently without the presence of an instructor. Schemes can be tailor made to suit particular training requirements and most trainees find the method interesting. However, there is no instructor immediately available to spur them on if they do lose interest and the preparation of good instructional materials can be extremely expensive, especially when its subject matter is constantly changing so that regular updates are needed.

Self-check

Distinguish between coaching, programmed learning, discovery training and job rotation.

Answer
Main points to be included:

Coaching:	one-to-one basis, flexible to suit needs of trainee, instant feedback, expensive, dependent on ability of trainer
Programmed learning:	trainee can work at own pace and alone, continuous feedback on progress, difficult and expensive to produce, trainee cannot ask questions
Discovery training:	high level of trainee participation, encourages independent thought, assesses trainee's ability to analyse
Job rotation:	planned progression through a variety of jobs so that the trainee acquires a broad understanding of the organisation.

Computer based training

As more firms employ computer assisted management methods it becomes increasingly attractive to base training on computer software packages. The program supplied in such a package will provide for instantaneous interaction between the package and its user and contain numerous exercises for testing the trainee's comprehension of the material it contains. Most programs are *menu driven*, meaning that users must themselves select, by choosing among options that periodically appear on the VDU, how they wish to progress. Thus, each section will be followed by a list of questions and multiple choice answers. If the trainee makes a mistake, the program scrolls back to the relevant part of the preceding text. Some 'adaptive testing' packages enable trainees to predetermine how much of the material they wish to learn. You might, for instance, only be interested in acquiring a brief overview of a subject, so that you would in this case select the option that provides just the fundamental principles of the subject, ignoring technical detail. Someone else might need to study the same package in depth and thus would choose an option to generate more extensive coverage. Training activities are therefore directly related to individual training needs.

A program might include access to a public or custom built data base (see Volume 3, chapter 3) thus enabling the trainee to ask factual questions. A few computer based training (CBT) packages adhere strictly to the principle of programmed learning whereby you are not allowed to progress until you have mastered the last section. You must answer questions correctly or perform a task (typing a letter for instance) before moving on to more difficult work. The program immediately indicates whether your responses are satisfactory and if they are not will tell you what you must do to improve your performance. Caxton's typing package *Touch 'n' go*[3] is a good example of this sort of program. It requires you to complete a series of typing drills, each more difficult than the last, within predetermined time limits. If you exceed the time allotted to a particular task or make more than a preset number of mistakes you are forced to do the same exercise again — the system is preprogramed not to allow you to continue until you have done so.

The advantage of CBT is that trainees can work independently and at their own pace, though much time can be lost in loading the program and becoming familiar with its operating system. To overcome the latter problem, audio tutors have been devised to accompany more complicated CBT programs. An audio tutor is simply a cassette that plays on a normal tape deck and tells you which keys to press on your desktop computer in order to run a package. It explains how to load the software and how to deal with particularly complex operations. Hence you spend the bulk of your time on the instructional material rather than reading a large and confusing operating manual.

CBT can be interesting as well as instructional, although considerable self-discipline is required to work all the way through a package — there are temptations to abandon the program half way through. CBT is particularly useful, therefore, when it is part of a wide training effort involving a variety of techniques of instruction.

Expert systems

An interesting development in CBT is the application of the concept of the expert system to the learning process. Expert systems attempt to mimic the human expert, applying the same knowledge and procedures to problem solving as would a highly skilled professional person (eg a medical doctor examining a patient). The facts and diagnostic processes contained in the package enable it to answer questions in a seemingly intelligent fashion. Packages themselves are divided into two parts: a shell which is a program to process information in a logical way, and a data base containing the information and rules about how it must be interpreted. The shell manipulates the data base according to a pre-set pattern, and various combinations of questions may be asked of the data. You ask questions in the form, 'what if ..., and ...., and if something else happens?' The answers should correspond to those of an expert instructor. Hence you can use the package to *diagnose* simulated problems and in so doing develop your personal knowledge of the subject and how best to investigate logically the problems that it involves. Expert systems have been applied to the training of telecommunications engineers (for fault diagnosis on printed circuit boards), to training operatives how to adjust complex electronic equipment and to training betting shop managers how to settle complicated bets (such as 'What are the odds if the number of runners in a horse race exceeds 12 and the race is a handicap and the chosen horse is placed third and ... etc).

New applications of expert systems to business are constantly being discovered. For example, cheap packages are now available to prepare short lists of job applicants for interview following the receipt of numerous completed applications. Users simply type-in key information taken directly from each candidate's application form and then specify various criteria (typing/shorthand speeds, possession of certain educational qualifications, number of years' experience of a particular kind of work, etc) deemed by users as crucial for successful performance in the job. Criteria can be altered at will and hence different sets of shortlisted applicants generated according to various sets of candidate characteristics.

Interactive video

An interactive video consists of footage of a simulated interpersonal communication situation (often a conflict situation) that maps out the background to how the situation arose, portrays actors assuming various roles, builds up to a climax and then stops abruptly leaving the viewer to provide the next step. Thus, for example, the film might show a production operative just about to lose his or her temper and, at the crucial moment, invite you to say how *you* would resolve the situation. Then you discuss your proposed solution with colleagues. Usually the video cassette is accompanied by instructional notes that relate the situation depicted and likely responses to it, to management theory. This technique supposedly enhances the realism of simulated problems, and intimately involves the trainee with the training material. It is based on the premise that the trainee will encounter similar situations at work and thus needs lots of practice in how to deal with them. Note that in a video the action may be slowed down or frozen to highlight critical events.

Video discs (as opposed to video tapes) have the advantage that random access is possible to any part of the film without having to search tediously backwards and forwards through a tape. Also, a disc can be linked to a CBT system that allows users to call up menus on a computer VDU showing the material stored on the disc and how to access various parts of the video. A combined video disc and CBT system enables film, graphic displays, text, questions and answers and a public and/or custom built data base to be incorporated into the same package.

Open learning

An increasingly popular mode of off job training is the open learning programme whereby a central organisation (usually a technical college or independent trainer) issues to trainees a package of learning materials (books, tapes, CBT programs, etc) and provides support such as tutor back-up, counselling, and face to face instruction at surgeries held on certain evenings or at weekends. Telephone contacts are also available for those (shift workers for example) who are unable to attend tutorials.

Group training

Group training encourages participants to learn from each other through discussing issues, pooling experiences and critically examining opposing viewpoints. Instructors guide discussions rather than impart knowledge directly — they monitor trainees' understanding of what is going on, ask questions to clarify points and sometimes (but not always) prevent certain members from dominating the group. An instructor should have a clear idea of the purpose of the exercise and what it should achieve. Several types of group training activity might be undertaken, including the following.

Case studies

Case studies simulate real life problems previously experienced or which are expected to occur in the future. Each member investigates and reports on an aspect of the case, and is expected to assess and criticise the work of colleagues. The aim is to encourage analytical approaches to problems and to develop participants' diagnostic abilities, focusing on general principles rather than administrative trivia. Casework utilises the existing knowledge and experience of participants. This creates interest and enthusiasm among group members, but equally can cause the exercise to fail if participants do not possess sufficient knowledge and experience to understand fully the implications of the case. Participants are offered a 'snapshot' of a work situation at a particular moment in time; they can analyse the situation at their leisure and they see that several different approaches might be possible. Hopefully, the understanding gained while slowly studying the case will later be transferred to the ability to analyse and *quickly* solve similar problems in the future.

Business games

These are simulated competitive situations requiring each of two competing groups to take decisions, the predetermined consequences of which are monitored. Participants must achieve objectives within preset environmental circumstances determined by the rules of the game. Elements of chance are incorporated through random occurrences beyond the control of the players. Although business games (and case studies) can be devised to correspond closely to real life situations, the classroom environment in which games are played or cases discussed is necessarily artificial and participants might not take the exercises seriously.

Role playing

Role playing requires each group member to act the part of a character in a certain situation. Often, the character played occupies a role opposite to that of the real life job of the participant. Thus, for example, a personnel officer might play the role of a trade union shop steward, a production manager pretend to be a salesperson or a purchasing manager could act the role of a representative of a supplying firm. Role playing forces trainees to see issues from alternative perspectives and points of view, albeit in artificial circumstances. Note, however, that flippancy of overacting will destroy the value of these exercises and participants often adopt stereotyped behaviour when playing certain roles (for example, a personnel officer pretending to be a union representative might change his or her accent, start banging on the table, begin to shout, and use other unrealistic interpretations of perceived unreasonable union behaviour). The great advantage of role playing is that mistakes can be made and corrected without serious real life consequences. Where possible, exercises should be filmed, preferably with instant playback. This records exactly how the players respond to various events and can be studied at length during post-exercise group discussions.

T-groups

T-group exercises (the T stands for training) leave participants to their own devices. There is no appointed group leader; the trainer simply informs members to look after themselves. Thus the group itself has to decide what to do. The trainer remains with the group as an observer, but does not intervene. Inevitably, a group structure emerges and group leaders appear. Members feel helpless at first, but through pooling their experiences and helping each other eventually create a cohesive, organised working group. Once the group has established a common goal it will appoint a formal leader. Haggling over the details of group structure will occur and sub-groups will start to form. Conflicts between sub-groups arise and are resolved. Individual roles within the group become clearly defined and a final consensus appears. The group becomes a distinct, independent entity. Four advantages are claimed for T-group training:

- participants recognise the need to learn from experience and from each other
- individuals observe how other participants react to offers of help and the extent to which various group members help each other
- since the group begins in a leaderless state, it has to make its own decisions about group leadership. This 'demystifies' the process of leader selection members learn how to delegate leadership tasks to those best suited for them
- members develop self-confidence in expressing their views. They exercise interpersonal communications skills, and in so doing come to understand the true nature of group dynamics.

T-group training is non-directive in character. Members are expected to *train themselves* and some individuals are better able to achieve this than others. It follows that those who are in fact capable of self-instruction, who recognise the training issues involved and are ready, willing and able to help the group define its purposes and clarify individual roles within its ranks, do not need T-group training! Moreover, the learning and adaptation processes encountered during T-group sessions are very similar to those experienced in many normal social group situations. People often find themselves having to take initiatives in newly formed social groups with vaguely defined purposes. Why then spend money on creating analogous situations in a classroom? Individuals who have undertaken T-group training often comment that although the experience was interesting, they learned little of practical value that could not be learned elsewhere at much lower cost.

Activity

You have been given a comprehensive summary of the range of training techniques available. Analyse the techniques used in your own firm and evaluate their effectiveness.

Different techniques lend themselves to teaching different skills and it is important to select the appropriate technique to meet the objectives of the training programme and the needs of the trainee.

Management training

Your firm might put you onto a management training course either to improve your supervisory and/or interpersonal skills or to prepare you for higher level work, in which case you need to be told how best you can equip yourself for promotion. Senior management should have prepared management development and succession plans and devised a training and planned experience scheme to remedy identified deficiencies. The programme will normally cover:

- background knowledge of the company, its trading environment, products, production methods, markets and personnel

- elements of management theory and practice, administrative procedures, the legal environment, specialist techniques
- analytical skills, organisation, delegation and control, time management
- interpersonal skills, communications, leadership and co-ordination, motivation of subordinates
- creative abilities, problem solving, capacity to initiate new activities.

Activity

Which training technique(s) would you recommend for the following cases:

— a clerical trainee who has recently been moved into the accounts department and will have to use a computer and software packages, such as a spreadsheet?

— a newly promoted manager who will be conducting staff appraisal interviews?

— a new recruit who will be expected to perform routine clerical tasks, such as manual PAYE?

Clearly there is no one right method and to a large extent it will depend on the resources of the firm. Rather than make recommendations, the criteria on which the choice should be made for each case are given below:

— the trainee will require some individual instruction on how to operate the computer and install the package. The technique selected must allow the trainee to learn the commands and practise using them. Access to an expert should be available

— the manager must play an active role and be encouraged to discuss the skills to be used. Feedback on performance is desirable. Individuals must be able to assess their own performance and that of others

— routine jobs do not change over time and simply require practice to perfect. While individual coaching might be needed initially, a detailed checklist approach may be employed.

Management training can occur on or off the job. On the job training is common where supervisors need instruction in existing administrative systems before being able to undertake routine duties.

Note, however, that some firms insist that managerial ability cannot be taught, and that management training courses are therefore a waste of time. They argue that few courses contain material that is directly relevant and immediately applicable to real life management situations, and that normal competition between managerial staff should ensure 'survival of the fittest'. Among firms which do train managerial staff, new approaches to training are increasingly common — firms wish to develop the initiative, self-reliance, leadership and interpersonal communications skills of managers as well as their technical abilities. Action learning is one way of pursuing these objectives. This is a training technique which seeks to develop the trainee's capacity for independent action through requiring that he or she collect and evaluate data relating to a real life problem, devise appropriate measures for dealing with the problem, then implement a solution and analyse the consequences of the results. The method is problem based and job specific, so instructors need expert knowledge of the problem being considered. Action learning will succeed only to the extent that trainees are genuinely curious about the tasks they are asked to analyse and perform, that they are capable of understanding the significance of what they are doing and are thus able to learn from experience. 'Coverdale' training[4] is a group training application of the principles of activity learning. Relatively simple tasks are undertaken by a group, using existing skills and under the direction of a specialist instructor who then leads discussion after the task's completion.

An interesting recent development in the supervisory training field has been the increasing use of outdoor management training, which assumes the existence of direct parallels between the personal qualities necessary for successful supervisory management and those cultivated through participation in outdoor pursuits such as rockclimbing, canoeing, sailing or orienteering. The essential demands of these activities: planning, organising, team-building, dealing with uncertainty, direction and control are the same, advocates argue, as those needed for management. In either situation, individuals must be able to identify relevant and feasible objectives and initiate and organise activities aimed at their achievement. Such duties require capacities for leadership, communications, coordination, and the motivation of subordinate staff. Creativity, and in particular the ability to implement quickly measures needed to solve immediate problems, is highly valued in commercial organisations.

Activity

Do management courses make better, more effective managers? Are managers born or made? Have the best managers worked their way up from the shopfloor? How would you respond to these questions?

There is no easy answer to any of these questions and there is an element of truth in each suggestion.

Experience can count for a great deal but individuals must also be open to new ideas and techniques. Management courses are not an end in themselves but introduce participants to new ideas and help them to acquire and develop the skills they will need. Group exercises and case studies will enable management trainees to develop their analytical powers and team work.

Outdoor development exercises supposedly demonstrate the importance of interpersonal cooperation, clarity of expression, trust and mutual dependence of higher and lower levels of authority, since nowhere is the effectiveness of a leader's style tested more rigorously than in physically challenging, tense, unusual situations where bad judgements will be ruthlessly exposed. Participants are forced to examine critically their individual strengths and weaknesses; they learn about themselves, their relationships with others and the true responsibilities of command. Outdoor training, its supporters argue, teaches accountability; there can be no hiding behind artificially and arbitrarily created status or authority structures on a mountainside or in the midst of desolate moorland. Concepts of delegation, appraisal, control and management style generally (job centred, task orientated, theory X, theory Y, systems approach or whatever) adopt dramatic new meanings in such circumstances. Confronted by difficult, physically arduous, outdoor problems the trainee soon realises his or her limitations, capacities and potential.

An important criticism of outdoor training is that it might not be relevant to managers involved in information technology whose management skills consist largely of aptitudes for identifying testable hypotheses and knowledge of operations research techniques. Outdoor activities will not teach managers how to formulate appropriate summary statistics, interpret complex data, construct models or predict outcomes and monitor (through a computerised management information system) the results. Another criticism is that it might encourage 'gifted amateur' approaches to management. Time spent on outdoor training might be better used for study of network analysis, CADCAM, critical path scheduling or other advanced management techniques. Note also that all outdoor goal achievement projects take place, necessarily, in artificial social (if not physical) environments.

Nevertheless, outdoor training is increasingly popular and participants usually enjoy the experience, but this is not surprising. The sort of person attracted to (voluntary) outdoor courses is usually the outdoor type who would choose to spend time on this kind of activity (rambling, orthodox sports for older people, excitement based hobbies) anyway. Participants are self selected, no-one is forced to scramble up a mountainside or shoot rapids in a canoe in order to gain promotion. Enthusiastic post-course evaluations from graduating trainees are to be expected.

Summary

Hopefully, you will now see the need for setting training objectives, developing training programmes for your staff and evaluating the effectiveness of courses attended.

You might find it useful to keep a record of the different types of courses available, both internally and externally and who they are best suited for.

In order to help you record and plan staff development, a simple chart might be used. Against each member of staff you can record training given with dates, performance (if known) and feedback about the course. This can serve as a quick reference when you discuss future training plans with staff.

Notes

1 Sex Discrimination Act 1975, s 6(2) and Race Relations Act 1976, s 4(2).
2 This is a sociological concept introduced by A Van Gennep in his book, *The Rites of Passage*, Routledge and Kegan Paul, London, 1960.
3 This is the typing tutor program of Caxton Software Ltd. It is available for most operating systems.
4 See N Rackham, P Honey and M Colbert, *Developing Interactive Skills*, Wellens Publishing, 1967.

3
Motivation

Objectives

At the end of this chapter you will be able to:

- analyse the reasons why people work and recognise the implications for motivation and performance in the workplace
- recognise the symptoms of lack of motivation in staff
- apply the principles of good job design to improve staff motivation
- identify the role of the manager in the workplace.

Employees are motivated in part by the need to earn a living and partly by human needs for job satisfaction, security of tenure, the respect of colleagues and so on. The organisation's reward system (pay, fringe benefits, job security, promotion opportunities, etc) may be applied to the first motive and job design to the latter. Much research has sought to discover the sources of motivation at work, but no definitive conclusions have emerged — it seems that many factors motivate individuals. Central to all theories of motivation is the concept of *need*, and how people seek to justify their perceived requirements.

Attitudes towards work

Controversy surrounds the question whether there exists in humans a natural instinct to work. An instinct is innate, it is

---

Activity

List as many reasons as you can why people work and what needs are satisfied through work.

Set your list on one side and we will refer to it again at the end of the chapter.

---

born within the person and does not have to be learned. Some theorists suggest that work is a natural activity and that left to themselves workers will normally work hard. Others assume that employees dislike work, will avoid it wherever possible and thus will require close and constant supervision.

In modern industrialised societies most people have to work whether they like it or not. Work provides income, social status and a means whereby individuals become involved with society. Work, usually, is a social activity, few people work entirely alone. The fact that work brings people into contact with others is itself a powerful motivator in making them want to work. Not only does unemployment cause reductions in workers' incomes but it also severs many of their links with society. Thus, social factors (as well as pay) are relevant to the incentive to work. Note particularly how physical working conditions are not necessarily related to workers' morale.

Few people would claim to have found the perfect job; all jobs involve some routine work or unenjoyable activities. Monotonous, uncreative work does however cause special difficulties, including the following.

Boredom

Boredom may result from continuous repetition of a simple task, or from the social environment in which tasks are undertaken. A task might be interesting, but the worker still feel bored if he or she must complete it in isolation. Equally, jobs can be trivial and repetitious, yet not create boredom because workers are able to communicate pleasurably with others. Workers who perform complex tasks typically become absorbed by them and are not bored.

Frustration

Workers experience frustration when they are prevented from exercising control over their work and are not able to achieve their (self-defined) objectives. Frustration can be caused by the lack of control over working methods or the speed of production, by having to do work perceived as meaningless, through not being involved in decision making or through workers not feeling that their grievances have been properly heard. A worker may react to frustration positively, by attempting to overcome the problem that caused the obstruction, or negatively. Examples of negative reactions are aggression (quarrels with colleagues, hostility towards management), apathy (lateness, absenteeism), unwillingness to assume responsibility, poor quality work, high propensities to have accidents and high rates of labour turnover.

Alienation

This is the feeling that work is not a relevant or important part of one's life; that one does not really belong to the work community. It is associated with feelings of discontent, isolation and futility. Alienated workers perceive themselves as powerless and dominated. Work becomes simply a means to achieve material ends. Great unhappiness can result from alienation, indeed, the mental or physical health of the employee can suffer. Alienation may result from lack of contact with other workers and/or with management, from authoritarian or paternalistic management styles or simply through the boredom of routine work. Its consequences are numerous: poor quality output, absenteeism, resistance to change, industrial disputes, deteriorating interpersonal relationships etc.

People usually work better when they feel they have a personal stake in the success of their activities — success not necessarily measured in financial terms. Money is obviously important, but many other factors are involved: staff might accept that they are well paid, yet still be dissatisfied with their jobs. Consider, for example, the highly-paid executive for whom a wage rise will mostly disappear in tax, or the person who automatically hands over the bulk of his or her earnings to someone else (a husband, wife or parent for instance), or the employee who already possesses a large private income. Proper pay and decent working conditions are obviously the foundations that underlie good relations between workers and the firm but thereafter other factors come to the fore. In particular, it seems that fair and equal treatment of workers and their involvement in the formulation of company policies greatly motivate employees.

Self-check

What factors might indicate a lack of job satisfaction on the part of your staff?

Answer
As a general rule of thumb, unacceptable behaviour signifies that all may not be well.
Poor job performance — in terms of quality, quantity or both
High absenteeism
High labour turnover
Frequent staff disputes and squabbles over minor matters.

The nature of work

Certain types of work provide employees with opportunities for creativity and the exercise of initiative (managerial work for example) and those who undertake such work typically derive great satisfaction from its completion. For others, however, work can be a drudge, neither enjoyable not satisfying, just something that has to be done. The latter situation is particularly unfortunate in situations where individuals are in jobs which are clearly unsuited to their abilities, aptitudes and perspectives. To the extent that people are well adjusted to their jobs, their morale, effort and efficiency is enhanced.

Individual differences

Each person enters the labour force possessing a particular stock of attributes. People have differing levels of ability, differing personalities, interests and temperaments. Individuals are dissimilar in their physical appearance, voice and manner. Certain people seem to possess natural aptitudes for particular tasks (those requiring manual dexterity or mental arithmetic for example) and individual personalities are unique — some people are introverted, others extrovert, some are sociable, others happiest when working alone.

Activity

Analyse your own attitude to work. Do you work to live or live to work? What aspects of work do you enjoy and what aspects do you dislike?

This is not an easy task but if you can understand your own attitudes, it may help you to appreciate the attitudes of your staff. We are all individuals, with our own needs and objectives, but at work we tend to be treated as part of a group.

Work requires social behaviour — cooperation, supervision, interpersonal bargaining, assessment and appraisal of others. Thus, social skills are needed to cope at work. From an early age children are socialised into the culture of work. They are prepared for the work experience through vocational education, careers guidance, school-to-work transition programmes, work induction and special training schemes. Whether the school-leaver eagerly looks forward to work as an exciting challenge or approaches work with fear and trepidation will depend fundamentally on attitudes towards and perceptions of work within the society in which the school-leaver has been brought up. People usually first learn about work through hearing their parents' conversations about their jobs and through observing parents going to and returning from places of work. Young children do not work as such, but their play often reflects themes derived from their parents' occupations. As they grow up they do increasing amounts of school work. They have no experience of specific types of occupation, yet attitudes consistent with occupational success are inculcated in them at school. Scholastic achievement is rewarded and success in competitive sports encouraged. Parents and teachers constantly exhort young people to do well in work-related activities and aspects of personality specifically relevant to occupational success (intelligence, initiative, ability to concentrate for long periods) are systematically developed. Discipline patterns in schools, moreover, are often justified against their value in training young people to fit into patterns of supervision and authority at work.

During these formative years individuals acquire self-identities which they carry into work. An individual's self-identity (or self-image) consists of a whole set of perceptions that a person has about him or her self. Such perceptions derive from individual experiences and personalities and offer a way of interpreting an individual's social role. Teenagers, for example, typically perceive their role as different to those of the middle-aged or retired and behave in accordance with the perceived requirements of that role (few old age pensioners ride motor cycles for instance, while teenagers rarely eat in restaurants frequented mostly by the middle aged). The way in which individuals perceive their social roles usually alters with respect to age, family circumstances and occupation. People see themselves differently as they get older, wealthier and as they are promoted at work. They act differently and expect others to alter their behaviour towards them.

Self-image is important for understanding attitudes towards work because the ideas people hold about themselves affect their behaviour. Individuals tend to act in ways that conform to their self-identities. Note however how self-perceptions can be entirely wrong. Often we view our own attributes and abilities in unreasonably favourable ways. Note also how easy it is for a person to confuse occupational status with genuine ability: promotion to a high ranking job for example does not necessarily mean that a person is intellectually superior to those who were passed over for promotion.

Self-image is important too for helping individuals choose particular lines of work. In selecting an occupation, adolescents are guided by the advice they receive from teachers and careers officers and by parental role models. Additionally, youngsters are likely to be attracted by jobs associated with characteristics which they perceive themselves to possess. A boy, for example, who sees himself as a gregarious type will probably not want a job that involves spending long periods alone. It follows that different types of work might be favoured at different stages of a person's life depending on age, family circumstances etc because perceptions alter over time. A 15 year-old looks at life quite differently to someone who is 25, married with children and paying a mortgage.

Self-image and occupation are to some extent interdependent. Many factors contribute to a final choice of job: availability, the nature of local industry, the example of older people and individual personality. Having taken a job, the employee might then begin to adopt outlooks and patterns of behaviour associated with that type of work. Newcomers to organisations often copy the behaviour of existing members and continued exposure to organisational norms will lead them to assimilate the norms and attitudes of the organisations to which they belong. Professionals similarly construct self-identities, but often identify more closely with the profession itself than with a particular firm. Usually, a professionally qualified person wants a career — a logically planned series of increasing responsible jobs — rather than a single post. Some professionals prefer to change firms frequently, relying on their professional expertise, abilities, and motivation to secure progressively senior posts; others choose to spend most of their careers in one large organisation which offers steady progression towards a senior management job.

Self-check

What is self-image and how does it influence one's attitude to work?

Answer

Self-image is an individual's perception of him/herself and will influence how he/she acts in any given situation. It frequently influences the choice of career as the individual will select the job which most closely matches the characteristics they perceive themselves as possessing.

Self-image often changes over time as one grows older. Having chosen a career, individuals may adopt the behaviour and attitudes of those around them.

As individuals are promoted they acquire new images of themselves. The self-identity of a supervisor for example is usually quite different to that of a middle management line executive, who in turn will possess a self-image different to that held by a person occupying a very senior post. Following promotion, managers will mix with people whose attitudes might contrast with those previously encountered, so that adjustments in attitude, behaviour and, ultimately, self-perception are required. Promotion brings a higher status, extra income and possibly a whole new way of life.

Managerial work

Activity

Define managerial work. What job titles do you associate with management?

Read on and compare your views with those in the text. Management is a broad term, covering a wide variety of tasks.

A job comprises a whole series of characteristics including skill requirements, education, training and experience needed, physical requirements for the type of work involved, the degree of responsibility assumed and working conditions. Other requirements might include the abilities to plan, coordinate and control the work of others, to withstand stress and qualities of initiative, reliability and willingness to work as part of a team. To be good at management you must learn to work with other people. You will have superiors and subordinates, through whom you will achieve results. It might be possible to avoid extensive contact with other departments but this is undesirable. Managers of the future need to be flexible and quickly responsive to change and the higher the level of management you achieve the more critically you will need to perceive *all* aspects of the firm and not just the needs of your own department. Senior management skills can be quite different to the skills acquired during early training: abilities to plan, coordinate and take strategic rather than operational decisions are paramount.

Many categories of employee now call themselves manager: supervisors, professional advisors, consultants and those who are concerned more with physical resources than people. There are, nevertheless, common elements in most managerial jobs. Perhaps the most common denominator is the unpredictability and variability of managerial work. Management typically involves doing lots of fragmented jobs. It involves therefore communication with others and requires an ability to appreciate the significance of their work. Henry Mintzberg pointed out[1] the contradictions that sometimes arise between managers' job specifications and the duties they actually perform. According to Mintzberg, the classical approach to management assigned to individual managers highly specific functional responsibilities — planning, organising, coordinating and so on, whereas other schools viewed the manager's role differently — as leadership, profit-maximisation, ensuring long run survival etc. Yet all management work, Mintzberg argued, has common elements, which he categorised under three headings: interpersonal, informational and decisional. In their interpersonal role, managers act as figureheads, leaders and coordinators. The informational role involves the collection, monitoring and transmission of information and the control of working groups. Decisional aspects of management work require individuals to initiate change, allocate resources, negotiate and handle disturbances. All managerial activity, Mintzberg commented, is characterised by pace, frequent interruption, variety, fragmentation of effort, the need for quick thinking and regular verbal communications with others.

Exactly *how* a manager undertakes such activities depends on the particular circumstances of the situation, on the manager's personality and the environments in which the manager and the organisation function. Management, argued Mintzberg, is an *art*, and as such, management skills can only be nurtured within individuals through self-analysis and appraisal, and through personal self-development.

Much controversy has surrounded the question whether management may be regarded as a bona fide profession. Without doubt, certain aspects of management have professional characteristics — they are intellectually demanding, require the exercise of discretion and application of expert

---

Self-check

How did Mintzberg categorise management work?

Answer

Interpersonal: figurehead, leader, co-ordinator

Informational: collection, monitoring and transmission of information, control of work groups

Decisional: allocation of resources, negotiations, coping with change

   He viewed management as an art, where the skills needed have to be developed over time.

---

knowledge and mistakes and bad decisions lead to serious adverse consequences for the firm. Yet the substance of management is extremely diverse. Management is necessarily a generic subject involving a great variety of fragmented jobs — if there is a single common denominator in managerial work it is the variability and unpredictability of tasks!

To qualify for true professional status, three conditions must apply. Firstly, professional activities should be based on an established and systematic body of knowledge, the acquisition of which requires several years of substantial intellectual training. Secondly, entry to the profession should be restricted to persons possessing certain predetermined qualifications and experience. Thirdly, carefully specified ethical (professional) standards should be maintained and codes of practice followed.

Management does not satisfy these criteria. No formal qualifications are needed to become a manager. Indeed many successful managers (especially entrepreneurs) have received only rudimentary academic qualifications. No generally accepted norms of management conduct exist (other than those imposed by government via legislation or regulatory bodies); and there are no uniform management principles to which managers are forced to adhere. Nevertheless, there is a strong case for treating management as if it were a profession. Modern managers must be encouraged to take a professional pride in the quality of their output — efficient and socially responsible management should come to be viewed as an end in itself and not just a means for earning a living.

Self-check

In your capacity as a manager, what functions do you perform? Do you regard yourself as a professional person?

Answer
There is little point in listing typical functions as they will vary depending on the nature and level of the post. However, tasks will include organising work and people, controlling resources, formulating plans etc.

While management may not qualify for professional status according to the textbook definition, the majority of managers will take a professional pride in their work. Today, greater attention is being paid to the need to train and up-date managers in order to ensure that they have the necessary skills to do the job.

Job design

Job design is the process of deciding which tasks and responsibilities shall be undertaken by particular employees and the methods, systems and procedures for completing work. It concerns patterns of accountability and authority, spans of control and interpersonal relations between colleagues. The purpose of job design is to stimulate the interest and involvement of the worker, thus motivating the worker to greater efforts. Jobs may be *enlarged* or *enriched*.

Job enlargement means increasing the scope of a job through extending the range of its duties and responsibilities. This contradicts the principle of specialisation and division of labour whereby work is divided into small units, each of which is performed repetitively by an individual worker. The boredom and alienation caused by the division of labour can actually cause efficiency to fall, thus, job enlargement seeks to motivate workers through reversing the process of specialisation.

Job enrichment involves the allocation of more interesting,

challenging and perhaps difficult duties to workers in order to stimulate their sense of participation and concern for the achievement of objectives. Extra decision-making authority may be assigned to workers or they might be given duties requiring higher skill levels or be required to have greater contact with customers and/or suppliers. Equally, existing single tasks might be combined into a composite whole or workers might be made responsible for controlling the quality of their output, or be allowed greater discretion over how they achieve objectives. It is essential to involve trade union or other workers' representatives from the very outset of any attempt to enrich jobs. Trade unions are naturally suspicious that in enriching jobs management seeks only to extract from workers more work for the same amount of pay.

The term *job extension* is used to embrace both enlargement and enrichment. Its underlying philosophy is, quite simply, that the wider the variety of tasks undertaken the more the worker realises the significance of the job in the wider organisation and the happier and more productive the worker will become. Of course, some jobs are more easily extended than others. Assembly lines in automated factories offer few opportunities for interesting work. In this case, higher pay and/or greater worker participation could be primary motivators. Note also that not everybody wants to assume extra responsibility. In situations where job enlargement is not possible, an alternative is to put workers through sequences of different jobs. Each job is boring, but monotony is relieved through regular job rotation. Thus, workers experience many jobs at different stages in the production process, even though the division of labour has been fully applied. Moreover, employee absences can then be covered from an existing pool of trained, experienced personnel.

To initiate a job design exercise you must first analyse the work that needs to be done using existing job descriptions and data from previous work study programmes. You should know which jobs are least interesting to the people who do them (and why) and what steps are necessary to make these jobs more interesting. Thus, you should interview subordinates individually (performance appraisal discussions offer convenient opportunities for this), confidentially and sympathetically in order to get the *feel* of their jobs. Unfortunately, people often exaggerate the

---

Self-check

What are the benefits to be derived from specialisation? How would you argue in favour of job enlargement over specialisation?

Answer
Benefits include — shortened training period, increased productivity and efficiency, lower labour costs as less skilled labour can be used.

Job enlargement gives an individual more duties and responsibilities. Studies have found that specialisation can lead to monotonous jobs, to the extent that the benefits of higher efficiency and productivity are not achieved.

---

difficulties and problems associated with their work, so you must pin interviewees down when describing their jobs; do not accept vague statements about tasks and responsibilities.

Having described subordinates' jobs, list the *interesting* duties — those which carry responsibility and which involve planning and self-control — associated with each position. Then specify exactly the changes necessary to make particularly boring jobs more interesting, eg the regrouping of activities (taking some interesting work away from certain individuals for reallocation to others), allowing workers to alter the pace or methods of their work or allocating broad rather than specific objectives. Participation in the setting of targets can also enrich employees' work, especially if the workers are encouraged to contribute completely new ideas.

Satisfied staff are easy to supervise, they are productive, cooperative and easy to please. Look critically at subordinates' physical working conditions. Can they be improved? Can you enhance the perceived status of subordinates, say by giving each of their jobs an impressive sounding title? Possibly, you can improve subordinates' sense of job security through frequently complementing their standards of work and you might perhaps reduce the amount of supervision you apply by removing various controls (time sheets, rigid directives on working methods, standard layouts for equipment and materials, etc). Can the staff be brought into contact with final customers, or even other departments which utilise their work? Much satisfaction can be gained from observing the pleasure of a customer when he or she is presented with a high quality finished product. Try to make your staff feel important, praise them and be seen to take a personal interest in their work.

Activity

Look closely at the jobs performed within your department. Identify those that are the most interesting and those that are the most boring. Can anything be done by means of job enlargement, job enrichment or job rotation to minimise the boredom factor?

You may well meet with a mixed reception if you try to implement any changes to working practices, but this should not be allowed to stand in the way of creating a more pleasant and satisfying working environment for the majority of staff.

If you have to criticise a subordinate, criticise an action rather than the individual and always precede the criticism with a compliment regarding some other aspect of that person's work. You may find the following a useful procedure for presenting a criticism:

- choose a private place for the conversation, do not dramatise and never cause the subordinate to feel that you will publicise the criticism to others
- show that a problem has been caused by the subordinate's substandard performance. Ask for a comment on the situation
- suggest a means of overcoming the problem and together examine the implications of the actions you jointly need to take
- sympathise with the cause of the subordinate's inadequacy, and offer *practical* help.

Job satisfaction in employees is not easy to measure because no standard measurement criteria exist: tasks which bore some people can interest others and people might work hard even though greatly dissatisfied with their work (in pursuit of high wages for example). Some firms issue questionnaires to employees asking them to list in rank order the tasks they find particularly tedious and/or unpleasant. Equally, employees might be invited to comment on the working conditions they regard as most attractive (security, good interpersonal relations, responsibility, control over work, etc). Results from such surveys may help in designing jobs, though many of the workers' suggestions will in practice be unattainable and again the problem arises that individuals will be subjective in their response, so that jobs designed according to the suggestions of one set of incumbents might not be suitable for the next.

It seems reasonable to assume that if employees are dissatisfied in their work they will take the maximum time off. Perhaps therefore the best indicators of job satisfaction are punctuality among employees, low rates of absenteeism and labour turnover. Other important symptoms are the incidence of invocation of grievance procedures and the frequency of arguments among the staff.

Self-check

What action do you take when you identify a lack of job satisfaction in a member of your staff?

Answer
Hopefully, none of you would take no action at all. Discontent can spread very easily and affect the performance of the whole section.

Essentially, you have to identify the root cause and if a remedy can be found, implement it.

Participation

Participation in taking decisions that affect individuals' working lives can greatly motivate them to increase effort. At the organisational level, participation may occur via works' committees, advisory groups and quality circles and through other formal joint consultation procedures. Essentially, joint consultation is a communications exercise; management retains control over the decision making process, but seeks to utilise the expertise, energy and initiative of the workforce in decision making activities. Management informs employees of its plans and opinions on various issues and invites comment. The advantage to management is that expert advice is obtained from employees who possess detailed knowledge of shop floor procedures and conditions. Also, workers who exert limited control over their environments are likely to cooperate with management and be receptive to change. Note however that workers will not be happy with consultative procedures if they are invoked only when difficulties arise, especially if financial economies are needed. Joint management/worker decision taking should extend to *all* aspects of the firm's work, not just the areas it finds convenient.

Suggestion schemes might be useful for motivating staff, though problems occur in deciding who is to receive the financial benefits that result from profitable recommendations. In general, the patent rights of a new invention belong to the firm that employs the inventor, not the individual worker. Also, once a suggestion has been submitted it becomes known to the firm and it might be impossible subsequently to prove the true identity of the inventor. Indeed, a firm might initially reject a worker's suggestion only to take it up after the worker has left the organisation without rewarding that person. Nevertheless, suggestion schemes are popular with both management and workers and firms introducing them often experience large benefits.

Participation, of whatever form, has advantages and drawbacks. The principal argument in its favour relates to its mobilisation of the talents, resources, experiences and expertise of junior staff who are positively encouraged to develop their decision making capacities. People can influence the events that determine their working lives — they feel involved, useful, valued and secure. Management is forced to think hard about the implications of its actions for the staff and analytical approaches to decision taking are encouraged. Further benefits could be greater willingness by workers to abide by decisions they helped to make and the fact that bad, unworkable, decisions are less likely because those who would have to implement them receive opportunities to point out potential difficulties.

Self-check

What is meant by participation?

To what extent is participation encouraged in your firm? Are there any ways in which you could encourage your staff to participate in the decision-making process of the department?

Answer

Participation is an approach to management, whereby employees are encouraged to contribute to the running of the organisation. This can range from formal joint consultative committees to suggestion schemes.

This is a difficult problem as it can be a matter of company policy and individual managers may not have the freedom to encourage worker participation.

Although this approach may bring benefits, all parties have to have a positive attitude. The workers must be willing and able to contribute and, moreover, believe that management will pay more than lip service to their contributions.

On the other hand, participation interferes with managerial prerogative, it delays decisions and can lead to inefficient working methods. Workers, moreover, rarely possess the administrative and problem solving skills needed for effective management. Other criticisms of participation include the following:

- much managerial information is confidential — often involving personal matters relating to individuals — which should not be disclosed to employees
- conflicts of interest between management and labour are inevitable, and are best resolved through collective bargaining. Workers cannot simultaneously represent their colleagues *and* be part of management
- participation does not alter fundamental financial realities. Businesses sometimes fail despite extensive prior consultation
- Workers sometimes adopt short-term and mercenary approaches to complex issues which really require long-term consideration.

If participation is to succeed, both management and workers must want it to succeed. Hostility from either side guarantees failure. At the departmental level, participation involves seeking advice from subordinates, exchanging information, joint determination of targets and joint planning and control of activities. For participation to work you need to be *seen* to be willing to share your decision making powers, yet formally established procedures are not necessarily most appropriate for achieving this objective, indeed they can be counterproductive if management representatives only grudgingly and reluctantly join a formal participation system. Ad hoc joint decision making together with regular briefing sessions might be more effective in generating feelings of involvement.

Note that some of your subordinates might not want to participate in decision taking and that others may not possess the skills and experience necessary to be able to do so. Do not force people to become involved in a participation scheme and recognise that even if they are willing to offer suggestions their contributions might not have much value in the early stages of the process. Joint decision taking implies shared responsibility for jointly determined decisions, and some employees (especially those who represent others, eg union shop stewards) may not be happy about this.

Promotion

Apart from improvements in pay and conditions of work, the most immediate incentive available to an employee is the possibility of promotion. If the firm has trained its staff adequately and ensured that their work experiences are sufficiently wide, internal promotion should present no problem. External recruitment should be necessary only for specialist positions or when no-one within the organisation possesses appropriate qualifications for a post. Promotion prospects offer significant motivation.

The criteria used in selecting individuals for promotion can be based on ability or seniority. Ability related systems accelerate the careers of exceptionally competent staff, whereas seniority based procedures ensure steady progression for all employees. Knowledge that promotion is reasonably assured can improve morale throughout the entire organisation. Promotion follows logically from training, performance appraisal, management development and management by objectives programmes. People can be selected for promotion directly, management simply appointing chosen employees to higher posts, or vacancies can be advertised within the firm. Direct selection is quick, inexpensive, and suitable where management knows the abilities of all its subordinates. Internal advertisement is appropriate in large firms where several candidates of about the same level of ability might apply.

Activity

How would you describe the promotion policy of your firm; ability-related or seniority based, favouring internal or external candidates?

Whatever the policy, it must be seen to be fair, objective and consistent. There will always be those who feel disgruntled and hard done by at being passed over for promotion, but you must be able to justify your decision if challenged.

Unfair discrimination in promotion upsets and demotivates staff and should always be avoided. Promotion should never be denied on grounds of race or sex. Indeed, discrimination in selection for promotion on these grounds is illegal under existing sex and race discrimination legislation. The Equal Opportunities Commission Code of Practice on avoidance of sex discrimination recommends (paras 25(c) and (d)) that promotion procedures be thoroughly examined to ensure that traditional qualifications are actually relevant to the job under consideration. It suggests, moreover, that promotion based on length of service could amount to unlawful indirect discrimination since women typically have shorter lengths of service through time out of the labour force taken for child-raising responsibilities. Where 'general ability and personal qualities' are the main requirements for promotion the Code insists that care be taken 'to consider favourably candidates of both sexes with differing career patterns and general experience'.

Organisations that operate in sensitive multicultural or multi-ethnic environments sometimes monitor the consequences of their promotion policies by checking whether certain groups are over represented among those who do not achieve promotion. Hence, if it is found that females, ethnic minorities or certain religious groups are prominent in the non-promoted category the reasons for this are isolated and remedial measures applied. Specifically, the following questions can be asked of the promotion system:

- what are the characteristics of non-promoted groups, and are there valid reasons explaining why individuals in these groups are not promoted?
- what contributions have non-promoted groups made to the work of the firm? Have they been adequately rewarded for their contributions?
- why do non-promoted individuals remain with the firm?
- what help can be given to non-promoted groups in order to help them qualify for promotion? What are the obstacles confronting non-promoted categories, and how can they be rewarded?
- what can management itself do to improve its knowledge of the backgrounds and difficulties experienced by non-promoted groups? How does management feel about these people?

Activity

What is your own attitude towards positive discrimination?

An analysis of those holding management positions within organisations frequently shows an under-representation of certain groups in society, ie women, disabled persons and ethnic minorities.

Positive discrimination, whereby preference is given to these groups, is seen by some as a means of rectifying the imbalance. Such a policy is fraught with problems as you may not appoint the most capable candidate and this can lead to resentment among staff.

A non-discriminatory promotion policy has numerous benefits: internal personal relationships between managers and subordinates improve, labour turnover falls (since able staff do not need to leave the firm to do higher level work) while efficiency should increase through utilisation in senior positions of the accumulated experience of long-serving employees. Additionally, there is little risk of the individuals promoted possessing unknown deficiencies, as occurs with externally recruited senior staff. On the other hand, outsiders can inject fresh ideas and apply new perspectives to existing problems, and external recruits might be of much higher calibre than internal candidates.

If you are called upon to recommend subordinates for promotion you should adhere to certain principles in making your selection. Do not overlook a suitable candidate simply because that person is performing excellently in his or her present job. It is unfair to block an individual's prospects simply because, through their hard work and personal competence, they have become indispensible in their current positions. In general, avoid promoting people who have only recently joined the firm. And always stand ready to justify your recommendations to subordinates, including those you feel are not yet ready for promotion.

Activity

Have you still got the list giving reasons why people work that you compiled in an earlier activity?
Would you modify it in any way?

Now try to identify the needs that you satisfy through work and put them into a hierarchy of importance. (This may prove difficult but try it anyway.)

Summary

You have been introduced to some of the theories of motivation and will appreciate that there can be no absolute answer to the question why do people work.

You will have your own views on how to get the best out of people but do not reject the ideas of others without first giving them some consideration.

Observe the people around you at work, particularly your subordinates, and try to keep a note of how they respond to different motivation techniques.

Several academics have made important contributions to motivation theory. Their work is described in an appendix at the end of the book.

Notes

1 Mintzberg, H, *The Structuring of Organisations*, Prentice-Hall, 1979.

4

Managing a Team

Objectives

At the end of this chapter you will be able to:

- define what is meant by a group and a team
- recognise the importance to individuals of belonging to a group
- distinguish between formal and informal groups
- operate as an effective team leader
- handle conflict situations.

Work is a social activity; few people work entirely alone. Groups emerge within work organisations through the specialisation of functions, through the creation of teams to handle projects or naturally in order to satisfy a social need. Groups may be formally established by management or they might arise informally and spontaneously among the workers. Formal groups are set up to perform specific tasks: decision taking, project completion, problem solving, communication and so on. The key issue with formal groups is how best to direct, control and coordinate their activities. Should management impose highly structured group processes, with explicit and rigid roles and conventions or should the group itself be made responsible for its internal organisation? Informal groups result simply from people intermingling in working situations. Workers establish customs and social relations among themselves; patterns of behaviour are constituted, informal rules, relations and working methods not shown in organisation charts or official staff manuals become entrenched.

Activity

You are aware of the difference between formal and informal groups. Consider your own department for a moment. How many formal groups can you identify? Are there any informal groups? If so, do the informal groups conflict in any way with work of the department?

We will return to the difficulties that arise when informal groups seem to work against the formal groups later in the chapter.

Roles

The concept of 'role' is crucially important for a person's self-perception of his or her occupational status and of the value of a job in comparison with those of others. Role theory concerns how individuals behave, how they feel they *ought* to behave and how they believe other people should respond to their actions. A role is a total and self-contained pattern of behaviour typical of a person who occupies a social position. Accordingly, people occupy many roles during the course of their lives — as husbands or wives, mother or father figures, as 'office boys' (or girls), supervisors, senior managers etc. Individual interpretations of roles within a group define the pattern of group interrelations, perhaps even the group's entire structure and organisation.

Associated with each role is a set of standards and norms of conduct that the role occupant (and others) expect from holders of the position. A supervisor, for example, might be expected to behave, perhaps even to dress and speak, in a certain manner. The term *role category* describes a complete class of persons occupying a particular social position ('leader', 'old person', 'mother', 'senior executive', etc). Role expectations are then attached to the role category. A role expectation differs from a social norm in that whereas a norm (ie a behavioural expectation common to all group members against which the appropriateness of individual feelings, conduct and performance may be assessed) applies to *everyone* in a group, a role expectation is specific to the individual.

People expect they will behave in a certain manner in a particular situation, and typically possess definite expectations concerning the conduct of others. Such expectations are important because they guide individual actions. For example, colleagues who have worked together for several years usually possess efficient, smoothly functioning relationships because they know exactly how their workmates are likely to behave — each person anticipates the other's reactions to various situations and then adapts his or her own behaviour in appropriate ways.

A self-perceived employment role might involve a certain appearance (for example, senior managers may want to dress differently to their subordinates, to 'look the part'), or a particular manner or means of expression (accent, intonation, style of language, etc) may be required. Manifestations of a role (such as a certain mode of dress) provide information to others about how they should act towards the role occupant. Such external signals provoke definite attitudes concerning how others inwardly feel they ought to behave in interactions with that person.

Through experience, individuals eventually form role categories into which people of the various occupational classes they encounter may be placed. A supervisor, for instance, may be expected to behave in an authoritarian manner, regardless of that person's personality, background or general approach to management affairs. These categorisations simplify social interrelationships, since it is not then necessary to analyse every situation the individual meets. Rather, the person merely assumes a certain mode of behaviour in the other party, using this preassumption to guide his or her her reactions to events.

Role set

The occupant of one role category (a supervisor for example) will have relations with a variety of *role partners*, eg the relations between manager and subordinates, parents and children, teacher and students etc. The totality of relations with

---

Self-check

How would you define role theory? What are the implications of role theory for the workplace?

Answer
Role theory is concerned with how individuals behave, their perception of how they ought to behave and how other people should respond to their actions.

We tend to associate a certain mode of behaviour with a specific role. We often expect people in authority to dress and act in a particular way. Therefore, if we are put in a position of authority, we will act accordingly. If an individual does not adopt the expected standards of behaviour, fellow workers find this very confusing and do not know how to respond.

---

the role partners of a person in a role category is called that person's *role set*. Other important role theory concepts are outlined below.

Role behaviour

A person's actual behaviour in a role may or may not conform to expectations. Behaviour in fact may deviate significantly from expectations or be quite irrelevant to the role. Thus, for example, a manager might be an extremely bad organiser and/or spend much time on non-productive, highly personal activities. Ideally, individual perceptions of 'correct' behaviour will correspond to senior management's views of what the person ought to be doing and thinking about the role. Sometimes, however, the perceptions of the individual and the organisation differ, possibly resulting in *role strain*.

Role strain

This (sometimes referred to as *role conflict*) occurs when the individual does not behave in accordance with expectations attached to a role because to do so would place too great a strain on that person. The role occupant may experience difficulties in meeting its expectations, or might encounter expectations which conflict — consider for instance the supervisor whose subordinates expect him or her to represent them to senior management but whose own superiors expect the supervisor to implement all management decisions regardless of their industrial relations effects.

The person who cannot live up to role expectations may experience feelings of inadequacy, embarrassment and guilt. Interactions with others become difficult and could eventually collapse.

Role ambiguity

An individual might be unclear about the exact nature of his or her role, the more explicit and specific the expectations attached to a role, the easier it is to conform to role requirements. Ambiguity in a role can cause stress, insecurity and loss of self-confidence. Newly-appointed heads of department, for example, might not be entirely clear about how much authority they possess.

Role bargaining

When an individual cannot possibly fulfil all the obligations associated with a role, he or she might seek to redefine the role's boundaries. This could involve either a direct appeal to other parties to alter their expectations, or the role occupant establishing a distinct set of priorities regarding role relationships.

Serious problems can occur when role occupants and others disagree fundamentally about the expectations of a role, ie about what is included in the role, the range of acceptable behaviour, whether a certain behaviour pattern is voluntary or mandatory and (importantly) which role obligations should assume priority. In setting role priorities, the individual may adopt any one of several means of approach. He or she might select for priority those role behaviours which:

● correspond to that person's perceptions of moral worth
● are expedient
● bring the greatest personal reward and/or avoid personal cost
● avoid controversy or unpleasant relationships with people the individual particularly respects.

Self-check

What factors might lead to an individual experiencing stress?

Answer
Where an individual cannot comply with the standard of behaviour expected of them. The individual feels under pressure to comply with the expectations of superiors and subordinates.

Where too much is expected of the individual in terms of what one is expected to achieve.

Where the nature of the role is ambiguous, leaving the individual unsure as to what action to take.

Groups

Whereas formal groups are deliberately constituted by management, informal groups develop without assistance or support. In a formal group, management selects members, leaders and methods of doing work. The group may be defined with respect to a task, function, status within the managerial hierarchy (such as members of the Board of Directors) or length of service with the firm (long serving employees might receive privileges not available to others and hence constitute an identifiable group). Formal groups are characterised by a high degree of managerial involvement in coordinating, controlling, and defining the nature of the activities they undertake.

Informal groups can form without management support. They are established by people who feel they possess a common interest. Members organise themselves and develop a sense of affinity to each other and a common cause. Often, it is an informal group that actually determines working methods and the quantity of work done. Hopefully, the aims of the informal groups that spring up within an organisation will correspond to the organisation's objectives, but they might not. Indeed, informal groups could form to oppose the wishes of management. A sensible management will thus recognise the importance of informal groups for organisational efficiency or their potential for disrupting organisational plans.

A further important distinction is between primary groups and secondary groups. A primary group consists of members who come into direct face to face contact with each other. Secondary groups are larger, less personal and lack immediate direct contact between members. Examples of primary groups are small departments within a firm, project teams, families, sports teams or other direct contact recreational associations. Membership of such a group often provides social and psychological support during times of stress. Secondary groups might be factories, communities, long assembly lines where workers do not come into contact with each other or geographical divisions of a company. These groups will be less solid and cohesive than primary groups, though interactions between members will still occur. Within primary groups, communications are rapid and direct.

Self-check

Why is it important for management to recognise the influence that informal groups can exercise?

Answer
Unlike formal groups, informal groups are formed voluntarily, often because the members share a common interest. They have the potential to act for or against the objectives of the organisation and management ignores such groups at their peril.

As you read on you will see the extent to which informal groups can influence standards of behaviour, working methods, output etc.

Group norms

Membership of a group helps a person interpret everyday events, identify his or her role in an organisation and satisfy social needs for involvement with others. The group supports and reinforces the individual's view of the outside world and this greatly encourages conformity to 'group norms'. A group norm is a shared perception of how things should be done or a common attitude, feeling or belief. Norms will exist about working methods, about how much work should be done (and how enthusiastically), about the quality of output, relations with management (and trade unions), how various people should be addressed and treated etc. Norms are particularly important in determining workers' attitudes towards change, since norms can create or overcome resistance to new ideas and working methods.

As norms emerge, individuals start to behave according to how they feel other group members expect them to behave. Initially, entrants to an existing group feel isolated and insecure and hence will actively seek out established norms to guide them on how they ought to behave. Norms facilitate the integration of an individual within the group and thus will be eagerly accepted by new members. They are soon internalised into entrants' personal value systems and help bind individuals to groups. In consequence, groups are often resistant to change. Members become set in their ways and attitudes and come to believe that the group norm is always correct, no matter what the circumstances. Any deviation from a norm has to be explained and justified by the individual to other members and if the deviation is not accepted by the group the deviant member is socially isolated.

Membership of a group provides individuals with companionship, social experience, opportunities for self-expression and social intercourse. Against these benefits, however, individuals must be prepared to modify their behaviour to fit in with group norms. The greater the value the individual places in group membership the more he or she will want to conform. Feelings of attachment increase and the power of the group to compel obedience to established norms is enhanced. Eventually, group

---

Activity

Ask yourself the question: how has my behaviour been influenced by groups, be it in- or outside the workplace?

Humans are by nature social animals and the desire to belong is deep rooted. There can be few people who have not undertaken acts of bravado in order to gain acceptance by a group, albeit the childish action of ringing a doorbell and running away, or scrumping for apples.

behaviour settles down to a fixed routine. New entrants are expected to conform and to demonstrate their willingness to abide by group norms. The group can then continue to function despite changes of personnel.

Conflicts and contradictions within the group now begin to emerge, caused (for example) by:

- new technology which demands new working methods and/or new divisions of labour among group members
- members perceiving group objectives differently
- breakdowns in communications between group members
- personal disputes
- changing expectations of what might reasonably be demanded from membership of the group.

Such conflicts create the need for readjustments in internal group relations, including perhaps the introduction of new group norms.

Group cohesion

Group cohesiveness is the degree to which members are prepared to cooperate, content to work together and share common goals. High cohesion results in high productivity and morale. A cohesive group will support, in thought and action, the continuing existence of the group and its present activities. Cohesion encourages conformity to group norms and causes stable behaviour within groups, but the increased pressures for conformity can stifle initiative. Several factors contribute to the creation of group cohesion, including how often its members come into contact with each other, members' enthusiasm for group objectives and the exclusivity and/or homogeneity of members of the group. The more frequently and intimately the members interact the more they will perceive themselves as a distinct group. If membership is selective, members feel a sense of achievement in being admitted and to the extent that members share a common background, education, age, outlook, ethnic or social origin etc they will be like-minded and share common perspectives.

External environments can also affect group cohesion. An environment consists of a multitude of physical, technological and social circumstances. If individuals see their environment as hostile they will feel great affinity to any group offering protection from external threat. Other factors conducive to cohesion are as follows:

- how easily members can communicate within the group. Poor interpersonal communications will inhibit the emergence of a collective sense of purpose. Note that a group is more likely to be internally cohesive the less contact it has with other groups
- the nature of the task to be completed. Individuals engaged on identical or very similar work are more likely to see themselves as a group than others. Incentive schemes can encourage cohesion; a group that is able to reward or punish its own members can exert great pressure on individuals to conform.

Self-check

What benefits does group cohesion bring?

Answer
— High staff morale and willingness to work together towards common goals
— Recognised and stable standards of work and behaviour
— Loyalty to the group and supportive atmosphere.

Cohesion is a most attractive feature in a working group, causing high morale, strong interpersonal relations and reinforcement of individual perceptions. The activities of a cohesive group are easy to coordinate since the group itself will monitor the efficiency of its operations. Members are encouraged to work hard in support of the group and may derive great satisfaction, even excitement, in so doing. Unfortunately, such enthusiasm might be directed against management, since powerful informal groups can arise to oppose management's wishes. Moreover, high group cohesion need not be associated with high productivity, low absenteeism and labour turnover, enthusiasm for work and other desirable characteristics, but rather the reverse. Cohesive groups might conspire to restrict output, perhaps even to disrupt the organisation's work.

Power and authority

Formal groups have appointed leaders. Informal groups have leaders who emerge naturally from the ranks of the group. Within a formal group, an unofficial leader might arise and function in parallel with the appointed leader. Unofficial leaders are important and their influence is sometimes formally recognised (for instance through the unofficial leader becoming a departmental shop steward). They exercise authority, albeit intermittently, but have no formal power as such. Formal leaders offer stability (appointed leaders are permanent, they remain despite changes in the structure of the group) and a focus for group identity. Usually, they can impose formal rules on individual members. Supervisors, for example, might be empowered to select individuals for better paid tasks, to recommend workers for promotion and might be authorised to suspend or dismiss subordinates. Often, leaders are appointed on the basis of their expertise in a function corresponding to that for which the group was formed. A typing pool supervisor, for example, is often a highly skilled and experienced typist. The chairperson of a problem solving committee typically has particular ability in the technical aspects of the problem area. Official leaders are responsible for communicating with other groups and for expressing the collective opinions of the group. In practice, however, unofficial leaders are frequently the people who actually direct and motivate others.

There are important differences between authority, influence and effective power. Influence is the effect of one person on the behaviour of others. It may be exercised by either formal or informal leaders and can operate through suggestion, persuasion, example or threat of sanctions. Authority is the *right* to control. In a supervisory context this might involve the determination of subordinates' workloads, taking decisions on behalf of the group, giving orders, possibly recommending pay rises or initiating disciplinary action. Formal authority is often accompanied by outward displays of status: different clothing (such as managers wearing suits while operatives wear overalls), separate canteens, different modes of speech and behaviour. These may even differ for each of several levels of authority within the managerial hierarchy. Lower ranks are expected to treat superiors with deference and respect. There is a clear system of command, coordination and control.

Power, in contrast, is a quality that other people *perceive* an individual to possess, giving that person the ability to influence the actions of others. An employee might have low occupational status and occupy no formal leadership role yet still exert enormous power within the organisation. Appointed leaders may or may not be powerful, depending on the following factors:

- their ability to coerce others into obedience through threats of punitive action
- personal charisma
- group members' willingness to accept the directions of appointed leaders
- the extent to which group members identify with the values of appointed leaders
- appointed leaders' abilities to satisfy group members' needs
- whether group members perceive appointed leaders to possess expert knowledge about the activities on which groups are engaged
- the extent to which members feel that a formal leadership position is legitimate, say because of seniority within the group
- control over information, resources and access to higher levels of formal authority.

Group activities inevitably change over time. It follows that those members who are able to understand, interpret and accommodate change will become powerful in the eyes of the rest of the group. Note how it is possible for powerful people, because of their ability to affect the behaviour of others, to act in innovative ways and initiate change.

Group members who possess much power but little formal authority are fortunate in that they do not have to take the blame when things go wrong. Appointed leaders, however, have to accept the consequences of their actions. If they make bad

Self check

Distinguish between power, authority and influence.

Answer
Authority is the right to control and make decisions. It is vested in an individual by a higher authority and is associated with the position held.

Influence is the ability of an individual to affect the behaviour of others and may stem from one's formal status or from one's personality.

Power is a quality that other people perceive an individual to possess. It may stem from one's personality or from one's position within the organisation.

decisions they are expected to pay. In consequence, official group leaders are often reluctant to take crucial decisions, either passing difficult problems upwards to higher management or ignoring them in the hope that other group members (those with power) will quietly sort them out. Responsibility, then, is a constraint on the exercise of authority, and might restrain the exercise of power.

Organisational culture

How groups form — their norms, working practices and patterns of interaction — depends in part on the culture of the organisation (sometimes referred to as *organisational climate*) consisting of its customary ways of doing things and its members' shared perceptions of issues affecting the organisation. A firm's culture evolves gradually, and employees may not even be aware that it exists. Organisational culture is important, however, because it helps define how workers feel about their jobs. A culture will have arisen within a specific environmental context and be related to particular organisational needs. The problem is that an organisation's needs and activities alter, while its underlying culture remains. Culture involves common assumptions about how work should be performed and about appropriate objectives for the organisation, for departments within it and for individual employees.

Charles Handy[1] distinguishes between four types of culture: power, role, task and person. One of these might dominate the entire organisation, or different cultures may exist in various parts of the firm. The *power culture* stems from a single central source, as in a small business that has begun to expand. Here, there are few rules and procedures and few committees. All important decisions are taken by a handful of people and precedents are followed. A *role culture*, in contrast, is highly bureaucratic. It operates through formal roles and procedures and there are clearly defined rules for settling disputes. Organisations dominated by a role culture offer security and predictability but, since they are rigidly structured, cannot adapt quickly to accommodate change (as can a power culture organisation). The *task culture* is job or project orientated and manifest in matrix organisation structures. There is no single dominant leader; all group members concentrate on completing the collective task. A task culture will encourage flexibility in approach and is ideal for an environment of change. Job satisfaction is high and there is much group cohesion. However, relationships are complex and control is difficult. A *person culture* might arise in an organisation which exists only to serve the people within it. Examples are partnerships, consultancy firms and professional organisations.

According to Handy, none of these cultures is better than the others. A culture arises, he argues, from historical circumstance, the existing environment, technology and the human needs of people within the organisation.

Activity

Analyse your own organisation. To which of Charles Handy's four cultures does it correspond?

Remember, there is no one best culture. However, by identifying the culture of the organisation, you may be able to explain how it is run.

Group structures

Well-constructed groups can greatly enhance employee commitment, job satisfaction and sense of purpose. Specialised skills
develop within groups; members collaborate, liaise, offer help
and advice to others and generally interact through their work.
Note, however, that working in groups is not always more
efficient than working alone. Frequent disturbances from colleagues and the need to consult before taking action can retard
progress and constantly irritate the individual worker. You need
therefore to seek ways of making group work enjoyable and
able to fulfil individual members' social needs. In particular, you
must prevent informal groups from taking over the functions
that official (management created) groups should undertake.

When creating groups (eg through establishing project teams
to achieve particular objectives) try to keep group sizes reasonably small. Groups of more than a dozen people require
extensive supervision and internal communications become
difficult. Much time is spent coordinating group activities and
decision taking is slow. Large groups encourage the emergence
of sub-groups and factions differentiated in terms of status,
length of service, opinions on social and work issues etc.

PARTICIPAT Encourage joint decision-taking within groups. Participation
improves morale and stimulates cooperation; it facilitates the
flow of information through the group and the emergence of
new ideas. Reassure group members that their contributions will
be taken seriously and that they are free to express opinions. Of
course, complex problems require careful and detailed analysis
and not all the group members will be capable of understanding
the issues involved. In this case you (or the group leader to
whom you have delegated official command of a subunit) should
inform all the group members of the nature of the difficulties
and how those members selected to handle these complex
CLEAR problems intend tackling them.
GOALS Define group objectives clearly and precisely. Members should
see the point of what they are doing and how it fits in with wider
organisational goals. Sound leadership is essential. As an
appointed group leader you have to motivate, direct, set
standards and monitor subordinates' performances. You allocate work to members, clarify issues and explain what needs to

be done, settle disputes among members, resolve grievances and generally keep the peace. A particularly important leadership role is that of introducing new members to the norms of the group. Newcomers, initially, feel anxious about their status and look to whoever they perceive as the group leader for clues regarding how they should behave. At first, formal rules will be followed to the letter, even if personal identities are sacrificed in the process. Then, as newcomers are gradually absorbed into the group, they learn to manipulate its conventions. They come to terms with other members and begin to assert their independence.

Groups function more efficiently if their leadership can be easily transferred. Critical dependence on a single person leads to the total collapse of the group when its leader resigns. Ensure, therefore, that someone is trained and ready to take over your group should you be transferred, promoted, temporarily absent or leave the firm.

Self-check

List the duties performed by a group leader.

Answer

Duties are likely to include allocation of work, motivation, monitoring results, settling disputes and grievances. The group should look to its leader for guidance, but should not be so dependent on the individual that it will cease to function, should the leader be absent for any reason.

Working groups can adopt one of three organisational structures: the hierarchy, the network, or the team. Hierarchies typically exhibit a pyramid form of authority and decision-making, with a distinct chain of command from the apex of the organisation to its base. There is a single group leader whose immediate subordinates themselves possess immediate subordinates through clearly defined spans of control. Each person is accountable only to his or her immediate superior in the hierarchy.

A *network*, in contrast, consists of a number of workers (or collections of workers, each with its own leader) who operate autonomously but nevertheless consciously seek to coordinate their activities. Members are jointly responsible for achieving the network's objectives, though each person takes independent decisions and there is no coherent chain of command. Rather, members are (usually) of equal rank and are accountable to a single central control. Networking is an increasingly popular form of business organisation, particularly when people prefer to work from home (computer software experts for example) and/or when highly specialised professional skills are involved.

A *team* is a special sort of group. All teams are groups, but groups do not necessarily behave as teams. The defining characteristic of a team is that its members cooperate and *voluntarily* coordinate their work in order to achieve group objectives. Team members are highly interdependent and each individual must to some extent interpret the nature of his or her particular role. Members feel especially upset, therefore, when they consider that a colleague has let them down, say by not doing a fair share of the work of the team. In a team, each person feels inwardly responsible for promoting the interests of the working group and personally accountable for its actions. Teams have leaders who may or may not be appointed by an outside body (higher management for example), but the authority of the leader of a team, as distinct from any working group, is fully accepted by all its members. The team leader represents the group to the outside world and is formally answerable for its behaviour. Within a team there will be a high degree of group cohesion, much interaction, mutual support and shared perceptions of issues. Team members will be willing to interchange roles, share workloads and generally help each other out. Typically, each team member will hold other members in high regard and will experience much satisfaction from belonging to the team. A working group can develop into a team and vice versa, a team can lose its coherence and begin to operate as if it were a network (with each member working independently and in emotional isolation from other participants) or as a hierarchy within which individuals will not initiate activity unless they are instructed to do so by a direct superior.

Team spirit is obviously desirable in a working group. To foster team spirit you need consciously to implement a participative management style. Try to adopt the following rules:

or bad often depends on the context of the incident — it is bad to ignore paperwork that is essential for the efficient functioning of the team but good to discard superfluous paperwork that would interfere with more important work. Thus, you ought not to criticise a member for failing to respond to letters and memoranda until you know the full circumstances of the events.

Define precisely the behaviour you believe needs to be altered, and how exactly you would like it to change. List the things the person is currently doing that you would like him or her to stop and all the things the person is not doing that you wish he or she would do. Arrange an interview with the person concerned and during the interview approach the issue circumspectly, focusing your conversation on the *effects* of the undesirable behaviour on the efficiency of the team.

Activity

Imagine the following situation. You have become increasingly concerned about the conduct of one of your male subordinates. His punctuality and sickness record is poor and when he does come into the office his work is below standard both in quantity and quality. The other members of his group have been carrying him for several months and morale is beginning to suffer.

What action would you take?

It is essential that you get to the bottom of this problem before matters get any worse. Clearly you will have to gather the evidence and speak to the individual to establish the cause of his unacceptable behaviour. You may be able to agree a course of action with him. If he refuses to recognise he is at fault and will not mend his ways, you may have to move him to another post, or consider disciplinary action. We will be considering disciplinary procedures in chapter 9.

Leading a team

Morale within your team will be enhanced if you know each of its members personally. You should know their names, something about their backgrounds and what they expect to achieve through involvement with the group. Make it known that you welcome initiative, new ideas and independent attempts to solve problems. Consult regularly with individual members and be ready to alter working structures and arrangements following the consultations. Treat subordinates as individuals, be aware of their strengths, weaknesses and potential. Keep everyone informed of the progress of the team and ensure that each member's contribution is fully recognised.

Activity

How well do you know the members of the team you lead?

It is important to know people's names and their work backgrounds. It is especially difficult when you meet people for the first time and it can help to break the ice if you know a little about them. It may be worthwhile keeping a personal record of what you know about each team member.

Participative decision-taking is good for encouraging team spirit. In certain circumstances, however, participation in decisions is not feasible, eg when highly technical and/or specialised matters are involved, or decisions need to be taken so quickly that consultation with subordinates cannot occur. Having taken a decision in such circumstances do not merely impose it on the group, but try instead to persuade the group that you have made the correct choice. Otherwise, try to suggest (rather than impose) solutions to problems. Invite comment and alternative views on issues and seek consensus on a common approach. Make sure that everyone understands the team's decision making procedures and whether responsibility for decisions will rest with you as the appointed leader or, in the case of democratic decisions (based ultimately on votes), with the entire team.

Symptoms of poor teamwork are easily recognised: absenteeism, latecoming, high staff turnover, bad temper, depreciatory remarks about other team members and so on. Staff lose confidence in the team's ability to achieve its objectives, comment is interpreted as criticism, the quality of work declines, staff lack effort and petty grievances arise. When this happens, undertake a complete review of the objectives and activities of the team. Look at physical working conditions, wage levels and relativities, terms and conditions of employment (do the staff feel secure in their jobs, for example) and interpersonal relations within the group. Examine also the status of the group in the hierarchy of the total organisation. Has it sufficient resources? Does senior management appreciate the work the team performs and does management understand the problems it faces? Consider introducing job enrichment programmes and reassess the adequacy of your own leadership style, especially the extent to which you allow subordinates to participate in decisions and act independently.

Self-check

List the symptoms of poor teamwork.

Answer
Symptoms are likely to be similar to those indicating poor motivation. Quantity and quality of work are likely to be affected by poor teamwork but these are unlikely to be the first signs that something is wrong.

Earlier signs are likely to be bad temper among staff, frequent squabbles, absenteeism, poor punctuality and high labour turnover.

Handling conflict

Conflict has positive aspects: it spurs initiative, creates energy and stimulates new ideas. Unfortunately, it can also cause the misdirection of efforts against workmates instead of towards the achievement of the organisation's common goals. Try to analyse systematically the sources of conflicts you experience especially if they concern personal rather than organisational problems.

Usually, conflicts at work arise in one of two categories: conflicts between your function and those of others or conflicts with higher authority or subordinates. To resolve conflicts you might appeal to higher authority to impose solutions, compromise or (assuming you are empowered to do so) impose your own will. The latter encourages retaliation and discourages the free interchange of information and ideas. However, imposed solutions are frequently better than compromises (even if the solutions established are not popular) since compromises satisfy neither party to a dispute.

It is often easier to deal with conflicts between other people than those involving yourself. Third party disputes can be approached objectively and without presumptions and you are better able to identify symptoms of distress. Look for breakdowns in communication and unwarranted arguments between individuals for unnecessary, perhaps even harmful, competition between functions and for inflexible, insensitive attitudes towards other employees. Further indicators of impending conflict are people deliberately withholding information from each other, abuse of colleagues behind their backs, excessively formal relations between individuals and unwarranted criticism of the quality of other peoples' work.

In seeking to resolve conflicts between colleagues, relate their behaviour to the objectives of the teams to which they belong. Objectives provide solid criteria for decisions when arbitrating disputes. Clarify each person's formal role as specified in the firm's organisation chart or manual and offer interpretations of peoples' roles where opinions differ. Define job boundaries and ask each side to detail *why* they consider the other's behaviour

---

Activity

How do you handle conflict situations at work? Do you have a procedure that you follow or do you improvise?

Conflict situations can be creative or destructive. In the former case, conflict will stimulate new ideas and discussion, whereas in the latter it will involve malice and be disfunctional.

As a manager, you have to consider each situation on its merits and decide whether and when to intervene. When you do intervene, you must be seen to be fair and the use of a simple checklist may help you. You must identify who is involved, what happened and why. Any solution must tackle the root cause of the problem or it will re-appear at a later date. Ideally, the solution should be acceptable to all parties, but more importantly it must be fair and reasonable.

to be unreasonable. Initially you should speak to the disputants individually, but in so doing ask each party to suggest items for the agenda of a meeting to settle the dispute. Ask each side to empathise with the other's position.

Choosing a team structure

Suppose you wish to construct a team of five persons (including yourself as leader) and that you need to devise a pattern of communications between team members to ensure that work is efficiently expedited within the team. Consider the possible team configurations shown in figure 4.1.[2] You are identified in each structure as number 1; your subordinate colleagues are shown as numbers 2 to 5.

In the *circle* you deliberately restrict your personal communications to persons 2 and 3, who each have one other contact. However, 4 and 5 interact, so that work originating with 4 might reach you via 5 and so take longer to complete. The *chain* is similar, but 4 and 5 have unique responsibilities which do not overlap. Both the *wheel* and the *Y* structures make you a central coordinator, except that with the Y, person 5 channels work through 4 and not directly to you. On average, work travels furthest through the circle and through the minimum number of people in the wheel. Thus matters requiring several comments and opinions might best be dealt with through a circle structure whereas routine tasks might be more efficiently handled in a section modelled on the wheel. In the wheel, work can be directed from any given member to any other member in just two steps. Contrast this with the chain wherein a problem originated by 4 that requires the attention of 5 must go through four intermediaries. If you choose the wheel structure you can process work faster, provided you can guarantee to identify the parties who will be interested in each piece of work. Against this, however, is the fact that your span of control is wide and your colleagues do not interact when processing work. In consequence, problems might not be properly considered by appropriate personnel and there will be little cross-fertilisation of ideas. You need to balance speed of transmission of work against the desirability of the involvement of relatively more people.

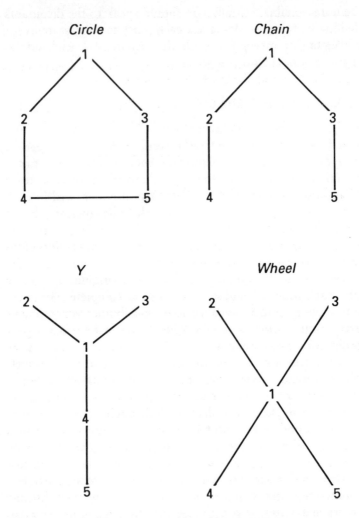

Figure 4.1 The possible configurations of team structures

You may, of course, devise further patterns of inter-action within each of the four basic structures, according to circumstances. In the circle, for example, 2 and 3 might need to interact or 3 and 5 might communicate directly in the wheel. Discuss the matter with colleagues and be prepared to experiment until you find the structure that best suits the needs of the team.

Activity

Four basic team structures have been outlined above. Examine you own team and decide which structure is the best fit.

You can see that each structure brings its own benefits and problems. It may be that a different team structure might suit your needs.

Working with a secretary

One vitally important but often neglected example of practical teamwork concerns the working relationship between boss and secretary. Depending on the nature of your work and the organisation of secretarial duties within the firm you might either have your own secretary working entirely within the department, or you might share a secretary with other managers in other departments. Whichever the case, your secretary is your communications link with the rest of the organisation and the outside business world and your working habits have to alter once you acquire a secretary. Two problems commonly arise: inappropriate structuring of secretaries' workloads and unwillingness to recognise the value of secretaries' contributions to the boss/secretary team — some managers with personal secretaries see them as appendages to themselves rather than as important employees in their own right.

Your secretary takes over much of your correspondence and effectively represents you to the outside world, thus creating your public image, an image that might be difficult to live up to and which possibly contradicts your own view of yourself. It is thus essential that you communicate well with each other and have a common understanding of how you will present your joint efforts to others. Together you must agree, perhaps tacitly, on the degree of formality of your relationship and about who will ultimately determine the style and layout of letters, reports and memoranda, bearing in mind that secretaries are invariably better qualified in these respects. Most importantly, you must agree about the way records are to be kept and the diary controlled within the office, and about which aspects of work the secretary is to be free to make independent decisions. Who for example will choose filing systems and other clerical procedures, determine the locations of desks, chairs and cabinets, the deployment of potted plants and so on?

Secretaries should perform those tasks they can do best, which today could involve acting as an information technology specialist, perhaps possessing a higher level of knowledge than the boss! Some supervisors resent this situation. It may not be easy to accept that the person who types letters, does the filing, etc is also capable of operating sophisticated business software that many supervisory managers cannot understand but without which they cannot work effectively. Bosses themselves now need to possess rudimentary keyboarding and software skills otherwise they are not able to function (eg by accessing computer stored data) when their secretaries are away.

Activity

If you have a secretary, what qualifications does this employee possess?

If you cannot list these qualifications, then try to get hold of the information, as without it you may not be making the most of the secretary's abilities.

Qualifications are likely to include shorthand, typing, word processing, office practice. Qualifications might include foreign languages, book-keeping, 'A' levels, degree, business studies, RSA Personal Assistant's Diploma, LCC Personal Secretarial Certificate.

More than ever before, boss and secretary need to work together as a team, which requires that both boss and secretary be able to make and take criticism without causing or perceiving offence. You must take your secretary into your confidence and provide all the information necessary to do the job effectively. It is easy to criticise whilst conveniently forgetting that you have not kept your secretary up-to-date with all the information available on the various projects with which you are involved. If you believe that a secretarial task should be completed in a certain way, then say so before it is finished. Standards should be established from the outset on both sides. If, for example, you are pedantic about the style of layout and typing accuracy of letters leaving the office it is unfair for you to imply that anything less than a high (predetermined) standard is acceptable, only to complain that work has not been completed according to specified standards when it is finished and presented for signature.

Always think twice before asking that work be repeated. Poor typing is a reasonable complaint, as is transcription that significantly alters the meaning of the text, but insistence that transcription *must* be word for word as dictated is unreasonable and unnecessary; it implies that the secretary does not have the ability to transcribe notes properly and/or is not competent to decide when a slight change in wording will improve the style of a document. People interpret tasks differently and so long as the end product is completed to a satisfactory standard within a reasonable time it is irrelevant and extremely annoying for either boss or secretary constantly to give opinions on the other's working methods. This does not mean that a secretary (or a boss) should never be criticised or that working methods should not be discussed, only that such conversations be planned and conducted dispassionately. The best time to do this is normally during periods set aside for dictation or for organising future work.

With the advent of word processing there has arisen a tendency for bosses to redraft work several times on the assumption that little effort is involved in retyping. This is a false assumption: files have to be found, programs loaded and points in the text needing amendment located. Further time is then absorbed in finishing the edit and printing the revised version. Yet in fact, the boss's retrospective feeling that a different wording might have improved the style of a document may have been little more than a passing fancy.

Too often, firms appoint overqualified secretaries to jobs that require only elementary office skills. Bosses frequently imagine there is a special prestige attached to employing a highly qualified person as a secretary, perhaps insisting that the secretary be a graduate and/or have high shorthand/typing speeds or speak several languages. Managers are attracted by

---

Self-check

Do you agree with the assumption that little effort is involved in retyping work since the advent of word processing?

Answer
If you agree with this statement, then perhaps you should gain some insight into how the word processor operates. Changes for changes' sake are a waste of everyone's time.

---

high qualifications in candidates for secretarial posts but fail to realise how bored a secretary possessing these high qualifications will feel when asked to perform unskilled clerical tasks. If highly qualified people are used as receptionist/coffee makers with little prospect of applying their knowledge they will quickly look for better jobs. Secretaries should not be appointed, therefore, until thorough job evaluation studies have been completed in the departments where they are to work and you should be realistic when recruiting secretarial staff. Ask yourself how you would react in a similar situation. Most bosses would not willingly remain long in positions bearing little relation to their job descriptions or which offered negligible opportunities for interesting work. When recruiting a secretary, seriously consider the precise role you wish the secretary to play and the skills levels and knowledge actually needed to perform that role effectively. The aim should be to utilise the strengths of the secretary as well as the strengths of the boss, and to establish rapport and good communications between the two.

You and your secretary must negotiate the secretary's workload. Managers commonly fail to realise that in allocating work to a secretary they are, in effect, structuring their secretaries' working lives. Bosses typically have many contacts and work interests beyond the boss/secretary relationship, yet secretaries are entirely dependent on their bosses for work. A boss who, for example, gives a secretary large amounts of copy typing may not appreciate the intolerable consequences that hour after hour spent before a word processor or the tedium that long uninterrupted periods spent on humdrum work can create. Serious problems occur when bosses become so reliant on good secretaries that they are reluctant to recommend them for promotion. By doing the job well the secretary becomes indispensable and thus can only advance by leaving the organisation! This prospect can frustrate and distress the secretary to such an extent that current performance suffers. It is obviously reasonable that well-qualified secretaries should have career aspirations and view each job as a means of enhancing their experience. Thus you should never interfere with your secretary's promotion prospects — doing so will simply encourage the secretary to resign.

Activity

What duties does your secretary perform? Are there any further tasks that you could delegate, leaving you free to tackle more complex matters?

A good secretary can often act as a competent assistant to the boss, relieving the boss of routine matters.

An important consequence of the introduction of information technology to the modern office is that today many secretaries work for several bosses. There are obvious advantages to this situation: secretaries are given a greater variety of work, are fully employed, accumulate wider experience, are more likely to use advanced secretarial and other qualifications and the system overcomes the not uncommon problem of secretaries sometimes being hired for their looks and the prestige they bring to a boss rather than for their actual contributions — incompetent secretaries cannot survive long when they have to work for many bosses. Against the system is the difficulty of coordinating the secretary's work and the conflicts of loyalty to various bosses that the situation creates. A one-to-one relationship enables a sort of unwritten boss/secretary contract to exist, so that for example you might tolerate the secretary's occasional absence or frequent latecoming in return for the secretary's willingness to work overtime whenever required. Secretary and boss might take turns to make the tea (bosses should remember that secretaries' time can be just as valuable as theirs at crucial moments) and clear and precise criteria for delineating the

decisions the boss shall take from those to be taken by the secretary can be mutually agreed — it is unfair to expect a secretary to
take important decisions that should be taken by the boss, even if
the boss happens to be out when crucial decisions are required.

Secretaries should always be present when the division of
their work is debated, and it is essential that in many-boss
situations the various bosses delegate to the one secretary some
interesting as well as routine work. Patterns of authority and
accountability within the many person team must be defined
exactly — secretaries sometimes resent being directly super-
vised by even a single boss and find the experience of being
administered by several bosses completely intolerable, especially
when the secretary exercises discretion about how much of each
managers' workload to assume. Rules are needed to ensure that
conflicting instructions are not issued, and the several bosses
must jointly realise that secretaries are *entitled* to job satisfaction. Tasks need to be varied and secretarial jobs enriched (by
increasing the importance of decisions taken) and enlarged
(through extending the range of the secretary's activities).

Summary

Managing a team is one of the most important functions of
management, particularly at the supervisory level, where most
of the manager's time will be devoted to supervising people.

You have been presented with the theories on how to
structure a group and build team spirit, on how to become an
effective leader and handle conflict situations, but how can you,
as the practising manager, utilise this information?.

Try to study the groups that exist within your own organisation and examine how they function. Identify how you, as a
leader, can influence these groups. Examine the policies of your
organisation on questions such as management style.

Notes

1 Handy, C B, *Understanding Organisations*, Penguin, Harmondsworth,
  1976.
2 The psychological implications of these alternative structures are
  discussed in Sprott, W J H, *Human Groups*, Pelican, 1958.

5

Performance Appraisal

Objectives

This chapter will help you to:

- understand the objectives of a performance appraisal system
- complete the documents used in performance appraisals effectively and objectively
- assess the performance of individuals
- conduct performance appraisal interviews in accordance with good practice.

Performance appraisal (PA) is the analysis of employees' past successes and failures, and the assessment of their suitability for promotion or further training. Most large organisations now operate formal performance appraisal systems, and the practice has spread to smaller businesses.

Activity

Does your organisation have a performance appraisal system?

If so, obtain copies of any documents used and any guidelines issued. You will want to compare these with the examples quoted in the text.

It began as a corollary to management by objectives (MBO) systems; but today, numerous firms that do not operate MBO still have performance appraisal programmes. In PA, managers' opinions of subordinates' work are stated openly and officially and may be challenged. Managers frequently make ad hoc judgements about employees, but are loath to discuss the grounds on which they are based. Performance appraisal replaces casual assessment with formal, systematic procedures. Employees know they are being evaluated and are told the criteria that will be used in the course of the appraisal. Indeed, knowledge that an appraisal is soon to occur could motivate an employee into increased effort aimed at enhancing the outcome of the assessment. Other advantages of PA include the following:

- it generates useful information about employees and the true nature of their duties. Unknown skills and competencies might be uncovered. This data can be incorporated into the firm's human resource plan and hence assist in avoiding compulsory redundancies, in career and management succession planning and in identifying needs for training and staff development
- manager and subordinate are compelled to meet and discuss common work related problems. Appraisees become aware of what exactly is expected of them, and of their status in the eyes of higher authority. Since PA forces superior and subordinate jointly to investigate problems, it guarantees the participation of lower graded employees in matters that affect their working lives. Subordinates should be better motivated in consequence of such involvement
- PA monitors the feasibility of targets set in management by objectives programmes. Feedback to higher management on problems encountered when implementing policies occurs. It creates a cheap and effective early warning system within the organisation's management information structure. Fresh targets — discussed with and endorsed by subordinates — are established for the oncoming period
- known and rational criteria are instituted to determine pay and promotion decisions. This is important in view of the introduction of laws (discussed below) that prohibit unfair discrimination and the fact that under the Employment

Protection Act 1975, a worker who is dismissed because of an unfavourable appraisal may demand, via an industrial tribunal, the production of all documents, correspondence and written criteria relating to the assessment and subsequent dismissal.

Activity

Based on your own experience, what would you say are the benefits of having a formal performance appraisal system?

Appraisal of staff takes place in all organisations, but in those organisations without a formal system, the appraisee does not know the criteria for assessment, nor does he/she participate in the procedure. Most formal appraisal systems are open, in so far as the appraisee has access to most of the information and discusses the assessment with the appraiser.

However, many of the benefits hinge on the ability of the appraiser to assess the performance and qualities of the appraisee.

Appraisal reviews are usually categorised into three types: performance, potential and reward.

Performance reviews

These are historical in nature. They analyse periodically an employee's past activities with a view to improving future performance. A review will investigate the appraisee's personal strengths and weaknesses and seek to discover fresh opportunities for improving efficiency. Reasons behind successes or failures are discussed and the factors preventing better performance are identified. There are three major methods of appraisal: the free report, the checklist and the analysis of critical incidents. The first requires assessors generally to evaluate the employee's overall performance without going into detail over specific issues. It is appropriate where only a few people are to be appraised and all of them are well known to management. The appraiser writes what is in effect an essay about the subordinate, structured in form, length and using criteria selected by the appraiser. Alternatively, an outline structure may be imposed, with suggested headings for such things as technical competence, communications ability, willingness to cooperate with others etc to direct the appraiser's thoughts and comments. Although a request for a free report compels a supervisor to think seriously about a subordinate's qualities, and although the appraiser can concentrate on those aspects of the appraisee perceived to be most important to his or her work, difficulties remain:

- many managers have difficulty in translating thoughts about a subordinate into a formal written report — their English might be poor (causing them to fear being ridiculed for making grammatical errors) and they might have forgotten about important aspects of the subordinate's past performance
- free expression requires careful preparation, and much time will be spent on drafting the essay. Managers are busy people, and might leave undone or treat superficially this time consuming and troublesome activity
- the chosen criteria might be ill-defined or inappropriate, so that comparisons between the performances of one subordinate and others are impossible.

Self-check

List the benefits and problems associated with a free report as a method of assessing performance.

Answer

Benefits: appraiser is free to choose what details to include, how much to say, and how to express his or her views

Problems: time consuming, requires appraiser to be literate, no well established standard practices, and free reports may be confusing for the appraisee.

The second method requires the assessor to report on each of several characteristics mentioned on a predetermined checklist in respect of each subordinate. Headings for assessment could include: punctuality, reliability, enthusiasm, productivity, speed of work, accuracy of work and so on. Often, however, assessors rate nearly everyone as average for most categories. Thus, the system might insist that only a specified proportion of evaluations be placed in central categories. The scheme may require that assessors award scores from one to ten for each attribute or assessors might allocate workers to various grades of ability (for example: poor, below average, average, above average, outstanding). Alternatively, assessors may be asked to place a tick alongside one of a number of statements about the appraisee's ability in a certain area. For example, in evaluating an employee's 'initiative', assessors might select from the following range:

- always needs to be told what to do
- frequently asks for instructions
- requires supervision only occasionally
- rarely requires supervision
- never requires supervision
- offers new ideas, initiates activity.

Without doubt, a prepared list of headings associated with a rating scale that requires the manager merely to place a tick in a box enables appraisals to be undertaken quickly, cheaply and with a minimum of effort on the appraiser's part but the outcomes may not be satisfactory. Hasty completion of such documents might lead to carelessness and unfair assessments and the list of factors considered may not be relevant to the subordinate's work. A vast array of characteristics might be evaluated, yet only some of them should be considered. Office workers for example do not need to to physically strong. Possession of a post-graduate educational qualification is not essential for effective performance in mundane, repetitive assembly line jobs. Apart from the headings for assessment previously mentioned (productivity, accuracy, initiative, and so on), an appraisal form might ask the assessing manager to consider the following attributes and characteristics:

- knowledge, skills and/or formal educational qualifications acquired and/or utilised during the review period
- abilities to delegate, plan, supervise, establish priorities, assume responsibility, cope with stress, exercise leadership
- personal qualities: appearance, personality, disposition, enthusiasm, compatibility with colleagues, physical makeup (health and strength)

- critical faculties: creativity; judgemental, problem solving and decision taking abilities
- interpersonal skills: verbal and written communication, willingness to accept new ideas, relationships with superiors/subordinates/clients.

Activity

Study the example of a performance review checklist given below. How useful would you find such a document? What do you think of the ratings used?

This system is used by many organisations as it standardises information while keeping writing to the minimum.

If your organisation uses a similar system, it would be interesting to compare the two, in the context of format, areas assessed, definitions used etc.

Example 5.1 A simple performance review checklist.

Job Title: Office Junior
Appraiser: Secretary to Head of Department

Please complete this form by circling the letter or ticking the statement which you feel best describes the appraisee. Use the following system for deciding your appraisal.

A = Exceptional performance consistently well above the standard required.

B = Good performance that displays an overall level of efficiency which generally meets and sometimes exceeds the required standard for the job.

C = Satisfactory performance, associated with an overall competence just sufficient to meet required standards.

D = Unsatisfactory performance which frequently fails to reach the necessary standard.

E = Poor performance that does not meet the standard expected.

1   *Technical Abilities (circle as appropriate)*
TYPING   A   B   C   D   E
CLERICAL DUTIES   A   B   C   D   E
(collating, filing, etc)

TELEPHONE MANNER (tick as appropriate)
  Always clear and polite   ———
  Usually clear and polite   ———
  Needs attention   ———

KNOWLEDGE OF SOFTWARE
  Fully comprehensive   ———
  Rarely asks for instructions   ———
  Sometimes needs help   ———
  Frequently needs help   ———

PERSONAL ORGANISATION
  Always well organised   ———
  Usually well organised   ———
  Sometimes confused   ———
  Unmethodical and disordered   ———

TIDYNESS   A   B   C   D   E

2 *Personal Qualities*
APPEARANCE
  Always neat and tidy   ———
  Usually neat and tidy   ———
  Needs attention   ———

PUNCTUALITY
  Invariably punctual   ———
  Usually on time   ———
  Occasionally late   ———
  Often late   ———

ATTITUDE TO WORK
  Enthusiastic   ———
  Satisfactory   ———
  Lacks effort   ———

INITIATIVE
  Requires very little supervision   ———
  Requires supervision only occasionally ———
  Sometimes needs to be told what to do ———
  Frequently needs to be told what to do ———

JOB KNOWLEDGE
  Fully comprehensive   ———
  Sound knowledge of most aspects of
  the job   ———
  Sometimes relies on others for information ———
  Knows only the basic elements   ———
  Unsatisfactory   ———

SPEED OF WORK   A B C D E

ACCURACY OF WORK   A B C D E

TRAINING UNDERTAKEN/NEW SKILLS ACQUIRED
      Specify details

DISPOSITION
      Copes easily with irate customers
      and stressful situations   ———
      Usually able to cope with
      difficult/stressful situations   ———
      Occasionally becomes irritable   ———
      Liable to fly off the handle   ———

ABILITY TO CONCENTRATE   A B C D E

RELIABILITY (DEPENDABILITY)   A B C D E

RELATIONSHIPS WITH SUPERIORS AND
COLLEAGUES
      Good   ———
      Satisfactory   ———
      Unsatisfactory (specify on a   ———
                   separate sheet)

INTERPERSONAL COMMUNICATIONS SKILLS
      Verbal
      Articulate and self-confident   ———
      Generally satisfactory   ———
      Needs attention   ———
      Written
      Good   ———
      Satisfactory   ———
      Needs attention   ———
      Cooperation
      Always works extremely well
      with other people   ———
      Normally co-operative   ———
      Can sometimes be difficult
      to work with   ———
      Uncooperative   ———

FURTHER COMMENTS
      Specify

These attempts to *quantify* employee characteristics are necessarily problematic. How for example can a subordinate's creativity be measured on a scale of 1 to 5? How, indeed, may creativity be defined in the first instance? The extremes, presumably, would be statements such as 'lacks new ideas' at one end, and 'produces many new ideas' at the other. But the *circumstances* in which new ideas are or are not created will not be included in the appraisal criteria. Numerous opportunities for appraiser bias exist and there is a strong tendency for appraisers always to select central ratings. Too much depends on the appraiser's interpretation of the various factors and of what the words fair, average or outstanding actually mean. Note, moreover, that since each appraisee is a unique individual, born and raised in a particular social, cultural and economic environment, then an appraiser's comments on one person's personal characteristics might not have meaning unless social factors are considered. Thus, for example, it would not be fair to classify (say) a black middle aged woman as someone who experiences difficulty in getting on with colleagues, while categorising a young white man as a good mixer if all the other employees in that section are young, white, racially prejudiced men.

Behaviour expectation scales

An interesting development in the checklist approach is the *behaviour expectation scale* sometimes referred to as the *behaviourally anchored rating scale* (BARS) which requires the assessor to select some aspect of a subordinate's behaviour that is considered indicative of his or her performance in a particular dimension of a job. For example, the superior of an employee being appraised under the heading *ability to cope with stress* would be asked to complete a form which begins with the words, 'I would expect this employee to behave in the following way:' followed by a list of statements from which the appraiser must choose. Among the statements might be:

- rarely exhibit symptoms of stress
- occasionally become frustrated
- show irritability when subordinates underperform

- act erratically under stress
- fly off the handle when provoked

and so on. Associated with each statement is a certain number of points indicating the relative desirability of the indicated behaviour, so that 'occasional frustration' might score three points, while 'flying off the handle' (which is much worse) scores seven. These scale values are said to be *anchored* against the typical employee behaviour that each statement represents.

BARS systems are complex, time consuming and difficult to administer. Specific problems include the following:

- selection of the categories of behaviour (called 'performance dimensions') deemed sufficiently relevant to the job to warrant assessment
- specification of examples of good and bad behaviour within a category
- deciding how many points to allocate to each example of behaviour (ie 'anchoring' scale points against appropriate descriptions of expected behaviour).

Checklist methods require much careful preparation and are expensive to administer. The third of the basic techniques is cheaper and simpler. It involves supervisors reporting and analysing critical incidents that have occurred in the course of an employee's work during the review period. Specific cases of outstandingly good or bad performance are isolated and discussed. This method tends to ignore the worker's overall average performance, since recent events may be overemphasised. Also, employees might feel they are continually being spied on by management. Note that under this system workers' supervisors assume additional authority over them because they have the power to overlook or record specific incidents.

The appraiser is forced to isolate and report significant aspects of the subordinate's work. In order to encourage superiors not to consider only the appraisee's performance immediately preceding the review, some critical incident schemes demand that appraisees report just two incidents from the review period: an example of outstandingly good performance, and one of outstandingly bad. *Causes* of the incidents and the roles of other employees in them are discussed in detail during the appraisal interview. Frequent occurrence of negative incidents could mean incompetence, lack of training, poor motivation, that the subordinate does not fully understand what is expected from the job or that the employee has been let down by others. Analysis of these incidents, hopefully, will uncover key aspects of an employee's general performance, though it might not: critical incidents are scrutinised but the overall ability of the subordinate may not be properly assessed.

Self-check

How does the analysis of critical incidents differ from the free report and checklist approach to performance appraisal?

Answer
The critical incidents approach isolates the two extremes of performance, ie outstandingly good and bad. These incidents are analysed and used to establish the strengths and weaknesses of the individual. Unless detailed records are kept, there will be a tendency to concentrate on recent events. The problem of prejudice on the part of the appraiser has to be recognised.

Potential reviews

The purposes of a potential review are to predict whether an employee is capable of taking on more demanding work and the speed at which he or she is capable or advancing. Potential reviews are necessary to:

- inform workers of their future prospects
- enable the firm to draft a management succession scheme
- update training and recruitment programmes
- advise employees of what they must do to enhance their career prospects.

The task is to match employees' abilities and aspirations with the firm's forecast requirements for managerial staff. A fundamental problem here is the tendency of superiors to assess subordinates according to successes achieved in their current jobs, rather than on their potential for higher level work. Someone who performs quite adequately at one level of management might perform abysmally if promoted to a more senior post. Thus, employees may be promoted on the basis of their achievements in successive jobs to the point where they cease to be effective and by then they already occupy senior positions where their incompetence causes enormous disruption. Potential reviews should be conducted therefore by people who are capable to recognising in others aptitudes for higher management work. Further difficulties arise when selecting the criteria to be used in assessing potential. These criteria should relate to the job specifications of the positions to which those under review hope to succeed.

A negative outcome to a potential review may damage the morale of the employee criticised and for this reason some firms conduct such reviews in secret. On the other hand, knowledge of a negative outcome could stimulate the employee to greater efforts and activities aimed at remedying deficiencies. Also, if the firm's manpower plan does not envisage promotion opportunities for a certain employee it is really in the employee's own interests to be advised to seek alternative work.

Activity

Appraisal will include an assessment of an individual's potential and suitability for promotion. Should an appraisee have access to this part of the assessment?

Here one faces a dilemma. A poor assessment may well undermine an individual's self-confidence, while a good assessment may raise an individual's expectations. The latter is not a promise of promotion but may be viewed as such.

While an individual may not have direct access to this information, he/she should be made aware of its content and have the opportunity of discussing the implications.

Read on for some further ideas on the subject of disclosure of information.

Arguments in favour of secret, or 'closed' potential review procedures include the following:

- if the assessor communicates to a subordinate the fact that the assessment of his or her potential is favourable the assessor might (unwittingly) imply that promotion will actually occur. Such a commitment may be inappropriate, yet the subordinate now expects advancement and will be depressed if promotion is not forthcoming. The subordinate will expect management to take positive action to further his or her career, and will feel resentful when this does not happen
- equal opportunity legal considerations place enormous pressure on the manager to classify all subordinates as 'acceptable' or 'average' in all circumstances, since the criteria used in an open potential review leading to a promotion (or non-promotion) decision may be deemed unlawful by a court or tribunal. Secret reviews enable appraisers to express frankly their true thoughts about subordinates.

Arguments in favour of open, non-secretive, systems are that:

- society increasingly expects openness and freedom of information (note that from November 1987, any personal records held in a computerised system must, under the Data Protection Act 1984, be available for inspection by the person who is the subject of the data)
- personal relationships between superior and subordinate suffer when the superior's opinion of the subordinate's potential is not revealed. Subordinates will not speak out during appraisal interviews. Free discussion will be inhibited.

Self appraisal and peer group evaluation

Appraisal might be more useful to the subordinate and lead in the long term to greater efficiency if it is conducted either by that subordinate or by a colleague of equal rank without authority to impose sanctions. Such appraisals may analyse issues more critically than when subordinates fear the career consequences of admitting mistakes. Subordinates state, using any of the methods previously discussed, how *they* regard their performances, the adequacy of the training they have received, effects of alterations in job content, perceptions of key objectives and future aspirations. They identify their own strengths and account for their failures and weaknesses suggesting ways in which the firm might better use their talents, skills and recently acquired experiences. There are, of course, problems with self-appraisal, including the following:

- many people are quite incapable of analysing themselves. It is unusual for individuals to assess their own competence in other walks of life. At school, college and during the early stages of a career the individual becomes accustomed to being directed and evaluated by others. The transition from appraisee to self-assessor might require skilled and detailed guidance by someone already competent in appraisal techniques. Most appraisees in lower level positions will have received no training in self analysis or appraisal
- to the extent that appraisals form a basis for future career development, appraisees might overstate their successes while ignoring their failings.

On the other hand, employees are compelled to think carefully about the adequacy of their contributions, about barriers preventing improved performance, their futures and the quality of their relationships with higher levels of authority.

Self-check

What is meant by self-appraisal?

Answer
This is where the appraisee is asked to assess his/her performance, strengths and weaknesses, potential etc. The main objection raised against this approach is that the individual will tend to overstate his/her abilities. Based on experience of self-assessment as used on YTS schemes, this is not necessarily the case. The YTS trainees were reluctant to use extreme ratings, but favoured the middle ground.

Reward reviews

It is a well established principle that salary assessments should take place well after performance and potential reviews have been completed. There are two reasons for this:

- the purpose of a performance review is to seek ways of improving efficiency. If salary is discussed it inevitably dominates the conversation to the detriment of fresh ideas for enhancing productivity
- salary levels are determined in part by market forces and union pressures independent of employees' abilities. Also, it may be necessary to maintain wage parity between grades and departments. These factors need separate consideration.

Appraisal interviews

As a manager conducting appraisals, you need to do four things: *assess* the situation confronting each appraisee, *diagnose* his or her problems, *improve* the capacity of the subordinate to improve performance and *monitor* the success of the action plan which the two of you agree. You need to listen, talk and re-assure. Use the techniques of counselling (particularly empathy and non-possessive warmth) discussed in chapter 6. Exude a quiet confidence in your ability to help the appraisee.

Begin the interview with an outline of its purpose and of the assessment criteria the company has chosen to adopt. The discussion should be serious and free from outside interruption. Be friendly: do not threaten, bully or even hint of adverse consequences resulting from the subordinate's behaviour. After some non-controversial remarks designed to put the appraisee at ease, offer an opinion of how well you think he or she has performed during the review period, focusing on the most positive aspects of the subordinate's work. Then, having congratulated the subordinate on successes achieved, ask whether he or she has any thoughts about how performance might be improved. This, hopefully, will elicit from the subordinate a statement on the problems he or she has experienced without your needing directly to point out that person's inadequacies. If it does not, bring up the topic of poor performance indirectly, concentrating on the *issue* rather than his or her personal failings.

You should now be in a position to be able to diagnose the causes of underachievement. Do not mention at this stage the potential consequences of continuing poor performance. Instead, root out the histories of specific failures. Ask questions, look for signs of distress or frustration as the subordinate describes particular issues. Always emphasise that your role is to offer constructive support, not condemn or discipline. Give the subordinate lots of opportunities to ask for your help and guidance, to air grievances and discuss anxieties.

Self-check

What are the objectives of the appraisal interview?

Answer
Evaluate past performance and assess strengths and weaknesses.
   Agree how weaknesses might be overcome in the future and establish goals for the next period.
   The main thing to remember is that it is preferable for appraisees to identify problems and possible causes themselves, rather than be fed with information by the appraiser.

Relatively unstructured interviews are probably better for these purposes. The subordinate should be able to challenge the accuracy or relevance of the assessment criteria as well as the fairness of initial targets and even your objectivity as an assessor. Try to adhere to the following guidelines:

- apply identical criteria to the assessment of each employee in a particular grade. Avoid favouritism, bias and stereotyping (the creation of mental images of certain categories of people and the expectation that all members of these categories will be exactly the same)
- ensure that all information is available and use it all in your appraisal
- be as objective as you can in interpreting information. Unfortunately, managers sometimes interpret data in ways which lead them to conclusions they have already decided to make, seeing only what they want to see, hearing only what they want to hear. Equally, managers can underestimate the difficulty of things they personally find easy and they sometimes notice and magnify in others their own personal faults.

In an ideal world, more than one assessor would be involved in each appraisal interview. Different managers perceive issues and subordinates differently and joint assessment should lead to greater consistency in procedures. In practice, however, the overwhelming majority of appraisals are conducted by a single manager, normally the immediate superior of the person being appraised. Immediate superiors should be fully conversant with their subordinates' work. Note that the targets for future activities agreed during appraisal interviews might usefully form an integral part of a department's general action plan. It is essential therefore that the subordinate's future progress toward achieving these targets be monitored since unrealistically high targets initially set during performance appraisals will inevitably result in underachievement.

Appraisal interviewing is difficult. It often involves the discussion of personal matters and, during an interview, both the appraiser and appraisee are likely to adopt roles which differ from the roles they normally adopt. Often, people play psychological games during an appraisal interview. One powerful and increasingly popular mode of analysing role playing behaviour is the method of transactional analysis, introduced in the 1950's by the American psychiatrist E Berne.[1]

Activity

If you conduct appraisal interviews, spend a few minutes thinking about how you structure them. See if you can answer the following questions:

— how long do you allow for an appraisal interview
— where do you conduct the interview and how do you set out the furniture
— how long do you spend preparing for the interview
— do you plan what you propose to cover
— do you have all the relevant documents to hand, ie appraisal form, past reports?

An effective appraisal system can bring many benefits to an organisation, but only if staff are trained in the techniques to be used.

Transactional analysis

Transactional analysis is a means of understanding inter-personal behaviour and, ultimately, for changing it. The theory asserts that each individual possesses three distinct *ego states*, referred to as the parent, the adult and the child. All three exist simultaneously within the person, though any one of them may dominate the other two at a particular time. According to Berne, these ego states are patterns of feeling and behaviour, common to all normal people whatever their ages beyond three or four years old. The child ego state develops in early infancy, but its characteristics (feeling, wanting, playing and manipulating) remain within a person throughout life and will manifest themselves from time to time, even in a person 50 years old. The adult is the thinking and reasoning aspect of an individual's personality. It deals with facts and with the development of skills. As people mature, they develop a parent ego state which they learn from others. This concerns attitudes towards right and wrong and how to care for oneself and others. Normal people are able to activate a chosen ego state at any appropriate moment, and any one may be used in communications.

Self-check

What are the three ego states identified by Berne?

Answer

Child ego: feeling, wanting, manipulating
Adult ego: thinking, reasoning
Parent ego: attitudes to right and wrong, how to care for oneself and others

These states exist simultaneously within the person and any one of the three may dominate at a particular moment in time.

On beginning an appraisal interview the appraisee, regardless of age or occupational status, will find him or her self in a situation similar to the childhood experience of entering the headteacher's study when at school. Accordingly, the appraisee might behave now as he or she behaved then. The child ego state is activated so that the subordinate feels, acts and speaks like a child, impulsively, exhibiting great conformity and with great deference to authority. Furthermore, it is highly probable that immediately following the subordinate's adoption of a child ego state, the appraiser's parent ego state will automatically be brought into action. Hence, the subordinate *is* in fact treated like a child, while in response the subordinate begins to behave towards the appraiser as if that person really were a parent. In the parent ego state, the appraising manager will establish standards, control, motivate and exude authority.

The problem is that both sides are in fact living out a fantasy rather than facing up to the reality of the situation. Adoption of these ego states does not assist either side to analyse problems objectively or to overcome difficulties. For effective communications, both parties need to be in adult ego states during the interview, asking sensible questions, speaking as adults and perceiving each other as adults. In the adult ego state, individuals are rational, unemotional, calm and collected. Decisions are based on facts, not on emotional reactions to the child or parent ego state of the other side.

Self-check

What impact can transactional analysis have on appraisal interview techniques?

Answer
It may serve to explain the behaviour of appraiser and appraisee. Think back to your last appraisal interview. It is quite natural for the appraisee to be nervous and apprehensive, so much so that the individual may feel as though he or she is back at school. If the appraisee acts in a child-like way, there is a natural tendency for the appraiser to adopt the role of parent and act accordingly.

Essentially, transactional analysis is a means for categorising social interactions into predetermined categories. Morrison and O'Hearne[2] suggest nine such categories for management situations: four relating to parent ego states, four to child and one to the adult. Of the four parent ego states two, the authors suggest,

are acceptable and two unacceptable. The first of the unacceptable parent ego state categories relates to *hurtful criticism*, ie
putting down the other person in a manner deliberately intended
to highlight his or her deficiencies and/or attempting to make
subordinates look bad or feel inferior. The second involves
dependent nurture whereby the superior intentionally puts the
subordinate into a vulnerable and defensive state thus forcing
the subordinate to look to the superior for guidance and
decisions. An implication that the subordinate has insufficient
experience, inadequate academic qualifications or technical skill
to undertake certain responsibilities is an example. Acceptable
parent ego states are *helpful intervention* whereby the superior,
via constructive criticism, prevents a subordinate from doing
something that will damage that person (or colleagues, or
indeed the entire organisation) now or in the future, and *support
nurture* which actively encourages the subordinate to express
respect and concern for other people and their values and to
care for their colleagues. An example here is a supervisor
encouraging subordinates to support a firm's equal opportunities
program.

Similarly, two of the four child ego states have positive
aspects and two should be avoided. The first of the acceptable
child ego states is *natural enjoyment*, ie taking pleasure in the
company of others, being companiable and having free and easy
relationships with colleagues. The second might be termed
liberal conformism and is associated with the practice of
deliberately telling other people what they want to hear in order
to make relationships easier and more comfortable for everyone
involved in a situation. Of the two unacceptable child ego states,
one is *excessive conformity*, which is a slavish mentality that
actually induces other people to take advantage of, even
persecute, the person concerned. The other is *revenge* whereby
the individual deliberately creates disruption, analogous to a
child throwing a tantrum.

Transactional analysis is especially useful for analysing interpersonal communications because it extends to the transmission
of non-verbal communications, body language, facial expression, posture etc, and the manner of delivery of a verbal message
(tone of voice, vocabulary, accent adopted and so on) helps
identify a person's ego state at the moment the message is

Self-check

List the acceptable and unacceptable categories for both the parent ego state and child ego state.

Answer

Parent ego state: acceptable helpful intervention, support nurture; unacceptable hurtful criticism, dependent nurture

Child ego state: acceptable natural enjoyment, liberal conformism; unacceptable excessive conformity, revenge.

This may well be a difficult topic to grasp. You may find it useful to associate each category with an example.

---

delivered. As a technique, transactional analysis focuses exclusively on the interactions that occur within a relationship not with the circumstances surrounding the relationship. This is advantageous because you can consciously seek to use the technique to improve your communications skills in performance appraisal and many other situations through deliberately aiming at behaviour within the ninth category — the adult. Here you treat the other party as a rational, sensible person who will honestly relate his or her experiences and feelings in a sensible way. Your joint decisions will then be based on evidence and logic rather than emotion.

Another useful insight that transactional analysis provides is the idea that each individual confronted with a trying experience (such as a performance appraisal interview) requires a certain amount of personal recognition presented in quite specific forms. An act of recognition of someone else's value is called a *stroke* and may be positive or negative. A simple compliment is an example of a positive stroke. Negative strokes are intended to be hurtful (criticism of a subordinate's work for instance) yet certain individuals actually seek negative strokes from others! This is because such people have developed a view of themselves of being inadequate or otherwise undeserving. They then look for external verification of the bad self-image: they want others to confirm the unfavourable view of themselves they have created within their own minds. Additionally, many perfectly normal interactions with other people will be interpreted as negative strokes by these individuals. Different people demand differing amounts of recognition. Each person is unique in this respect and you should thus attempt to ascertain the degree of attention required by each of your subordinates.

Conditional strokes are rewards to a person for behaving in a manner that the strokegiver wishes. Thus, a compliment to a subordinate for having remedied a deficiency (frequent late-coming for instance) about which you previously complained is an example of a conditional stroke. Unconditional strokes on the other hand are presented to the individual person and are not specifically related to a particular act or mode of behaviour; they are expressions of appreciation of the total worth of the person and hence are extremely useful for starting an appraisal interview — they put the subordinate at ease and encourage his or her enthusiastic participation in what follows.

Although many interpersonal communications may be allocated straightaway to appropriate ego state categories, some transactions are not what the participants anticipate. A *complementary* transaction is one where the person who responds to an initiating action (a remark for example) in a manner that the other person expects. If you adopt a parent ego state when addressing a subordinate you expect that person to adopt a (complementary) child ego state in response. Conversely, a *crossed* transaction involves an unexpected and/or undesired reaction; for instance, when the initiating communication is of the parent variety and is met with a patronising and casually dismissive response. This might occur in the context of a disciplinary interview, for example, when there is basic disagreement about whether someone has actually done wrong. *Ulterior* transactions involve more than two ego states simultaneously and are often associated with symptoms of distress. They occur when someone is fundamentally unsure of his or her own position and how to relate to other people. Berne suggested that communications can be expected to proceed smoothly provided all the transactions are complementary.

Performance appraisal interviews should, therefore, be structured in a way that elicits adult responses from both parties. Informality is almost certainly the best way of achieving this,

Self-check

Give an example of each of the following:

Negative stroke
Conditional stroke
Crossed transaction

Answer

Negative stroke:	deliberate hurtful criticism
Conditional stroke:	praise given where an individual has overcome a problem identified at an earlier interview
Crossed transaction:	where the reaction of an individual is not what was expected

focusing initially on management's rather than the appraisee's inadequacies, in not specifying targets sufficiently precisely, not providing sufficient resources etc. Then environmental factors affecting performance might be discussed, leading up to consideration of particular aspects of the subordinate's performance and its consequences for the organisation as a whole. Any interview technique that causes the appraisee to assume a defensive position may trigger in that person the adoption of a child ego state to the detriment of the efficiency of the appraisal. Thus, the parties should already know and, if possible, trust and respect each other. The appraisee should be given plenty of time to prepare for the interview and its outline structure (in terms of topics for discussion) should be known in advance. Free discussion should be encouraged, avoiding argument but encouraging the subordinate to volunteer possible solutions to problems and openly express his or her personal hopes for the future.

Equal opportunities considerations

In assessing the performance of a subordinate, the appraiser will inevitably rely in part on subjective evaluations of the subordinate's personal worth. If, as a supervisor you are instructed to assess someone who reminds you of the secondhand car

---

Self-check

What benefits can transactional analysis bring?

Answer
Transactional analysis is a means of understanding human behaviour. Appraisal interviews work best where both parties involved act in an adult way, exchanging views and ideas. If one accepts the concept of transactional analysis, the appraiser can interpret the ego state of the appraisee by means of body language, responses etc. Indeed, the appraiser can create the environment whereby the appraisee feels relaxed, does not feel threatened and can respond on equal terms. The degree to which you can adopt this approach will depend on the degree to which you believe in its philosophy.

---

salesman who recently sold you a dodgy car or of the woman who last month borrowed £50 and never paid it back then you will take an instant dislike to the appraisee the moment he or she walks through the door. Our perception of another person depends crucially on our experiences of other people who exhibit similar characteristics as that individual or on images of that type of person which have been implanted in our minds. We organise information presented to us into preformed categories and we use predetermined criteria to distinguish good from bad. Often, opinions about someone else rest not on direct observation, but on hearsay and/or knowledge of who that person is and prejudices once formed are difficult to eradicate. An appraiser will possess a stereotyped perception of what the ideal occupant of a particular job should be like. A typical salesperson, accountant or personnel officer or whatever, will be expected to exhibit certain characteristics. A subordinate who does not fit into the stereotype might therefore be unfairly treated.

Consider for example the problems that might arise when a male appraiser, unsympathetic to the idea that women should be involved in management, evaluates a subordinate female manager. The male superior may bring to his assessments inappropriate interpretations of female characteristics, aptitudes, and managerial abilities. Traits identified as desirable in a man might be considered undesirable in a woman. Frequent loss of temper, for example, could be interpreted in a man as positive assertiveness, in a woman as inability to cope with stress. Male assessors might value in women certain characteristics: supportiveness, overt sexuality, maternalism, that are not only irrelevant to most management jobs but which influence men's interpretations of observed female behaviour. A man who believes that women possess innate strengths and weaknesses fundamentally different to those found in men may well apply double standards in his evaluations. If for example he considers women to be emotional he will tend to notice emotional aspects of a woman's behaviour while ignoring them in men.

Lack of confidence in a woman manager's career commitment may cause male appraisers to interpret femininity in manner as incompatible with suitability for senior posts, because femininity, according to this view, is associated with perceptions of innate female characteristics (excessive concern with domestic issues, questionable loyalty to the organisation) that make women inappropriate for top level management work. Consider in particular the checklist technique of performance appraisal with headings for qualities such as: initiative, decisiveness, enthusiasm, creativity, commitment, cooperation, consistency, self-confidence etc. A man who perceives women as supportive, sensitive, and good at human relations may assume (wrongly) that possession of these 'feminine' personality characteristics will necessarily affect a woman's possession of checklist factors. For instance, a man may assume that problem solving ability is directly related to personal assertiveness, or that sensitive, caring people (ie women) are not suitable for command. In consequence, women who are not 'feminine' will gain favour in the prejudiced male appraiser's eye. Obviously, a man who believes (perhaps unconsciously) that women are not suitable for senior management will be impressed by females who do not behave in feminine ways. The male superior will admire and promote those of his female subordinates who behave as if they were men, while steering 'female' females towards areas regarded as more suitable (ie less demanding) for women, eg personnel or welfare work, but which offer fewer opportunities for advancement through line management.

Women managers often complain moreover that male superiors

Activity

Take a minute to consider your own attitudes and judgements. Can you honestly say that you are without prejudice and that you do not stereotype people based on first observations?

Prejudice can take many forms, but once formed is often deep rooted and difficult to eradicate. Take the general attitude towards male nurses, female lorry drivers etc. We tend to stereotype people within the first few minutes of meeting them.

As a good manager you will try to guard against this when dealing with people and give fair, objective assessments. Legislation on equal opportunities will not alter attitudes overnight. It is a long, slow process of re-education.

---

sometimes alter their perceptions of female subordinates' activities to correspond with preconceived stereotypes of how women behave. In particular the 'softer' management styles adopted by many women can be interpreted in comparison with male workmates as unassertive and lacking initiative and without doubt the reserved, unobtrusive, approach to leadership (highly effective in some circumstances) has caused some women to be categorised as uncommunicative and introverted. Thus successes might wrongly be attributed to the influences of overtly visible male colleagues. Conversely, the modest, unassuming woman will find that she carries all the blame when things go wrong. Too often, male superiors see men's successes as due to innate ability while women's achievements are attributed to chance. Male superiors might perceive selectively aspects of female subordinates' behaviour that correspond with initial prejudices. A man who believes that certain undesirable traits, emotionality, inconsistency, illogicality, lack of commitment, are common in women will observe and record incidents in a woman's performance of her duties which confirm these suppositions while not noticing other incidents that contradict such preconceived views. Thus, women subordinates' actual behaviour seen through prejudiced eyes supports, even reinforces the original bias. Unfortunate events in a woman's career are recorded; occasional mishaps that happen to a man are ignored or; if serious, soon forgotten.

Further problems with performance appraisal

In a well known critique of the use of performance appraisal, Douglas McGregor[3] records the extreme reluctance with which many managers undertake their assessment responsibilities, preferring to treat subordinates as professional colleagues rather than as inferiors upon whom they are entitled to pass judgement. People, McGregor asserts, dislike 'playing God'. Typically, they are fully cognisant of their own biases and thus rightly seek to avoid situations where prejudice could arise. Subordinates may resent their personal qualities being commented upon, seeing the appraisal as a patronising exercise designed to humiliate or to punish past inadequacies in their work. Appraisal, moreover, requires concentration, diligence and competence in the appraiser. Training in appraisal techniques is required, followed by extensive guided experience in their practical application. In fact, few managers receive significant amounts of instruction in appraisal methods and even managers who are properly trained might not possess all the information needed to undertake fair appraisals. They may be out of touch with current working practices or be unfamiliar with environmental problems that interfere with subordinates' work.

Apart from managers mistrusting the fundamental worth of an appraisal scheme, they may also resent the extra work associated with its implementation. Thus, the appraisal process if seen as a ritualistic chore; to be completed as quickly as possible and in a manner that causes minimum repercussions.

Legal aspects

The Race Relations Act 1976, s 4 (2) states that it is unlawful to discriminate on racial grounds in appraisals of employee performance. Likewise, the Sex Discrimination Act 1975, s 6 (2) (a) makes it unlawful, unless the job is covered by an exception[4] to discriminate directly or indirectly on the grounds of sex or marriage in the way they *afford access to opportunities for promotion, transfer or training*.

Thus, a performance appraisal system could be deemed

Activity

Examine your own views on performance appraisal. Do you agree with McGregor?

Your views will be coloured by personal experiences. Any appraisal system is only as good as those who operate it. It is essential that appraisers receive adequate and regular training in the techniques of assessment and interview. How much training have you received and how useful was it?

Since appraisal takes place in some form or another, it is preferable to have a formal, open system, where the appraisee has access to the information, participates in the system and has the right to challenge incorrect or unfair assessments.

---

unlawful by an industrial tribunal, with consequent compensation to aggrieved parties and forced changes in the scheme. Both the Equal Opportunities Commission and the Commission for Racial Equality issue Codes of Practice covering these matters. A Code of Practice has no legal force in its own right, but a tribunal or higher court will examine closely whether and to what extent an employer has followed the provisions of the relevant Code when adjudicating a case, and the employer who has failed to adhere to a Code is in a much weaker position than one who has! The CRE Code (sec 1.19) recommends that staff responsible for performance appraisals should be *instructed* not to discriminate on racial grounds, and that assessment *criteria* be examined to ensure they are not unlawfully discriminatory. Similarly, the EOC Code of Practice (sec 25) requires:

- that not only should assessment criteria be examined, but also that performance appraisal schemes be regularly monitored to assess how they are working in equal opportunity terms
- that the eligibility criteria for access to training, promotion or other benefits be periodically reviewed to ensure there is no unlawful indirect discrimination
- specification of the relationship between performance appraisals and promotion, and investigation of reasons for exclusion from the appraisal system of any group of workers predominantly of one sex
- that when general ability and personal qualities are the main

requirements for promotion, care should be taken to consider favourably candidates of both sexes possessing different career patterns and general experience

- that policies and practices regarding selection for training and/or personal development should be examined for unlawful direct and indirect discrimination. Causes of imbalance in training between the sexes should be identified. Age limits for access to training and staff development should be questioned to ensure they are not unfairly discriminatory.

Activity

Try to get hold of copies of the Codes of Practice issued by the Equal Opportunities Commission and the Commission for Racial Equality. Study the content and assess the degree to which your appraisal system complies with the Codes.

Arguably, it is not appropriate for men to interpret and grade women managers' qualities of initiative, assertiveness, self-confidence, leadership ability etc because men and women sometimes approach these facets of personality in different ways and even a male manager who is not inherently biased may experience difficulty in empathising with the softer, more persuasive management styles that many women apply. Women appraisees moreover are often older than male colleagues of equivalent rank and their role as child-bearer will have resulted in career interruptions preventing them from undertaking formal management training and planned experience programmes at the same time as male contemporaries. These problems led the EOC to issue a Model Equal Opportunities Policy[5] which recognises the difficulties that can arise from male superiors ascribing particular personality traits to the criteria to be used in assessing a person's success in a managerial job. 'It is essential', the Model Policy states (sec 4(1)), 'that managers do not make pre-assumptions that individuals because of their sex possess characteristics that make them unsuitable for employment'. Among the many examples of inappropriate preconceptions quoted in this document are the assumptions that women:

- lack commitment
- have outside interests which would interfere with work
- are unable to supervise others
- possess limited career intentions
- are unwilling to undertake further training.

However, the Model Policy suggests few remedies for such mistaken ideas, stating (sec 5(9)) merely that staff should be 'encouraged' to discuss their career prospects with departmental heads and that written promotion procedures stating who is responsible for promotion decisions should be made available to all employees.

Summary

This chapter has tried to identify good practice in performance appraisal, and to give the reader insight into some aspects of human behaviour.

It is time for you to analyse your own organisation's attitude to performance appr isal.

If a system exists alr ady:

— examine how it operates, who is involved, how much training is given
— evaluate the documents used
— evaluate the interview techniques used
— ascertain the attitude of staff to the system; is it regarded as a waste of time, a meaningless ritual, biased etc
— based on what you have read, is there any way that the system might be improved?

If there is no system:

— has one ever been operated, and if so, why was it stopped
— how is the performance of staff assessed
— what is the attitude of staff towards a system being introduced
— what system might suit the needs of your organisation?

Notes

1 Berne, E, *Games People Play*, Penguin, London, 1964.
2 Morrison, J H, and O'Hearne, J J, *Practical Transactional Analysis in Management*, Addison-Wesley, Reading, Massachusetts, 1978.
3 McGregor, D, *An Uneasy Look at Performance Appraisal*, Harvard Business Review, Vol 35, No 3, 1957.
4 Certain jobs are exempt from sex discrimination legislation. Examples are employment (a) mainly or wholly outside Great Britain, (b) with a church that operates a sex bar, (c) in the armed services, or where sex is a 'genuine occupational qualification', eg actresses, jobs in single sex institutions, etc.
5 *An Equal Opportunity Policy*, Equal Opportunities Commission, Manchester. Revised version, October 1985.

6

Counselling

Objectives

This chapter will help you to:

- understand the benefits that counselling can bring to a modern business
- become an effective counsellor in the workplace.

Counselling is the process of helping people recognise their feelings about issues, define their problems, find solutions to problems, and/or resolve troublesome dilemmas. It is a difficult and exhausting function, yet one that few supervisory managers can, or indeed should, avoid. When asked to define the word *counselling* most people think first of the social and medical services, of a doctor/patient relationship, perhaps even of the psychiatrist's couch! Actually, counselling is a duty undertaken by anyone who has a working relationship with others in a helping capacity, and many supervisors do in fact counsel extensively without ever realising that this is the case. In counselling, you use your own personal experiences, knowledge and understanding — things you have already learned — to assist someone else to reach a decision, alter behaviour or learn to live with a situation. Think of all the supervisory management situations where the need for some form of counselling might arise.

Other counselling situations might arise when listening to grievances (directed perhaps as much against fellow employees

Activity

You have seen that counselling is a process of helping people to overcome problems, and that it can occur in the workplace.

In supervisory management, you are in the front line and your main function is to deal with people. Try to identify two different situations where you have undertaken some form of counselling.

It is highly likely that the situations you describe will involve personal problems which affect an individual's work. You may have been unable to resolve the personal problem yourself, but were able to refer the individual to specialist help.

Study the examples outlined below.

Example 6.1.

A recent recruit to your department (a young man) is unhappy in his work. His output is satisfactory, but he does not seem able to establish meaningful relationships with working colleagues and rarely communicates with them. He is well qualified, industrious and makes valuable contributions to the work of your section. Without warning, he resigns. You arrange a termination interview to establish his reasons for leaving and to enquire whether and in what circumstances he would be willing to stay. He arrives for the interview. How do you proceed?

Example 6.2

A valued female subordinate, 20 years older than yourself and with longer service to the firm, is persistently late in arriving at work. Your superiors insist that something be done. You feel she might have a personal problem she is keeping to herself, so you ask her to come and see you.

Example 6.3

A black woman is transferred to your section. All the other staff in your section are male and white. She is sexually and racially harassed and registers a formal complaint. You identify the person who orchestrated the campaign of abuse and arrange for him and the aggrieved woman, to see you separately.

Example 6.4

Your firm operates a management by objectives programme, directly linked to a formal performance appraisal system. One of your subordinates has significantly underachieved her targets. An appraisal interview is due.

as against management) or when handling disputes and inter-departmental conflict, in your role as a trainer of subordinates and in staff development generally, in how you deal with people accused of theft or other improper behaviour or in helping subordinates cope with personal problems or with stress. Details of techniques dealing with all of these issues are described fully in other chapters. Here I explore methods for handling their one common component: the need for counselling.

Activity

You have read the examples given in the text. What action would you have taken, what questions would you have asked?

Read on and you will find some ideas. Compare these with your own, but remember that there is no one right answer.

What counselling is

The essence of a counselling relationship lies in the nature of the help offered to someone who must take what to him or her is a difficult decision. In Example 6.1 above the young man must decide whether to leave the firm, abandoning thereby what might have been a promising career; the woman in Example 6.2 must decide whether to continue arriving late and thus incur the displeasure of higher management (and possibly disciplinary action) or whether to deal directly with the source of her unpunctuality. The racist employee in Example 6.3 must decide whether his prejudiced views are compatible with continuing association with the employing firm and, if they are not and he wishes to remain with the organisation, whether he can adjust his views to fit in with the reality of the new situation. Counselling activities can range from giving straightforward advice, to lengthy and detailed consideration of vexatious issues. Usually, the ideal outcome would be an adjustment in an individual's perception of a work situation and his or her role within it, followed by a change in behaviour which overcomes the initial problem. The aim is not so much to impose a solution, but rather to induce people independently to learn how to sort out their problems and take appropriate decisions. This may lead to a change in objective circumstances — as for example when the persistently late employee overcomes her problem by switching to public rail transport instead of travelling by car and thus being held up in traffic jams caused by major roadworks on her route into work, or when the unhappy recruit leaves the firm for another, more suitable, job — but it need not. The employee who, for instance, has suffered a serious heart attack can never return to heavy manual work. What of the trainee who, having attended a course paid for by the firm, fails an examination and thus does not qualify under the rules of the company's training and management development scheme for any further promotion? Or how about employees who are demonstrably and irrefutably incapable of undertaking higher level work and who must learn therefore to accept the fact that they will never progress in a particular occupation? These latter examples require individuals to alter the ways they *feel* about themselves; to adjust their self-identities in accordance with the realities of the situation.

First, you must decide how you can help: how you can assist a person better understand a situation, personal motives, the alternatives that exist and the implications of various courses of action. You need a private room removed, if possible, from the environment of the factory floor or general office and it is essential that the conversation not be audible to people passing by or standing around the door or in an adjoining office. If people being counselled even suspect that their comments will be overheard, then serious discussion of deeply felt personal matters will become impossible. Choose a room without a telephone or if there is one disconnect it for the period of the interview. Make sure you will not be interrupted by secretaries, colleagues or intruders from other sections. Sit alongside the person you are speaking to rather than across a large desk and, generally, avoid status differentials: do not, for instance, sit on a better quality chair than your subordinate or if you normally wear a white coat or other overall possessing status significance take it off during the interview. Much will depend on the state of mind in which the counsellee approaches the interview. Either you will have directed that person to see you at a certain place and time; or preferably you will have engineered a conversation wherein the contentious issue circumstantially arose so that you were able to express your concern and suggest, congruently, that the two of you get together to explore some problem in greater depth. Always see people individually, even if more than one subordinate is involved and never attempt to counsel 'on-the-job' at the place of work.

Self-check

It is important that you create a friendly and relaxed atmosphere, where the member of staff feels that he/she can talk to you confidentially.

List the action you can take to ensure a conducive environment.

Answer
— private room with no interruptions and where you will not be overheard
— remove any barriers between you and the member of staff, such as furniture, demarcations of status
— arrange for tea, coffee or soft drinks to be available
— allow the individual to smoke
— do not rush the individual and do not make them feel you have something else to do.

Counselling methods

Counselling involves two people, a formal interview, a purpose and a problem. It is a dialogue between equals (even though the equality of status might cease the moment the interview ends) where one guides the other towards a choice or acceptance of a fact. The correct choice, often, is obvious to an outsider: the male worker who, for instance, has suffered a major heart attack *cannot* return to heavy duties, and *must* therefore seek an alternative occupation. He must recognise the reality of the new situation and its lifestyle implications. Yet individuals frequently are unable to summon up the courage to take indisputably necessary but traumatic decisions. The worker in this case knows intuitively what he must do, but perhaps cannot accept within himself that his job and lifestyle must change. What you need to do here is help this man express to *himself* an acknowledgement of his new status. You should try to get him to explain to you, and hence to himself, why he cannot bring himself to explore alternative work possibilities. Hopefully, your conversation will lead to the emergence of thoughts, new ideas and helpful suggestions not previously expressed or acknowledged — about how best to cope with rather than change this irreversible situation.

There are three schools of counselling theory. One school advocates *non-directive* counselling, another suggests a *directive* approach, while a third, the *situational*, contingency or eclectic school, asserts that since each case is unique, valid generalisations are normally impossible. The three approaches differ more in emphasis than in substance[1]. All agree that the basic aims of counselling are to enable people to recognise and analyse their problems and, if possible, solve them; or if the problems are intractable, to resolve the situation (ie learn how to live with it). Opinions differ however over how much direction to a counselling interview the counsellor should impose.

As an illustration of how a counselling interview might proceed, suppose that your organisation operates a detailed management by objectives system, and that you are about to interview a female subordinate who has seriously underperformed. Your objective, obviously, is to improve the subordinate's efficiency or at least discover why she cannot reasonably be expected to improve (it may be that factors beyond her or the firm's control have prevented her achieving the targets set). To achieve this objective you must:

- establish whether the cause of under-achievement is a temporary or long term problem and, assuming it is short term, how best you can help your subordinate through this temporary crisis in her career
- identify as quickly as possible any outstandingly difficult barriers to improvement and, if appropriate and if there is no issue of confidentiality involved, refer these matters upwards for further action
- create a solid basis for future good communications between the two of you so that you can assist in her normal career development.

Activity

While each case will be different, it is useful to devise a checklist, along the lines of the one given below. If you have your own ideas, devise your own checklist and use it for the next month or so.

Checklist
— establish objectives — what you hope to achieve by the end of the interview
— establish the root cause of the problem, is it short- or long-term
— agree a course of action aimed at overcoming the problem
— if necessary, agree a review at a future date in order to monitor progress
— ensure that the individual is encouraged to come to you should further help be required.

You need to understand and know how to apply three necessary conditions for successful counselling. These conditions, empathy, congruence and non-possessive warmth (discussed at length by Carl Rogers in a highly influential book on counselling technique[2]), are today generally accepted as essential for successful counselling work.

Empathy

Empathy means seeing and trying to experience a situation as it is perceived by someone else. You have to try and enter into and share your subordinate's feelings about the issue. If you are to do this effectively, you must not prejudge her behaviour, make assumptions or question the propriety of her motives. Empathy differs from *sympathy* in that the latter implies pity, which is most definitely not the impression you want to create. By sympathising with your subordinate's underachievement you make her feel worse about having failed. An emotional barrier is created between the two of you (sympathy is a selfish emotion; easily recognised as such by the other side) and offering sympathy will not help your subordinate identify what has gone wrong, or help you understand her feelings. Also, excessive displays of sympathy will encourage the subordinate to exaggerate her difficulties and distort her account of their causes. Feebly sentimental commiseration with increasingly embellished excuses can lead her on to the point where fantasy rather than an actual situation is being described. Avoid, therefore, comments such as 'how dreadful', or 'that's appalling', or 'what an awful thing to have happened'. Concentrate instead on determining the facts. A good way to test the extent of your empathy with the other party is for you occasionally to interrupt the conversation (when there is a natural break in the flow of her remarks) and make the comment 'You feel ... (now fill in your interpretation of her perceptions and emotions: anger for example) ... *because* ... (insert here your interpretation of her reasons for feeling that way)'. This simple device will convey to your subordinate the fact that you understand her view of the issue and is preferable to gratuitously sentimental statements. It is important that you seek to empathise with the subordinate's actual feelings rather than what you believe she ought to feel. Perhaps, in your opinion, she ought to experience remorse for having neglected some particular employment duties — she might have messed up a major contract, mislaid important documents, offended a valuable client, or whatever — but *she* may see things in a totally different way. Try to share the counsellee's entire world, without making ethical or moral judgements about her behaviour. Do not ask impertinent or leading questions (which imply a particular response, eg 'Well Mary, your production figures last quarter were pretty appalling weren't they?') and never create the impression that you want to 'interrogate' or dominate the counsellee. Rather, you hope that she will volunteer additional information.

Self-check

What is the difference between empathy and sympathy?

Answer
Sympathy is associated with pity and may encourage the individual to exaggerate problems, while doing little to help him or her to analyse what has gone wrong and thereby find a solution.

Empathy is where you are able to put yourself in the individual's place and see the situation through his or her eyes. You do not pre-judge.

An effective counsellor can empathise with an individual without displaying excess sympathy.

Congruence

This, in the context of counselling requires you to recognise your own personal feelings as they relate to the issue and to share these feelings with the other side. It has been described, aptly, as the 'transparency of self'. There is a danger that as you counsel, you end up satisfying your own needs for self-expression and understanding rather than those of your subordinate. You might use the interview to gratify your own emotional demands; to exploit your position of authority in the interview, to dominate the subordinate; to try and impress her with your knowledge and importance. On the other hand, you might be overprotective, pandering to needs *within yourself* to be liked and appreciated. Recognise this problem. Accept that the urge to satisfy some emotional needs which have not been adequately satisfied in your private life will inevitably spill over into your supervisory work.

Congruence does not mean that you must always agree with the counsellee. On the contrary, if you feel strong emotions in response to something she says, express them to her openly. The important thing is not to confuse your own feelings with those of your subordinate. If you begin the interview in a depressed or angry state of mind, say because that morning you had failed to obtain extra resources from the firm's budget committee, do not attribute your feelings of anger or depression to your subordinate's remarks. You are angry with your own short-comings at the meeting of the budget committee, not with her.

Non-possessive warmth

According to Rogers, the effective counsellor will exude a genuine sense of concern for the other party. You should be seen to care. Thus, you should not appear bored or irritated, stare out of the window while talking, make insensitive remarks or otherwise exhibit discourtesy or disrespect. Recognise that your subordinate is a unique individual, a sentient, rational being possessing emotional as well as contractual rights: the right to express herself, to disagree with you and have an independent point of view, to have you listen attentively to her opinions. Accept the woman as she is. If her underachievement is in fact due to avoidable errors do not reinforce her sense of failure through haste and insensitive criticism of her mistakes. Do not condemn, appear shocked by or sceptical of her excuses (even if you are). Your subordinate should not feel threatened by the interview. If she does, if she fears that the interview will expose her inadequacies and do harm to her career, that her knowledge, skill and competence will be questioned and found wanting then she will probably respond in negative and hostile ways. Non-possessive warmth will enable you to discuss serious matters with your subordinate, without her anticipating your rejection of her statements or feeling that you will ridicule or condemn her behaviour. Beware of critical remarks — they serve only to create anger and the blame they imply may be totally in-appropriate. Do not threaten, moralise or act aggressively; even a reserved and reasoned response to a comment can provoke hostility, since it may be interpreted as condescension on your part.

A problem arises here in that the better you are at exuding non-possessive warmth the more intimate will be the confidential information you receive from the counsellee, perhaps more intimate than you really want, and involving perhaps confidences about the behaviour of colleagues and other subordinates.

If you feel uneasy about confidentiality you should at least begin the interview with a declaration of just what exactly you would regard as sufficiently serious to warrant a report to your

Activity

What do you do if, for example, you are told 'in confidence' that the reason your subordinate's output figures for nightshift working are so poor is that the man she works with and who is responsible to another section has a daytime job and sleeps on a camp bed he has installed behind shelving in a corner of a warehouse instead of working as he should? What if you are told 'in confidence' that someone is pilfering from the stores; that there are non-existent people on the company's payroll, etc?

Comment

This is a difficult question. My view is that all comments offered during a counselling session should be absolutely confidential. Some people disagree with me on moral grounds, arguing that if one hears, say, that a criminal offence has been committed, or even that company rules have been deliberately abused, then one has an ethical duty to make a report. My approach in these circumstances would be to urge the *counsellee* to make a report, stressing that the misdemeanour is likely to be discovered anyhow and that she will cover herself against adverse consequences when that happens by submitting a report now. Also, if she transmits the information herself there will be no danger of misinterpretation or misrepresentation of her own role in the matter during subsequent enquiries. Yet I would leave the final decision entirely to her. I would offer suggestions about how best her report could be drafted, and I would 'prepare the ground' for her by seeking a sympathetic hearing from senior management, but I would not feel that my role as supervisor and counsellor was compatible with my providing a free espionage service to other sections of the firm.

superiors, pointing out that it might be necessary to transmit such information in order to *solve* a problem. In difficult circumstances, specify your own ethical position, and the legal position if your knowledge of an event makes you an accessory to a crime (for instance, if stolen goods are involved) but never encourage a person to reveal confidences with the intention of reporting, without the other party's permission, details of what you hear. You will never be trusted again by that person or indeed by any other of your subordinates. Note that if you adopt a non-confidentiality approach you need to state not only which particular issues you deem it appropriate to report to higher management, but also whether any opinions or sentiments expressed by the subordinate during the interview (for example, derogatory comments about senior managers) might also be reported.

Directive versus non-directive counselling

Your effectiveness as a counsellor will depend critically on your ability to establish a meaningful relationship with the counsellee. In the past, non-directive methods have normally been recommended by counselling theorists (Rogers included), though today the drawbacks of non-directive approaches are increasingly recognised. In our illustrative example of a management by objectives interview, a non-directive interview would assume that;

- only the subordinate herself is capable of defining accurately the real reasons for her underachievement, so that only she can find (with your help) appropriate solutions to the problem,
- the most efficient way of getting to the heart of the problem is to encourage the subordinate to talk about what she, and only she, wants to talk about,
- you accept the situation entirely as it is, not as you would like it to be. You are looking for explanations of events rather than immediate change. The relationship you establish with the subordinate itself causes her to become aware of her shortcomings and to seek improvements,
- there is no point in pushing your subordinate towards a solution of the problem which she does not wholeheartedly accept within herself.

Unfortunately, non-directive methods are difficult to apply in circumstances where the counsellee does not really desire a deep relationship with the other side. Your subordinate may not want your help or feel that you have anything constructive to offer towards overcoming her problem. You have therefore an uphill struggle in establishing a worthwhile relationship in the first instance, let alone developing the relationship in mutually beneficial ways.

With a *directive* or 'task orientated' counselling technique you take the initiative in suggesting to the subordinate ways of approaching the problem. You outline to her the implications and possible consequences of various courses of action, and you may even suggest a range of solutions to be considered. The subordinate takes the final decision, but in doing so is following a path clearly charted in advance by yourself. You encourage the counsellee to reply on your expert knowledge and experience of similar situations. If the subordinate is reluctant to discuss matters with you, then on the basis that people generally respond well to personal information, you tell her something about yourself and how you see the world. You relate an anecdote, perhaps tell a joke, you state your perception of the purpose of the interview and what you hope it will achieve. This helps the counsellee to relax and establishes common ground for the discussion. But do not say too much about yourself, or the conversation will soon switch to a discussion of your problems instead of hers. In effect, you predetermine the boundaries of your relationship, and what you expect from it. The counsellee responds to *your* cues and is gradually encouraged to release emotions and sentiments that were previously suppressed. She is confronted with interpretations of her problems that she might not have thought of before, and thus might alter her inward perceptions of the significance of various events.

Activity

You have read the pros and cons of non-directive and directive counselling methods. Which approach do you adopt when counselling staff?

You may favour either approach but which one is appropriate will depend on the personality of the individual and the circumstances.

The non-directive approach is dependent on the relationship between the two parties and requires that the counsellee is willing and able to identify and resolve the problems.

With the directive approach, the counsellor takes the initiative and will often suggest causes and solutions.

A major problem with counselling is that you never know at the outset of an interview how long it will take. It could be 10 minutes, 3 hours or all day and extra sessions may be required. Nor do you know at the outset just what it is the counsellee will want and expect. An open door policy on counselling might lead to people coming to see you just because they want to natter or, insidiously, because they want to run down colleagues who have incurred their displeasure. You need therefore to learn how to recognise when you are being abused. Non-directive counsellors will never specify in advance how long an interview is to last, whereas a directive approach might begin with a statement of how much time you have. In either case, however, you should never appear restless, hurried, bored or to be watching the clock. Rather, you need to project a quiet confidence in your ability to help your subordinate solve her problems, all she need do is trust in your guidance.

The counselling interview

During the interview, you will have to give one hundred per cent attention to the counsellee. There is no respite and counselling interviews lasting more than an hour or thereabouts are emotionally and physically exhausting, so never begin a counselling session when you are already tired — you will not be able to stand the pace. First thing in the morning or immediately after lunch are probably the best times. Counselling is very tiring, so do not take on too many interviews in any one day and give yourself plenty of time to recuperate, relax, think and reflect between each session.

Begin the conversation by establishing a common ground. Make a non-controversial remark about something with which your subordinate is sure to agree. Express your gratitude at her having turned up. Then proceed to some straightforward questions requiring only short, non-analytical answers. Do not ask any critical or personal questions at this stage and check with yourself to ensure you have not stereotyped the person prior to the conversation. Have you already categorised her as neurotic, overambitious, greedy, unreliable, dishonest or in some equally unflattering way? At first, be less concerned with seeking factual explanations as with rooting out how your subordinate *feels* about the issues. As the tempo of the conversation increases you will need to create pauses — breathing spaces — during which you can gather your thoughts and think ahead. This is an important element in the skill of listening, it is essential that the other party believe that you are listening attentively to what she has to say and listening is not as easy as it may first appear. The counsellee may be confused, have a poor command of English, repeat herself, ramble and speak in a clichéd manner. In counselling, you spend a lot of time listening and the things you hear may bore you, irritate, offend and annoy, but you must not show that this is the case. Look at your subordinate while she is speaking, do not yawn, do not look at documents (though you should of course have briefed yourself fully on the facts of the situation prior to the interview — you should *never* have to ask the counsellee to remind you of the circumstances of the interview), do not look at your wristwatch or otherwise appear disinterested. Your aim is to create a structure for the conversation; to break it up into component parts that can be easily digested and which have meaning to you both. Several measures might help you in these respects:

- interrupt occasionally and repeat something your subordinate has said or intimated but rephrase the point in your own words. This acts as a check on your understanding of what she is saying and will stimulate her to expand the point. Having an important point restated will help your subordinate define precisely the true nature of an issue or problem, and it reinforces the relationship she is creating with you. It is a good technique to use immediately after a strong emotion has been expressed, or when a complicated personal matter arises. It shows that you and the subordinate are 'on the same wavelength'
- practice empathy. As well as listening to your subordinate's words, try to experience for yourself the emotions behind them. Try the 'You feel ... because ...' approach previously outlined. Careful observation of your subordinate's method of delivery can help you here, her tone of voice, how she is sitting, whether she is nervous, angry, has clenched fists, looks dishevelled when discussing a particular issue, her body language generally — all might indicate how she feels

- As the interview develops, use open-ended questions (ie which cannot be answered with simple statements or yes/no answers). Such questions are prefaced by the words 'who, what, how, or why', eg

   'How did you feel at that time?'
   'What made you decide to do that?'
   'I can see that the incident deeply worried you, why was that?'

   Open-ended questions are good for eliciting feelings and attitudes, and for encouraging your subordinate to expand a point

- identify and accommodate natural pauses in the conversation. The need for a pause may be indicated by the counsellee becoming tongue-tied, repeating herself, or her insisting that she was correct about a specific point (here she is looking for confirmation of the propriety of an action). Pauses enable you to map out the interview, to digest the information presented and link it together into a coherent whole. When you read a book, you can flick forward a few pages to get a quick preview of what is to come and you can refer back to information on previous pages which will be the same now as it was the moment you first read them. Not so with a conversation. You are not able to predict accurately the points that will be raised or how they will be presented, you do not know that your subordinate will become angry, upset, reticent or whatever until it actually happens and when a point is repeated it might be repeated in an entirely different emotional context and manner than when it was first mentioned. Thus, pauses are essential to *punctuate* the flow of information. You can use them to sum up the information so far advanced, to ask detailed questions, or to suggest parallels or ask for examples. If you find a particular statement difficult to understand, say so — explain that you find the point complicated and confusing and ask your subordinate to expand. This will help her realise which aspects of the problem an independent listener finds interesting and significant. Note however, that your subordinate will find it difficult, at least initially, to talk about embarrassing or unpleasant incidents — short silences will be needed to enable her to formulate in words explanations of events and feelings she has not previously discussed. Do not criticise statements made immediately following a lengthy pause, and never point out contradictions in your subordinate's interpretations of events.

Self-check

You have been given some guidance on good practice in conducting counselling interviews. Draw up a checklist of do's and don'ts. Compare your list with the one given below.

Answer

Do: allow time for the interview, ensure that you feel fresh, establish common ground as quickly as possible, establish a rapport with the individual, listen to comments made, have the facts to hand, recap from time to time, encourage the individual to talk freely.

Don't: display outward signs of boredom such as yawning, clock watching, criticise statements made, point out contradictions, make fun of or anger the individual by remarks made, talk too much or too little, make copious notes.

If you are nervous about the interview, if you lack self-discipline, or if you do not take your counselling duties seriously you will find that you, and not the subordinate, do most of the talking. You will discuss your own feelings and problems, not hers! The problem is that in the rest of your supervisory work you are accustomed to exercising leadership, giving orders and generally behaving in personally assertive ways. Passive listening may be alien to you, since all your training and past experience makes you want to respond. Instead of listening creatively via the conscious identification of points needing expansion, or of wide generalisations that require more detailed explanation, you might either dominate a conversation or, realising this to be inappropriate, sit in complete silence waiting for the counsellee to speak. The latter approach will unnerve and disconcert your subordinate, as it is unlikely that she will have previously experienced situations where she is expected to speak for more than a couple of minutes (at most) without interruption. Your perceived lack of response to her presence may cause her to assume she is not getting her message across and she will tend to repeat points and her conversation will begin to meander. So you must interject occasionally, if only to reassure her that you understand what she is saying and wish her to continue to speak. Look at her while she is talking. You can nod, smile occasionally, make brief comments such as 'I see' or 'that's interesting' or otherwise use your body language to acknowledge her efforts. At the same time, however, your interruptions should not imply that you approve or disapprove of a particular statement — you should never 'take sides' during a counselling session. Nor should you become emotionally overinvolved with the counsellee — if you do you will find that your emotional reactions inhibit your ability to evaluate the situation objectively and take proper decisions.

Resist also the temptation to offer analytical interpretations of the subordinate's feelings. It is she who knows how she feels about an issue, not you and your analyses might be completely wrong. Even if your interpretation is correct, an outright presentation of it may so confuse and frighten the counsellee that she is unable constructively to contribute further to the discussion. If is better for your subordinate to work things out for herself.

Is counselling really worthwhile?

Instead of counselling, why not assess the situation yourself, decide what is to be done and issue directives? After all, counselling is a draining activity, requiring much preparation, self-discipline and intense concentration. It absorbs time (often the hours that otherwise would be the most productive of the day), exhausts the counseller and can be extremely depressing. You have to absorb and be seen to absorb large amounts of information, you have to learn how to recognise symptoms of tension and distress, you are immersed in other peoples' problems and complaints. You need patience, alertness and the capacity to offer sound advice to people with whom initially you did not have a close relationship. The fundamental problem is that you are trying to do a highly personal job in an *impersonal* way. Your perceptions of events inevitably depend on your own

experiences. It is impossible to remove personal value judgements entirely from a counselling interview, particularly when
sensitive issues arise and during moments of stress. There is
within individuals an information filtering system that repro-
cesses facts and opinions which they do not wish to accept — we
see what we want to see and hear what we want to hear;
unwelcome facts wash over us like water off a duck's back.
Other questionable aspects of the value of executive managers
counselling (rather than merely directing) subordinates include
the following.

- 'Parkinson's Law' applies to counselling. Problems can
  expand to fill the time that is made available for dealing with
  them. Yet, at the end of the day, intractible problems remain
  unresolved. Many situations simply cannot be altered. True,
  your counselling efforts may teach your subordinates how to
  discuss their problems, analyse their feelings and describe
  their inner selves, but they might not alter their behaviour!
  Inducing them to change their ways might require firm
  directive action on your part, reinforced by the threat of
  sanctions
- arguably, counselling approaches to personal problems
  encourage the malingerer and encourage the inefficient to
  look for excuses rather than confront directly the sources of a
  problem. More commonly, the emotional overprotection you
  provide to counsellees causes them to become dependent on
  you and to lack initiative; they become incapable of standing
  on their own two feet
- provision of a counselling service might undermine the
  authority of the employing organisation. Open door counselling may encourage individuals to complain about colleagues,
  terms and conditions of employment and superiors but, as an
  executive manager, you are an integral part of the management hierarchy of the institution that your subordinates are
  complaining about. In effect, you are being asked to subvert
  the firm's authority system on behalf of those who for some
  reason or other feel aggrieved. Loyalty problems persistently
  arise in counselling situations. Consider for instance our
  earlier example of the manager conducting an exit interview
  with the recruit who decides to quit. You establish a good

relationship during the interview. At first, he tells you that his resignation is due to some immediate incident but, as the discussion develops, you discover that other factors are involved. He has been abused, bullied, picked on, made to perform demeaning duties and so on. No wonder he dislikes the firm. Yet if you are to ask him to withdraw his resignation you need to remove the source of the unfair treatment and this necessarily will disrupt the status quo. You will have to counsel his colleagues and immediate superior and you will not be able, ultimately, to avoid taking sides.

In view of all these difficulties, is counselling really worthwhile and should it be undertaken by line managers rather than more specialised staff? The answer to both questions, I believe, is 'yes'! I reject totally the proposition that effective counselling is such a skilled activity that line managers have no right to involve themselves in this pursuit. You will necessarily be required to counsel occasionally as a *normal* part of your supervisory work. Confronted with a problem, individuals want to talk, to discuss the matter with someone who will not condemn their feelings or actions out of hand. People develop their own peer group counselling networks to lend comfort and support to individuals when things go wrong. Subordinates with problems *will* go to someone for help and advice. How much better it is if the person they turn to is you. You will know everything that happens on the shop floor, and your personal influence on subordinates' actual behaviour will increase. This is particularly important if you are a newly appointed manager who is not familiar with a group. Once you are identified as the person to turn to when problems arise then, if you take care to structure your counselling interviews in appropriate ways, your personal authority within the group is guaranteed. Other benefits from counselling include the following:

- through analysing their own feelings and the causes of their actions, subordinates learn valuable problem solving skills that have many collateral applications
- even if a problem is unalterable, perceptions of it can change and, in consequence, workers' morale may improve. The process of learning to accommodate a situation itself creates a sound base for later attempts at altering behaviour

- managements which ignore the counselling function are more likely to have employees who feel that higher authority is uninterested in their activities and welfare. Many grievances which otherwise could create significant industrial relations problems may be resolved through counselling, which can defuse potentially explosive industrial relations situations
- counselling will develop your overall interpersonal management skills. You will become more perceptive, cognisant of the problems of others, and better equipped to define precisely the substance of your managerial role. Your subordinates will feel you are treating them as colleagues rather than inferiors.

Summary

You may well be undertaking counselling duties without recognising them as such, but for counselling to be effective, the counsellor must adopt a suitable approach and frame of mind.

While an open-door policy may help to resolve human problems before they grow too large, it can be very time consuming on the part of the manager and may encourage people to bring petty grievances to his or her attention.

Analyse your own attitude to counselling. Do you regard it as an integral part of your management role, or is it a duty you are required to perform?

Notes

1 For a good survey of counselling theory, see: Brearley, G and Birchley, P, *Introducing Counselling Skills and Techniques*, Faber and Faber, London, 1986.
2 Rogers, C, *On Becoming a Person*, Houghton Mifflin, Boston, 1961.

7
Job Evaluation

Objectives

At the end of this chapter you will be able to:

- apply the principles of job evaluation to your workplace
- prepare detailed job descriptions
- explain the legal requirements, particularly as they relate to work of equal value.

Job evaluation concerns the appraisal of the relative values of jobs compared to other jobs undertaken within the organisation, focusing on the *characteristics* of each job rather than on the personal attributes of the occupants of specific positions. Its purposes are firstly to establish a hierarchy of graded posts according to their objective worth to the business (so that individual occupants of these posts may be fairly rewarded), secondly to remove pay anomalies and petty differentials and thirdly to reduce the number of separate grades of pay.

Since jobs differ in so many respects, numerous problems arise in assessing their relative importance. A 'job' consists of a whole series of tasks, responsibilities and obligations, including the skills, knowledge, training and experience needed for its effective completion, physical stamina and mental agility required, qualities of initiative, reliability and ability to withstand stress, capacities for planning, controlling others and coordinating, the nature of the environment in which the work is completed and so on. Ideally, jobs should be ranked according to objective criteria known and understood by all who work in the organisation. Management, therefore, should seek to establish a rational basis for measuring the values of jobs, and for relating these values to wage payments.

Why have job evaluation?

To avoid interminable grumbles, formal complaints and invocations of company grievance procedures by employees who feel undervalued and underpaid in comparison to colleagues whose jobs they consider to be lower valued, management must rationalise and justify wage differentials. Job evaluation, if it is done properly, avoids inequitable job structures thus removing the source of disputes over pay relativities. Also, clearly defined job hierarchies facilitate the implementation of rational promotion systems that specify precisely all the qualifications and personal attributes needed for an individual to advance to the next higher grade. All jobs of equivalent value will be equally graded and rewarded, regardless of their departmental locations.

Self-check

How can job evaluation help to resolve arguments over pay differentials?

Answer
One of the most common complaints from staff concerns pay, and in particular one person's pay in comparison with another's.

Job evaluation attempts to rationalise pay differentials and assess job content in such a way that, although actual tasks may vary, jobs of similar value are equally graded and rewarded.

Apart from 'good employer' considerations, there are important legal reasons why firms should possess demonstrably fair job evaluation systems. Under the 1984 amendments to the Equal Pay Act[1] any person is entitled to the same remuneration and conditions of service as a member of the opposite sex who is doing similar work, or *work which is of a similar value*, as judged under a *job evaluation exercise.* If a job evaluation has not already been undertaken within the organisation the employee has the legal right (regardless of length of service, current grade or whether part-time or full-time) to apply to an industrial tribunal for an order (which is legally enforceable) that a job evaluation be carried out by an independent expert appointed by and reporting to the tribunal. This evaluation will consider the effort, skills, responsibility, need to take decisions and so on attached to the post and the demands made on the individual worker in this job compared to jobs done by the firm's other workers. Apart from the report submitted by the independent expert appointed by the tribunal, reports may be submitted to the tribunal by each side based on job evaluation studies undertaken by their own (paid) experts. These are presented as evidence in support of each party's case. The tribunal's decision is legally binding: wages *must* be increased and jobs regraded if the tribunal orders that this should occur. Moreover Article 119 of the Treaty of Rome (which overrides UK domestic law) explicitly demands 'the application of the principle that men and women should receive equal pay for equal work'. An EEC Council Directive (75/117/EEC) of 10 February 1975 defines specifically what is meant by the principle of 'equal pay for equal work':

for the same work to which *equal value* is attributed ...
In particular, where a job classification system is used for determining pay it must be based on the same criteria for both men and women and be so drawn up as to exclude any discrimination on grounds of sex.

The practical implications of this Directive can be interpreted in several ways and various interpretations are currently being tested in the courts, but the crucial importance of job evaluation and the increasingly close scrutiny to which job evaluation techniques may be subjected by an industrial tribunal is clear.

Yet another reason why management should take job evaluation seriously is the likelihood that British industry in the future will move away from nationally determined, nationally applicable, rates of pay and working conditions towards locally negotiated agreements. Widening regional variations in unemployment rates, incomes and living standards create pressure for parallel local variations in wage payments, with lower rates applicable in poorer areas. To the extent this occurs, individual firms will need to rank and reward jobs at plant level rather than simply apply national collective agreements. Each firm will have to establish its own, unique, job hierarchy.

Activity

Does your organisation have a job evaluation system? If so, it will be useful to find out how it has been implemented.

Under the 1984 amendment to the Equal Pay Act, any person is entitled to the same pay and conditions as a member of the opposite sex who is doing similar work, or work of similar value. If your organisation has not conducted a job evaluation exercise, an independent expert may be appointed to undertake such a study should any dispute arise.

Two cases have been well documented in 1988, both concerning women claiming that they were entitled to equal pay to male colleagues, employed on work of similar value. The first case concerned a female catering assistant working for a shipbuilding firm, while the second concerned a group of female workers at a mail order firm. The implications of the outcomes of these cases are considered later in the chapter.

Devising a scheme

Working groups typically possess their own ideas about what constitutes fair payment. If jobs are officially ranked in an order that directly contradicts workers' perceptions of fair play, then discontent, hostility and conflict with management is likely to ensue. Common criteria, equally applicable to all employees, should be used and wages directly related to each job's contribution.

The first thing to do is a detailed analysis of all the jobs undertaken within the organisation. Information from previous work study and/or organisation and methods exercises might be used, together with new or supplementary information gleaned from direct observation of employees' current activities, or from

---

Activity

A pre-requisite for any job evaluation exercise, is to gather detailed information about the jobs undertaken within the organisation.

You will find below, recommendations as to how you should gather the information and how it should be presented.

Study the next few pages carefully and the sample job description given.

---

questionnaires issued to and interviews with, individual workers. As a manager responsible for preparing job descriptions for the work done in your department, you might proceed as follows:

- list the job titles and functions of all your subordinates, then specify to whom each of your subordinates is accountable and how many people each subordinate controls
- write down all the duties that you regard as important for each post. Then ask your subordinates to keep daily diaries which detail all the tasks they undertake during (at least) a full calendar month, specifying the resources and equipment controlled, and the frequency and purposes of their contacts with other employees
- compare these diaries with your original listings of functions. Identify major discrepancies and seek clarification from the people concerned
- write out a complete description of each job, stating:
  — what is done, and the purpose and relative importance of each task
  — how things are done
  — who the job incumbent comes into contact with in the course of the job
  — the experience, skill, knowledge and special qualities required
  — how frequently the incumbent must do each task (rarely, occasionally or often)
  — the physical environment/special working conditions in which the work is undertaken
  — any special circumstances or requirements (overnight

travel, lifting heavy weights, for example) that might be encountered.

To define the relationship of one job to others, write out lists of points of similarity and difference between jobs, particularly in relation to the demands made on the employee, and to the pay, working hours, holiday and sick leave entitlements etc relevant to each position. Specify also the availability of overtime and/or bonus payments and how they are calculated. Note the significance of the frequency with which certain tasks are undertaken. One job might require taking important decisions (that would cost the firm dearly if they went wrong) two or three times a year. Another job might involve taking such decisions two or three times a week. It is useful therefore to divide a job description into sections for: routine tasks; non-routine tasks; tasks which are only rarely undertaken (when deputising for an immediate superior for example). Likewise you should spell out the judgemental and *managerial* abilities expected from job incumbents: ability to plan, coordinate, organise, etc. Finally, you should state briefly the performance standards expected from the holder of the post. Your completed job description for a particular position (an office junior in an advertising department for instance) might look like the following.

Example 7.1

JOB TITLE:	Office Junior
PURPOSE OF JOB:	To provide routine clerical support to senior members of the advertising department
RESPONSIBLE TO:	The Head of Marketing Department's Personal Assistant
MAJOR DUTIES:	Photocopying and collating
	Sorting and distributing mail
	Typing routine correspondence
	Taking telephone messages
	Using a mailmerge package
	Filing hard copy and making entries to a database
	Maintenance of records and files

	Collection and collation of statistical information
	Tidying up at the end of each working day
TRAINING:	Standard two day company induction. Four days on-job training within the department. Day release for up to one year for secretarial training will be made available
OCCASIONAL DUTIES:	Receiving visitors and making coffee
	Preparing graphs, bar charts and pie diagrams using standard graphics package
	Taking minutes in departmental meetings
	Drafting correspondence
	Making appointments for senior managers
	Making travel arrangements
REGULAR CONTACTS:	One other office junior in the public relations department
	Head of marketing department's PA
	Three senior advertising department executives
	Secretaries to heads of departments of personnel and production
	Mail room supervisor
	Gate receptionist
EQUIPMENT USED:	Amstrad PCW
	Rank Xerox photocopier
	Voicebank telephone system
	Locomail and Tasword word processing packages
	Cardbox database
	DR graphics package
NECESSARY SKILLS:	30 wpm typing (no shorthand)
	Ability to audio type and to load and use simple software packages

	Knowledge of organisation of the marketing department
WORKING ENVIRONMENT:	Busy open plan office of 17 people
	Will have own desk, chair, word-processor and telephone
	Moderate noise
	No more than three hours exposure to word-processor per day
	No unusual physical demands
SPECIAL REQUIREMENTS:	Non-smoker
	Must be willing to work up to one hour's overtime twice per week
	Punctuality is essential
GENERAL:	Incumbent should be numerate, well organised, capable of self-direction and able to exercise initiative
	He or she needs to be well-spoken and capable of dealing with irate customers over the telephone
	Willingness to obey instructions promptly and efficiently more important than judgemental/planning skills

There are, of course, difficulties associated with the process of collecting information for accurate job descriptions. Workers who are aware that their activities are being recorded might deliberately go slow. They might exaggerate when asked to list their duties and responsibilities. As a supervisor, you might not fully understand the true nature of your subordinates' work, or you might underestimate its difficulty. Subordinates might be deliberately vague when replying to your questions; workers may put forward large amounts of irrelevant and confusing information. Non-existent duties might be listed. The importance of an individual's contributions may be overstated.

Activity

Let us try to put the theory into practice. Take two different jobs within your department and prepare detailed job descriptions for each.

When you are happy with the end result, read on and you will discover how to rank or grade the two jobs.

Job evaluation techniques may be *analytical* or *non-analytical*. The latter category comprises two major methods: ranking and grading (sometimes referred to as 'job classification'). Analytical methods normally involve the allocation of points to the constituent features of each job. The greater the total number of points awarded the higher status (and wage) of the post.

The ranking system

This is the most basic of the methods. Management (or a ranking committee that includes workers' representatives) makes an overall assessment of each job, taking account of all aspects of the work. It is a subjective, impressionistic evaluation which does not attempt to quantify the relative significance of particular aspects of a job. Ranking is quick, easy, and cheap to apply, but it does not evaluate the individual demands of a position; and this, as will shortly be explained, can lead to very serious legal consequences. The 'whole' job is compared against other whole jobs and is ranked according to its perceived importance. To apply a ranking system you will need to define (at least) three 'benchmark' jobs at the top, bottom and in the middle of the hierarchy. Then you should examine the job descriptions of each post and slot them into the hierarchy according to their relationships to the benchmark jobs and to each other. Note the need for you to be able to justify a particular decision and remember always that you may have to present your justifications to an industrial tribunal.

The grading system

Management predetermines a number of grades into which all jobs are fitted. The lowest grade is usually reserved for unskilled workers; the highest for senior management. Job specifications are examined (perhaps by a committee) and assigned to an appropriate grade. Typically, there are no more than six or seven grades; otherwise grades become meaningless. Too few grades, on the other hand, create large differences in skill and other requirements within each grade.

To apply this system, you will have to write grade as well as job descriptions, so you need to decide the differences in skill, responsibility, complexity, physical effort etc that will distinguish one grade from others. Then you compare the job description for each post with the predetermined grade descriptions and allocate jobs to whichever grades seem most appropriate. Jobs are evaluated against existing grades, not against each other. In view of the enormous importance of grading decisions to the incomes and prospects of job holders, the final allocation might be better undertaken by a committee consisting of the organisation's personnel officer, union representatives, a work study officer and, sometimes, an outside consultant as well as yourself. Use of outsiders can lend credibility to a system. It creates an impression of genuine objectivity, even though allocations might actually be determined on subjective grounds. Allocations imposed in secret by individual managers are unlikely to be accepted, or reasons for the allocations believed.

The points system

Management prepares lists of factors deemed relevant to all jobs to be evaluated. Typical factors are:

- required technical expertise
- academic qualifications
- responsibility for equipment/cash/assets
- difficulty of tasks
- supervision of others
- initiative required
- dexterity
- energy and stamina

- physical strength needed
- need to concentrate
- numerical ability
- ability to withstand stress
- training needed
- leadership
- judgement
- ability to solve problems
- experience necessary
- degree of monotony
- decision taking
- need to communicate
- need to delegate/seek advice
- physical conditions
- interpersonal skills (eg interviewing/counselling)
- need to control grievances

Other factors may be considered according to circumstances. Of course, not all factors are equally relevant to all jobs, so weightings are introduced according to the perceived importance of a factor in a particular job. Thus, for example, physical strength may be considered twice or three times as important for a labouring job than for other types of work. Each factor is given a points value. The more demanding the job in relation to a particular factor the more points are awarded for that characteristic. The task of deciding how many points actually to award for each factor to each job might be undertaken by a committee as outlined above. Once this has been done, total points awarded for each of the factors are aggregated to give a final score for the job. In consequence, jobs are compared against common criteria and thus can be rewarded according to pay scales designed to correspond to various ranges of points.

Practical problems

All systems, ultimately, are subjectively determined. Unions are fully aware that job evaluation undermines their capacity to negotiate with management about the determination of wages. Accordingly, unions will from the outset seek to ensure that none of their members will be made worse off through their jobs

---

Self-check

Distinguish between ranking a job, grading a job and awarding points.

Answer

Ranking system: establishes a hierarchy of jobs, defining what constitutes at least three benchmarks. Each job is evaluated as a whole and ranked accordingly.

Grading system: the organisation decides on a set number of job grades and establishes the criteria for each grade in terms of skills, responsibility etc. Job descriptions are prepared and compared with the grade description in order to determine the grade for the job.

The points system: the organisation decides on a list of factors to be evaluated and allocates a points value to each. Since not all factors are equally relevant to all jobs, weightings are used. Each job is given a final points score which is used to determine pay etc. Two jobs with identical points scores may be said to be of equal value.

    Do not worry if you find this somewhat confusing. Job evaluation techniques are in their infancy and very complex.

---

being evaluated and that there is no unfair discrimination or imposition of irrational differentials. Thus, collective bargaining between management and unions to determine final rankings will occur and compromises will be negotiated. What then is the point of attempting formal analyses in the first instance?

Complicated jobs with multifaceted characteristics are especially difficult to evaluate precisely. How can 'experience' be valued; how do you actually *measure* the effects of stress or unpleasant physical working conditions? Is an enthusiastic worker in a particular grade worth more than one who is recalcitrant?

A major problem is that since a job evaluation scheme is unlikely to succeed without the endorsement of workers' representatives it is usual, at the stage of initial consultation, to guarantee that no-one will be made worse off through introduction of the system. This results in the continuation of existing anomalies and consequently in increased resentment among staff whose jobs are allocated to the same grade as people they know to be earning much higher wages. Very often, individuals are paid according to what they have achieved in the past — on their previously acquired (and possibly outdated) qualifications, skills and past experiences, rather than on what they are worth now. Appeals procedures and pressure for parity during the early stages typically result in 'levelling up' of wage rates, so that instead of creating systematic pay scales related to jobs rather than people, the firm simply ends up paying out more in wages. In principle, overpaid incumbents of posts within a particular grade should eventually disappear through natural wastage, but their successors, who will be paid at lower rates than previous incumbents, may bitterly resent what they perceive as a downgrading of the positions. Borderline decisions between grades are inevitable, and are sure to generate dissatisfaction regardless of the direction of the allocation. An upwards movement of a borderline case may be seen as devaluing the higher grade. A downwards regading will create the existence of an overpaid individual in the lower grade.

Activity

As stated in the text, job evaluation exercises do have their problems. If your organisation has conducted a job evaluation exercise, how did it overcome the difficulties?

Apart from the obvious problem of valuing factors, most of the problems are likely to be human ones, where people are reluctant to lose differentials.

Following the completion of an extensive (and expensive) evaluation exercise there might be a skills shortage in one or more occupations within a particular grade. Suppose for example that a fair, detailed and comprehensive study determines that a certain calibre of carpenter shall belong to the same grade as a certain type of plumber but that there is a shortage of carpenters. The firm will not be able to recruit the carpenters it needs unless it pays market rates. It must offer a premium over and above the standard grade wage in recognition of market forces, hence making a mockery of the formal, systematic approaches used in the initial grading calculations. Inevitably, other classes of worker belonging to the carpenters' grade will feel resentful.

The temptation is to fiddle the grading points allocated to the scarce skill in order to reclassify workers possessing that skill into a higher classification, but this will create even more resentment. Alternatively, management might frequently regrade all categories of employee in attempts to keep up with current changes in market forces. Thus, the personnel department will regularly scrutinise newspaper advertisements for similar jobs in other firms, will approach recruitment agencies for details of current wage levels available elsewhere, examine labour turnover rates for various categories of employee and periodically restructure the grading system as external economic conditions alter. Yet this overrides the original intentions of the grading scheme, namely the provision of stable, objectively defined grades, protecting the individual worker against arbitrary decisions, creating pay differentials that can be maintained and defended and easing the administration of the wage payment system. Employees will quickly realise that their grading is determined by supply and demand and not at all by the stated evaluative criteria. The extra administrative burdens of regular regradings, together with the cost and inconvenience of operating complex appeal procedures, can easily outweigh any financial benefits anticipated from the programme.

Legal considerations

Since 1 January 1984, any person has been able to claim equal pay relative to a member of the opposite sex employed by the same firm who does work of *equal value* as determined by a 'proper' job evaluation study. This legislation was designed to enable women who perform jobs not usually done by men (typists, office cleaners etc) to claim fair rewards for their contributions. Hence, a woman need not identify a man who is doing identical work for the firm on higher wages, she just has to demonstrate that her job is *worth* the same in terms of its

---

Self-check

How might the supply and demand of labour affect job gradings and pay?

Answer

If labour with certain skills is in short supply, you may have to offer a rate of pay above that for the job as determined by the job evaluation exercise in order to attract applicants.

In teaching there is a shortage of mathematics and science teachers. In order to attract people into the profession it is felt that financial incentives should be offered, in terms of extra allowances, payment of removal expenses, help with accommodation. Such a remedy does not comply with the underlying philosophy of job evaluation.

---

demands. Such demands might relate to the effort, skill, responsibility assumed, working conditions or decision taking capacities required for effective performance. The comparability of these demands with those embodied in a job done by a member of the opposite sex will be established via a formal job evaluation study.

The revised Equal Pay Act is explicit in its insistence that a job evaluation be done using *analytical methods*. Under the Act, the study should have been undertaken with a view to evaluating;

in terms of the demands made on the worker under various headings (for instance, effort, skill, decision) the jobs to be done by all or any of the employees in an undertaking or group of undertakings.

In other words, the study *must* use analytical methods: overall ranking or classification will not be regarded as satisfactory. This is a point of great significance for employers, since it means that any non-analytical study is open to challenge. Specifically, the law as it stands[2] requires the complainant whose job has been rated as *unequal* by an analytical study to demonstrate that there was a fundamental flaw in the analytical techniques adopted. If no such defect can be shown the complainant will not be allowed to present her (or his) case to an industrial tribunal and the matter will rest. If the job evaluation was non-analytical there is no need to demonstrate a flaw in the method. It is automatically assumed that the study was inadequate and that it did not meet the requirements of the Act and in consequence, it cannot be used as a barrier against a claim in an industrial tribunal — the aggrieved party may simply ignore the fact that the evaluation occurred and can proceed directly to the tribunal without having to prove the study was faulty.

I said earlier that managements commonly agree in advance that no-one will be made worse off via job evaluation but that subsequent incumbents of certain posts will be paid at the rate appropriate to a lower grade. This again can cause legal complications, because if the next person occupying a particular position is of the opposite sex to the last (overpaid) post holder then he or she can lodge an equal pay claim in relation to his or her predecessor (or successor — the situation applies in reverse if a job is upgraded for the next incumbent) provided the essential nature of the work has not substantially changed. Note that changes in job titles and/or job descriptions are not relevant as far as the courts are concerned — they look only at what people actually do not at what they ought theoretically to do.

Today, any job evaluation is liable to be subjected to rigorous independent external inspection. Employers are not legally obliged to conduct their own job evaluation studies, but if they do not and if an employee feels that she or he has been sexually discriminated against then, following a complaint to an industrial tribunal, it is extremely likely that an outside expert will be appointed by the tribunal to compare analytically the complainant's job against others within the firm and if the independent expert assesses (say) a woman's work to be equivalent to that of a man then she *must* be paid equally.

If an employer does conduct an analytical study, its findings may be challenged. In order to do this the claimant needs to show that the evaluation and/or the criteria used within it were 'irrational', 'biased' or sexually 'discriminatory', or that a member of the opposite sex is doing the same or 'broadly similar' work for higher wages. Each case brought before a tribunal is, of course, judged on its individual merits.

Self-check

Why is it important to use analytical methods in conducting a job evaluation exercise?

Answer
By law, since 1984, non-analytical methods are deemed to be inadequate and can therefore be ignored. With an analytical study, the aggrieved party has to demonstrate that there was a fundamental flaw in the technique used before the case can be brought before an industrial tribunal.

If you read on, you will find what principles have been established.

To date, the following substantial principles have been established:

- if a job evaluation is not to be regarded as containing a 'fundamental error' (ie if it is to be a 'proper' job evaluation) then it has to be:
  — thorough in analysis
  — capable of impartial application
  — complete and
  — it must take into account all 'factors of importance'. Failure to consider a relevant factor will render the study improper
- if women or their union representatives do not participate in the execution of the evaluation exercise then the study may be 'irrational'
- to be a proper study, the evaluation must be consistent, ie not undertaken casually by different people at different times in a 'subjective' and 'unprofessional' manner
- errors in job descriptions cause a job evaluation to be irrational. An example of an error is a listing of duties that is out of date, inaccurate or otherwise irrelevant.

Measuring equal value through analytical job evaluation

Even if an analytical job evaluation fairly demonstrates that two jobs done by members of the opposite sex differ in content, a claim can still be made if the jobs have equal value in terms of the effort, skill, decision making, etc., required to undertake them but they are not equally paid. The amended Equal Pay Act emphasises that the relevant yardstick in determining equal value is whether the jobs are equivalent with respect to the *demands made on the employee* when doing the job rather than the perceived value of the work to the employer. In other words, it is the nature of the *work actually done* that matters.

Activity

The information in the next section gives guidelines for you to follow, should you be asked to compare two jobs within your department from the point of view of equal value.

You may find it useful to devise your own checklist and have some examples to follow.

To investigate whether two jobs in your section are of equal value (bearing in mind that if they are and if they happen to be undertaken by members of the opposite sex, your firm could be open to legal action if they are not paid equally) you should firstly list all the common elements in the two jobs, secondly list all the differences between them, and thirdly assess the extent to which such differences can be set off against each other in terms of the demands they make on the worker. Then, list all the differences which in your view cannot be offset and for each difference specify why the difference is important and why exactly it causes one job to be more valuable (in terms of the demands made on the worker) than the other. The Equal Opportunities Commission's guide to the amended Equal Pay Act[2] offers a number of examples of possible similar and dissimilar demands made on the workers undertaking two hypothetical jobs.

Finally, write out an *explanation* of the pay differential between the two jobs, remembering always that at the end of the day you may have to justify the difference not only to an aggrieved subordinate but also to a court of law.

Cases that go before tribunals are judged on their individual merits, though all rely heavily on the results of independent analytical job evaluation studies. Already, such studies have

Example 7.2 Similar Demands

Job A	Job B
Responsible for contact with public	Responsible for staff
Lifts heavy weights occasionally	Lifts small weights continuously
Diagnoses machine faults	Analyses written reports
Checks stocks and orders replacements	Checks work done by subordinates and allocates tasks
Uses drilling machine	Uses typewriter
On feet most of day	Has to concentrate on numbers

Example 7.3 Dissimilar Demands

Job A	Job B
Drives a van	Examines customer complaints
Sweeps up	Chooses fabric for new designs
Decides shift rosters	Responsible for packing and despatch

determined[3] that the work of a factory nurse was of equal value to that of a skilled fitter, that a secretary's work had equal value to a scientific assistant's, that an administrator's job was equal to a data analyst's, and that the demands made on a seamstress were of equal value to those made on a fork lift truck driver. Other pairings have involved quality controllers and technical trainers and the comparison of catering assistants with drivers. There are no limits on the jobs that can be compared and every organisation must today be fully cognisant of this when devising job evaluation procedures. The EOC suggests six categories of factors for analysis in evaluation, and it seems to me entirely appropriate and sensible to adopt this categorisation, as it stands, when conducting internal evaluation studies. Procedures are then seen to be fair, and subsequent disputes may be resolved in the context of this common categorisation and of course, an independent expert appointed by an industrial tribunal to conduct an investigation will refer to this categorisation anyhow. The EOC groupings are reproduced below.

Activity

Compare the factors specified in Table 1, with those used by your own organisation in job evaluation.

Since your procedures may be subject to scrutiny by independent experts, it may be worthwhile adopting a similar approach.

Table 1 Job evaluation factors divided into categories[4]

Section 1 Factors with a time dimension

Length of service	Experience
Age	Qualifications
Education	Knowledge
Breadth of know-how	Depth of know-how
Training period	Level of skill

Section 2 Factors with a security dimension

Responsibility for cash or assets	Discretion
	Responsibility
Confidential data/information	Accountability
Effect of decisions	Decision-making
Supervision of subordinates	Planning

Section 3 Factors with a relationship dimension

Safety of others	Cooperation
Creating new business	Supervising
Personal appearance	Communication
Contacts: internal/external	Coordination
Human relations responsibility	Expression
Public relations responsibility	Accuracy
Caring	

Section 4 Factors with a physical activity dimension

Responsibility for equipment	Heavy lifting
Technical expertise	Physical hazards
Spatial ability	Physical effort
Responsibility for product	Operational knowledge
Responsibility for standards	Physical skills
Unpleasant working conditions	Safety of others
	Visual concentration
Knowledge of machinery, tools and materials	Stamina
Responsibility for materials	Versatility
Procedural know-how	Fatigue
	Monotony

| Scanning and location of details | Dexterity |
| | Typing and keyboard skills |

Section 5 *Factors with a mental activity dimension*

Numerical calculation	Knowledge
Numerical ability	Problem solving
Mathematical reasoning	Initiative
Originality	Ingenuity
Judgement	Mental effort
Complexity of job	Planning
Verbal comprehension	Concentration
Verbal expression	Memory
Information ordering	

Section 6 *Factors with a sensory activity dimension*

Differentiating sounds	Differentiating tastes
Differentiating smells	Visual concentration
Aesthetic appreciation	Tactile sensitivity
Artistic/musical creativity	

Jobs that are not equal

If following a job evaluation study you decide that two jobs in your section are *not* equal then you must be able to justify your conclusion. Again I would advise you to set out your arguments and rationalisations using the language, techniques and approaches embodied in relevant legislation and which will be applied in disputes that go before a tribunal.

A person may claim equal pay if he or she does 'like work' to that of a member of the opposite sex or if that person does work which is of equal value. Like work could be work involving near identical duties, or it might be work that is 'broadly similar'.

Broadly similar work

Under the Act, jobs are not broadly similar if there are many and/or large differences between them and if the differences occur frequently. Broadly similar jobs will have lots of common elements and insignificant differences. Thus for example shop assistants working in different departments of a store, and male and female cooks working in the different canteens of the same firm, have been adjudged to be doing work of a broadly similar nature. Pay differentials are justified only is there are differences of 'practical importance' between the two jobs (ie important differences directly related to the tasks performed), or if there is a 'material difference', relating to the *people* involved. 'Practical' differences concern work done, whereas 'material' differences concern the personal qualities or circumstances (such as age, length of service, a skill or academic diploma) of the job holders. Material differences must be genuine and not related to sex and must fully account for a pay difference. Thus, if a worker is paid more on account of additional 'experience', the experience claimed must demonstrably exist, result in better performance and completely justify the extra payment. Similarly, practical differences that result in a member of one sex being allocated to a higher grade must *demonstrably* result in more and/or better work.

Unequal value

All the individual components of a job need to be examined before it can be concluded that it is not of equal value with another, and the methodology and evaluative techniques used may be legally challenged. A complainant may demand via an industrial tribunal production of internal documents, memoranda, letters, notes on file, etc relating to a specific decision, and a tribunal order that such evidence be produced is legally enforceable. Even the points awarded to a particular aspect of a job may be disputed in a tribunal. And an evaluation that allocated different numbers of points to a man and a woman for the same 'demand' under any of the headings mentioned in Table 1 above will be deemed discrimination unless the difference is *demonstrably* justified. Thus, for example, if a man and a woman have equal numbers of subordinates, they should both receive the same points under a 'supervision of subordinates' heading unless it can be proven that there exist substantial differences in the nature and quality of the supervision afforded. Similarly, a woman might complain that the need for intense mental concentration in her job has been awarded fewer points than demands for physical strength in the job of a man. She would argue that the two demands are of equal value even though they are different in form. An evaluation, if it is not to be deemed discriminatory by a tribunal, must consider all the 'important' elements of a complainant's job and must not allocate extra points to factors that are more typical of a job undertaken by a member of a particular sex.[5]

Note the requirement today for employers to be prepared to *explain* and *justify* the results of job evaluation exercises. The first line of defence against an equal value claim is to argue the existence of a 'material factor' which explains a difference in pay, but the case for a material factor must be carefully and closely argued and there is much confusion about just what exactly a material factor is. It is unclear, for instance, whether male/female pay differences based on skill shortages relating to certain jobs normally done by a particular sex represent a material factor, or whether the possession of an academic qualification by the higher paid party is a material factor. In the latter situation, it might be possible for the complainant to overcome the material factor argument through identifying some other attribute (extra responsibility for subordinates, need for greater concentration on the job, etc) which might offset the lack of that particular academic qualification.

Summary

Job evaluation is a means for ensuring fair and equitable rates of pay and conditions of service.

Since the Equal Pay Act 1970, women have been entitled to equal pay with that of a male colleague, provided that they are doing the same or similar work. However, in many cases, there are no men with whom to make the comparison.

The introduction of the concept of equal pay for work of equal value is seen by many as a watershed. Many employers feel that it will open the floodgates and lead to substantial rises in the wages bill. Consider some of the examples quoted in the text; the work of a seamstress is of equal value to that of a fork lift truck driver, the factory nurse with that of a skilled fitter. Opponents of the equal value concept feel that it is being applied too liberally.

The onus is on the organisation to explain and justify its job evaluation system. Perhaps you should try to assess how fair your organisation's system is. Would it pass an investigation by an industrial tribunal? If not, perhaps the matter should be looked into before it is too late.

Notes

1 These were introduced via the Equal Pay (Amendment) Regulations 1983, and came into force on 1 January 1984.
2 For details see: Equal Opportunities Commission, *Equal Pay for Work of Equal Value*, EOC, Manchester, 1985.
3 Ibid para 61
4 Ibid Annex A
5 Two recent House of Lords judgements have greatly strengthened a woman's legal position when claiming equal pay for work of equal value. The first of these has established that 'tokenism' is no longer a valid loophole through which employers can escape their responsibilities under the new legislation. Previously, some employers had intentionally segregated their workforces in the following way: (a) all women were allocated to certain departments on wages considerably lower than those of men doing work of a similar nature but in other departments; (b) men were given higher grades and allocated to separate all male departments where they received higher wages than women workers in the (nearly) all female sections; (c) just one solitary man was employed to do 'women's work' in each female department, and this man was paid the low wage applicable to female workers.
Suppose for example that an employer hires 500 women and one man to do a particular type of work on wages lower than the wages of men doing similar work in the same establishment. The 500 women might complain that their work has equal value to that of higher paid male workers; but the employer could simply reply that since a (token) man is being paid *exactly* the same wage as the women then, by definition, discrimination cannot have happened! This loophole meant that until 1988, claims for equal pay in organisations practising tokenism could not even be initiated in industrial tribunals. Following the House of Lords ruling this option is no longer available to employers.
The other test case decided that perks and fringe benefits paid to a woman cannot be offset against the higher wages paid to a man who performs work of similar value. Hence, it is not lawful to pay a man (say) £400 a week wages and a women (say) £300 per week wages plus £100 in fringe benefits for equally valuable work — the actual wages must be the same. This ruling has led to bitter complaints from employers' associations which point out that whereas firms are currently being forced to increase the wages of certain grades of female employee, firms are *not* able to reduce the value of contractually agreed or well-established customary perks paid to women employees for fear of actions for breach of contract. In consequence, female workers might end up with effectively *higher* total remunerations than male colleagues doing similar jobs.

8

Handling Grievances

Objectives

At the end of this chapter you will able to:

- understand the legal requirements of a grievance procedure
- undertake the duties of a supervisor within a grievance procedure
- identify the major causes of grievances and take appropriate action.

The Employment Protection (Consolidation) Act 1978 (see chapter 1) requires that all contracts of employment, which by law must be issued to employees within 13 weeks of starting work, contain details of the employer's grievance procedure (EPCA, s 1(4)(b)). This does not mean that an employer *must* have a grievance procedure; only that if it exists then its particulars must be communicated to employees via the contract of employment. The mechanism for invoking the procedure should be set out, stating full details of to whom the employee should complain and the process of appeal should the employee not obtain satisfaction. If a firm does have a grievance procedure but the worker is denied knowledge of its existence, then he or she can refer the matter to an industrial tribunal which can order that details be revealed. These revealed details then bind the firm 'as if' they had been included in the original contract of employment. However, tribunals cannot interpret the meaning of words used in describing procedures (s 11(1)-(7)).

Activity

Have you had to participate in a grievance procedure? If so, it will be useful to refer to any notes you may have made at the time. If there are no written records you can refer to, write down a brief summary of what happened.

It will be useful if you can compare your personal experiences with the theory outlined in the text.

Invariably, departmental managers and supervisors are closely involved in grievance procedures. Indeed, many procedures explicitly state that the worker's immediate supervisor should be approached in the first instance. If the grievance remains unsettled, then typically the worker will nominate a representative (often a trade union representative) who takes up the case. The union representative will discuss the matter with the supervisor and, if settlement is still not forthcoming, with higher levels of management. It is important to establish at an early stage whether the worker's representative may be any person, including for example a solicitor or a full time national union official, or whether the choice of representative is restricted to fellow employees within the firm. The former situation is preferable from the worker's point of view since more specialised and perhaps effective representation will then be available. Local shop stewards, who frequently represent workers in grievance procedures, often lack the knowledge and experience needed to conduct tense and complex negotiations.

The need for formal procedures

Serious discontent can arise from seemingly trivial incidents. Often, grievances relate to personal relations within a section, though they might equally emerge from almost any aspect of the employee's work: terms and conditions of employment, holiday arrangements, status and authority, treatment by superiors, working conditions etc. No organisation is so well managed that its employees never need to complain and even if the firm is objectively a good employer, staff may still *feel* that complaints are justified. Well constructed grievance procedures enable firms to resolve complaints quickly, fairly and without industrial action. Formal procedures minimise the risk of inconsistent decisions. The employer is *seen* to be trying to be fair and, of course, the absence of formal procedures will severely prejudice an employer's case if the grievance eventually results in legal proceedings.

A grievance procedure is an established set of agreed rules for enabling management, the aggrieved employee and his or her representative to settle a complaint. The rules will restrain both sides from behaving irresponsibly, provided both sides are committed to their application and have confidence in their impartiality. This presupposes that employees have knowledge of the rules and how they should be interpreted.

Self-check

Why have a formal procedure for handling grievances?

Answer
— establishes who should be involved, the sequence of events and what written records have to be kept
— helps to ensure consistency in dealing with grievances
— matters more likely to be dealt with quickly and objectively.

Activity

Familiarise yourself with your own organisation's grievance procedures. If no formal procedure exists, try to discover what the common practice is when handling grievances from staff.

There are several advantages to formal procedures, including the following:

● each side has a common understanding of how a grievance will be received and processed. Indeed, the very act of drafting agreed procedures normally involves consultation with employee representatives and will include a wide ranging discussion about the *nature* of the grievances likely to arise
● since promotions, resignations, transfers and retirements of

staff mean that the managers and union officials who deal with grievances change periodically there is need for continuity in procedures — made possible by the existence of written rules

- written rules clarify important matters such as who has authority to take decisions in settlement of disputes, the time scale for registering a grievance, how an appeal should be lodged, and so on. The procedure should also specify whether witnesses may be cross-examined, and whether documents may be produced to support a case. Each side might be required to provide the other with copies of all documents relevant to the issue (letters, internal memoranda, notes on file, etc)
- subsequent misunderstandings about what was discussed and agreed during the hearing of the grievance will be minimised if the hearing is recorded and follows a set of formal rules
- employees have the security of knowing that whenever major problems arise they can air their concerns to the highest levels of authority within the organisation. Management is compelled to consider the consequences of its actions in the context of their possibly resulting in invocations of the grievance procedure.

The case for informality

Although informal application of ad hoc custom and practice can lead to ambiguity and inconsistent decisions, it may in some circumstances be more efficient than a formal procedure. Formalisation reduces flexibility, since precedents established through following formal rules must be adhered to in future cases. A mini legal system will build up around the procedure with its own protocol, norms, case law and rules of interpretation. It becomes impossible to turn a blind eye to certain practices, no matter what the circumstances. Managerial prerogative is necessarily affected by the existence of a grievance procedure, since departmental managers and supervisors, who occupy 'front-line' positions in management's contact with the work force, are liable to have their decisions challenged. Grievance procedures can be used tactically as part of a wider industrial relations offensive (a union might for example instruct its members to invoke the procedure whenever possible in order to inconvenience the management and hence pressurise it into conceding a pay claim) or vexatiously in order to draw attention to a secondary issue. Moreover, formalisation does not remove the underlying causes of grievances, it merely changes the forum in which grievances are discussed. Grievances might be dealt with faster and more equitably if they are settled on-the-spot without formal provision for appeal to higher authority.

Self-check

Can you envisage instances when you would not invoke formal grievance procedures?

Answer
Formal procedures can be time consuming, and perhaps should be reserved for serious problems. Each manager will have to use his or her own judgement, but if the grievance can be dealt with personally, on the spot, then there may be a case for not following procedures.

A grievance procedure

The earliest authoritative and detailed guidance on the drafting of grievance procedures was contained in the Code of Industrial Relations Practice issued by the then Department of Employment under the Industrial Relations Act 1971, and most schemes began with and have evolved along the lines suggested by that document. The Code was not law but, as with all other government sponsored Codes of Practice, courts and tribunals would enquire whether it has been followed when adjudicating cases. Courts and tribunals take a dim view of organisations that do not adhere to government recommendations on the conduct of procedures. This particular Code embodied three principles in relation to handling grievances: that workers should have a contractual *right* to seek redress for grievances relating to their employment; that unions or other employee representatives be involved in the drafting of procedures; and that grievances be dealt with promptly and fairly — which implies that the *principles of natural justice* (see chapter 9) should apply. The Code recommended that the following details be specified:

- how and at what level a grievance should first be raised
- time limits for registering grievances and lodging appeals, and provisions for extending these limits by mutual agreement
- the stages of the procedure. For example, that initially the grievance be discussed with the complainant's immediate supervisor then, if it is not resolved, with an appropriate company director, and that it should then be put before (say) a three person tribunal comprising a national trade union official, a representative from an employer's association, plus one other person mutually acceptable to both sides and that the tribunal's decision shall be binding.
- availability of representation to the complainant and whether external representation is allowed.

Usually, the union representing the aggrieved party must agree as a condition of its involvement not to initiate any form of industrial action until all stages of the procedure have been completed and a failure to agree formally recorded. The latter situation cannot arise if both parties agree in advance to be bound by the decision of the final appeal body. Procedures should also specify any matters that management is not prepared to discuss, such as matters not related to the immediate workplace, or questions involving wages and terms and conditions of employment and any restrictions on the right to use the procedure (for instance, if the employee must have worked for the organisation for some minimum period before being allowed to raise a grievance).

Equal opportunity considerations

The Sex Discrimination Act 1975, s 4(1)–(3) makes it unlawful:

to victimise an individual for a complaint made in good faith about sex or marriage discrimination or for giving evidence about such a complaint.

'Victimisation' means treating someone less favourably than others simply because that person is claiming a statutory right or is helping someone else to do so. Likewise, the Race Relations Act 1976, ss 2, 4(2) prohibits discrimination in the operation of grievance procedures invoked by individuals complaining of racial discrimination and/or harassment. The Act is particularly concerned to prevent employers from disciplining workers who raise grievances concerning discrimination. Also, the Commission for Racial Equality's Code of Practice (sec 1.22) (issued in 1984 under the 1976 Act) insists that employers not:

> ignore or treat lightly grievances from members of particular racial groups on the assumption that they are oversensitive about discrimination

Moreover, trade unions are obliged under the Race Relations Act (s 11(3)) to offer the same help to members of all racial groups in the processing of grievances. Both the CRE code and that issued by the Equal Opportunities Commission (in respect of sex discrimination) strongly recommend that internal company grievance procedures be fully utilised before taking a discrimination matter before an industrial tribunal.

Activity

List what you consider to be the major causes of grievances.
    As you read on, tick off the causes on your list as they appear in the text.

Causes of grievances

Grievances can result from external circumstances, such as the employer imposing detrimental working or other conditions or treating a particular employee less favourably than others, or from internal feelings of unhappiness within the individual, even though no formal employment rule or obligation has been breached (interpersonal conflicts for example). Externally created grievances may be remedied through altering environmental circumstances: restoring a contractual right, improving conditions, increasing a benefit, or whatever. Grievances resulting from the worker's hurt feelings might best be resolved through counselling.

Often, grievances result from misunderstandings rather than fundamental conflicts of interest and it may well be that a simple statement of facts will suffice to solve a problem. Minor complaints might similarly arise from breakdowns in communications, petty jealousies, inter-personal rivalry or inter-departmental disputes. These difficulties are usually settled quite easily by increasing the flow of information through the organisation, by defining more carefully the authority and responsibilities of people and departments, and by generally promoting co-operation between sectional interests.

More serious grievances emanate from deep felt anger and frustration within the individual. 'Frustration' occurs when someone really wants to achieve a goal but something interferes with progress towards its accomplishment — the individuals knowledge, skills, opportunities or available resources are not sufficient to attain desired outcomes, and in consequence the employee feels deeply aggrieved. Such feelings typically result from a belief that failure to perform well is not the individual's fault but rather the result of external intervention. The sense of frustration is greater the more important to the person is the unachieved goal; paradoxically therefore the highly motivated, hard working, enthusiastic and ambitious worker is sometimes more likely to raise a serious grievance!

Individual reactions to frustrating situations depend considerably on individual levels of tolerance and the extent to which procedures for dealing with them — counselling facilities, performance appraisal interviews, participation in management by objectives exercises etc — exist. If there are no such facilities; if frustration is 'bottled-up' within the person, then he or she might fly off the handle following the most trivial incident, possibly an event totally unrelated to the issue causing the frustration. Examples are when an innocent conversation between two managers is wrongly interpreted as collusion to usurp the authority of a third party, when offers of help are seen as criticisms of a person's competence, or when accidental failure to pass on a message is regarded as deliberate withholding of vital information.

Anger is one manifestation of frustration, resulting from attempts to overcome difficulties that have been blocked in some way. The energy that should have been used in achieving the frustrated objective is instead dissipated in a rage against the cause of non-attainment. Not only can this lead to grievances from the frustrated individual, but also to complaints from that person's colleagues and/or subordinates who suffer his or her angry outbursts. Moreover, frustration often leads to quarrelling and malicious gossip, usually directed against external (and perhaps completely innocent) parties. Confronted with these problems, senior management might react with tighter control, by imposing additional rules and generally enforcing stricter discipline — precisely the inappropriate measures that will create yet further grievances.

Activity

How do you deal with grievances?
  Whatever approach you choose to adopt you must:

— take the complaint seriously
— be seen to take some action
— ascertain all the facts you need to make an objective decision
— keep a record of what took place.

Dealing with grievances

As an executive manager you will almost certainly be involved at some time or other in grievance control. Never ignore or trivialise grievances presented to you, however petty they might at first appear. Workers do not raise grievances they do not perceive as important. You need to be *seen* to be taking complaints seriously. Avoid giving the impression that matters will be 'swept under the carpet', so always reply quickly, formally and in writing whenever the procedure is invoked and visibly investigate the facts. If the grievance concerns pay or working conditions then ask your personnel department for copies of relevant contracts of employment and other documents and request from personnel an official interpretation, in writing, of contentious issues. Factual matters relating to pay, health and safety, overtime availability etc should be dealt with in purely objective, factual ways. Where interpretations are necessary, exercise discretion in favour of the complainant. If this results in criticisms from superiors, get them to issue to you a formal instruction that in future you must exercise discretion in a downwards direction. Then you can show this instruction to the aggrieved party or, if it is not in writing, you can refer the complainant to the person who issued the directive.

A grievance interview must be handled in a different manner to a disciplinary interview. In the first place, there is no presumption of any party's 'guilt'. Your task is to establish the facts and, assuming the complaint is valid, to remedy the grievance. If the complaint fails, you must convince the complainant that your decision is fair and based on objective criteria. Thus, you must be strictly neutral in your approach. Do not try to 'perform well' during the interview — aim for a satisfactory outcome rather than an impressive display of your negotiating skills. Note also that initially you will be dealing with the complainant on a one-to-one basis. It is within *your* authority to reject a grievance in the first instance but as someone else will adjudicate an appeal against the decision, it is essential that your first response be based on hard, factual evidence, preferably backed by witnesses and written documents. A major problem confronting supervisors in these situations is that senior management often expects supervisors to 'fob-off' legitimate complaints from workers and will take into account a supervisor's ability to do this successfully when appraising his or her performance. You will have to be somewhat devious here, since you must 'knife-edge' between the need to satisfy senior management's requirement that you minimise the frequency and consequences of grievances and the complainant's legitimate demand for fair treatment. Two devices can be used to ease the dilemma:

- tell each side (senior management and the aggrieved party) that the other side has requested a formal written statement of the other's position
- if a statute, contract, or Code of Practice covers the point at

issue make this fact known (discreetly and in confidence) to the complainant and then tell your superiors that the aggrieved party is demanding statutory or contractual rights or the application of a government sponsored Code of Practice the breach of which could land the firm in serious difficulties. Then claim that it is the complainant and not you who is pressing for a satisfactory response from senior management. Whenever you ask for guidance, do it in writing (copy to the complainant) and say you have been asked to seek guidance by the aggrieved party.

Another important difference between grievance and disciplinary interviews is that you cannot prepare for the former because you will probably have little prior knowledge of the nature of the grievance until it has been explained. Thus, grievance management requires good listening skills, and a flexible approach. You must, however, be fully conversant with the rules of procedure governing the situation, and you should have a copy of these rules beside you during the interview. One way to conduct a grievance interview is as follows:

- ask the complainant to state the background to the case and (importantly) what he or she would like to see done to resolve the problem. Listen sympathetically. Try to empathise with the aggrieved person. Your task at this stage is to understand why the worker has complained
- explore the facts. Take a note of the names of witnesses to incidents and of any documents that might help resolve the case
- attempt a preliminary definition of the nature of the problem. Identify any company rules, policies or procedures the breach of which might have caused the complaint. Ask the complainant whether he or she agrees with your interpretation of the problem. If there is disagreement, isolate the differences of opinion. State your position as clearly and simply as you can
- either, suggest a solution to the problem or, if you believe the grievance is unfounded, explain carefully your reasons for rejecting the complaint. Do not expect a coherent response; angry people are rarely lucid when venting their displeasure. Inform the complainant of the procedure for appeal and the

time scale for this. Never threaten or even imply victimisation of the worker for questioning your decision
● record your decision or a failure to agree in a written statement approved by the complainant. A 'failure to agree' should highlight the contentious issue.

The extent to which you can settle grievances 'on-the-spot' depends critically on how much authority is delegated to you by senior management. Obviously, you are not entitled unilaterally to decide on major policy issues or establish important precedents when ruling on complaints, but you should be able to implement routine decisions. Some grievance procedures err in that although they specify a departmental manager or supervisor as the person to whom a grievance should first be taken, this person is not allowed to settle matters without first obtaining permission from higher authority. Thus, confidence in the supervisor is undermined and much time is wasted in explaining problems to people unable to do anything about them. Sometimes, individual grievances raise questions of fundamental principle that can only be resolved through collective bargaining. There is need, therefore, for a mechanism for transferring such matters to another forum, where different procedures apply.

Interesting situations arise where there is conflict between the complainant and his or her union in relation to the validity of a grievance. For example, management and the union might have negotiated an agreement whereby certain groups will be made worse off as part of a wider terms and conditions deal. A member of the disadvantaged group might complain, yet be denied union representation. Then, you might uphold the complainant's position in opposition to the policy of the complainant's union! Also, union representatives themselves attribute various degrees of enthusiasm to the grievances they handle, depending on their attitudes, experience and the difficulty of the case. A racially prejudiced union representative for example might not wholeheartedly support a member belonging to an ethnic minority group. Cases which are difficult, complex and/or emotionally harrowing might not attract the same degree of union support as other, easier, cases. It may be that union representatives have warm and friendly relations with management generally, and do not wish to prejudice this relationship

> **Self-check**
>
> As you cannot prepare for a grievance interview, apart from familiarising yourself with any rules of procedure, it is recommended that you follow a blueprint. Identify the five stages suggested in the text.
>
> *Answer*
> Stage 1 — Allow the complainant to state the reason for the complaint
> Stage 2 — Ascertain all the facts, in particular the names of witnesses, documents etc listen to the evidence
> Stage 3 — Give your summary of the complaint based on information supplied, company regulations etc. Ensure that the complainant agrees with your summary. If not, identify differences
> Stage 4 — Decide whether to accept or reject the grievance. Give your solution and inform the complainant of the appeal procedure
> Stage 5 — Make a written record of events.

through becoming involved in contentious, confrontational, issues in support of individual members' grievances.

The extent of union involvement should be predetermined by the written procedure. Some systems exclude union representation from the first stage of the procedure, on the grounds that complaints can often be settled more quickly and effectively through relatively informal discussions between complainant and supervisor, without any outside interference. Other procedures allow for representatives to present the complainant's case from the outset, arguing that representatives are more objective, unemotional and thus better able to articulate a case in a lucid and coherent (and hence more efficient) form.

Failure to agree a remedy for a grievance might result in the matter being put to arbitration, with both sides promising in advance to accept the arbitrator's decision. Typically, unsettled complaints relating to the interpretation or application of existing agreements are considered suitable for arbitration, but not matters that have wide implications for management or the complainant's union. External arbitrators can bring fresh perspectives to vexing problems, and both sides 'save face' in the event of an adverse decision. Thus, a union representing the aggrieved person can blame the arbitrator for an unsuccessful appeal rather than carry responsibility for not having pursued the member's grievance with sufficient vigour. The written procedure should specify whether arbitration is to be allowed, at which stage and whether it can be invoked unilaterally by one of the parties or whether mutual agreement is required.

Summary

A grievance procedure enables members of staff to bring complaints to the attention of management. Unless tackled quickly and fairly, grievances can lead to frustration and ill-feeling.

While there is no legal requirement for an organisation to have a formal grievance procedure, it makes good business sense to adhere to the Codes of Practice that have been drawn up.

You are now in a position to evaluate your own organisation's grievance procedure and in particular, compare what actually happens with what should happen.

9
Dismissal Procedures

Objectives

At the end of this chapter you will be able to:

- identify the legal requirements for disciplinary actions
- identify the legal requirements for dismissal procedures
- distinguish between unfair and wrongful dismissal
- carry out the tasks of a supervisor and act in a fair and reasonable manner when invoking disciplinary and dismissal procedures.

Workers who behave improperly, perform unsatisfactorily or who lack effort are subject to disciplinary action. Sanctions include demotion, suspension and, ultimately, the sack. Motivated employees usually exercise effective self-discipline, though control is often improved if workers receive clear, precise and comprehensive instructions about what they are expected to do. If an employee is not prepared to abide by rules specified in a contract of employment, the question arises whether it is worthwhile continuing the employee's association with the firm.

Departmental managers and supervisors are invariably involved in the implementation of disciplinary and dismissal procedures, and there are perhaps four questions of interest from their point of view.

- what authority does the departmental manager have to ensure that organisational rules and decisions are obeyed, and what

practical steps can he or she take to counteract improper behaviour
- what considerations (legal or otherwise) are relevant in deciding whether to pursue a particular course of disciplinary action
- how should the disciplinary procedure operate, including the right of appeal
- what sanctions short of dismissal should exist, and in what circumstances might they be applied?

Activity

What authority do you have to take disciplinary action against a member of your staff who behaves improperly or whose performance is unsatisfactory?

You should know exactly what action you are permitted to take and what procedure to follow. It is unlikely that you will have the authority to dismiss someone, but you may be the one who initiates proceedings.

The law also lays down rules that have to be followed. You must be familiar with the law, as failure to comply may result in a claim for unfair dismissal being accepted by an industrial tribunal.

The role of the individual manager

Taking disciplinary action is necessarily unpleasant and it is important therefore to establish at the outset precisely who is responsible for enforcing regulations. First, identify the source of the rules. Is there an up to date rule book? If so, are its procedures clearly defined? How should disciplinary incidents be recorded? Note the important distinction between formal and informal warnings when documenting disciplinary events. In law, an unrecorded 'informal' warning *cannot* be used to justify disciplinary action following a repetition of the offence. Informal warnings are precisely that, ie off-the-cuff reminders not to behave in a certain way. Vindication of disciplinary sanctions requires detailed cataloguing of misdemeanors as they occur and the issue of formal *written* warnings outlining the likely consequences of continuing errant behaviour. Moreover, miscreants must be informed that incidents have been recorded.

Self-check

What is the difference between formal and informal warnings?

Answer
Informal warnings are not officially recorded and therefore cannot be used as evidence when justifying disciplinary action.

Formal warnings are usually made in writing and give a clear indication of the action that will be taken should the unacceptable behaviour continue.

You can see how important it is to use the correct format.

The sanctions that each level of management can impose should be clearly specified in a written procedure. Often, the only person possessing formal power to dismiss is the organisation's chief executive, although he or she will obviously be guided by the advice of others. You might be expected to draft regulations, determine standards of behaviour and job performance, interpret rules imposed by higher management, clarify 'custom and practice' in relation to unwritten rules and explain to employees the firm's expectations of their behaviour. Almost certainly, you will have to negotiate with workers' representatives (usually shop stewards) when disciplinary problems arise and you must therefore be fully conversant with the details of company rules and procedures as well as the facts of individual cases.

Serious difficulties can arise from conflicting pressures on managers exerted by different departments in respect of disciplinary issues. The personnel department, for instance, might want you to ignore a shop steward's persistent latecoming or absenteeism because of the industrial relations difficulties that your disciplining this employee might create. Senior managers may overturn your decisions. Deals might be struck between the personnel officer and union representatives behind your back. Other sections may fear the consequences of disrupted production schedules should you take action against certain individuals. Yet, it is *you* as executive manager, not they, who must live with the detrimental effects of indiscipline. Colleagues may not appreciate the practical problems created by (say) absenteeism, persistent latecoming, petty pilfering, deliberate idling, messing about etc.

Activity

How conversant are you with your organisation's disciplinary and dismissal procedures?

While you may not be able to quote the procedures chapter and verse, you should be able to lay your hands on a copy of the rule book. Since rule books are often lengthy and complex, it may be a good idea to devise your own crib sheet, or perhaps an index of the elements you need to refer to in the book.

Legal constraints

There are many restrictions on the right to dismiss. In general, dismissal is the termination of employment by,

- the employer, with or without notice, or
- the employee's resignation, with or without notice, when the employer behaves in a manner that demonstrates refusal to be bound by the contract of employment. This is termed 'constructive dismissal', it means the employer is behaving so unreasonably that the worker has no alternative but to quit, or
- the failure of the employer to renew a fixed term contract.

Dismissal without notice is known as 'summary' dismissal. This might occur when a workers' behaviour makes impossible the fulfilment of a contract of employment. Examples are theft, persistent drunkenness, violence, abusiveness to colleagues or customers, wilful disobedience, or incompetence that immediately causes damage to the employer's business.

There is an important difference between 'unfair' dismissal and 'wrongful' dismissal. The former can only happen when the person dismissed is an 'employee' (in the sense defined by the

1978 Employment Protection (Consolidation) Act, which deals with these matters) of an organisation and certain eligibility criteria apply. At the time of writing, a worker is able to claim unfair dismissal only if he or she has worked continuously for an organisation for at least two years full time, or two years part time doing at least 16 hours a week or five years part time doing at least eight hours a week. Continuity means the absence of gaps in the worker's service of more than a week, although holidays, time off for sickness (up to six months at a stretch), and 'normal' layoffs (teachers' long summer vacations for example) do not break continuity. A series of short term contracts, issued one after another, will build up a worker's continuity to exactly the same extent as a single contract for a longer period. Thus, a worker employed on (say) renewable one year contracts is regarded in law as equivalent to someone on a permanent contract after the appropriate number of years have elapsed. Note, however, that a recent case has established the principle that separate concurrent contracts with the same employer cannot be added together to create the total number of hours needed to be covered by the 1978 Act. Thus, as the law stands at the moment, a contract for eight hours a week in one division of an organisation cannot be added to a concurrent contract for eight hours a week worked in another part of the same employing firm to give the 16 hours per week needed to claim a redundancy payment or to initiate an unfair dismissal case after two years' service. These details are important and you should always check the current position with an up to date text on employment law[1]. If there is any doubt about eligibility to claim unfair dismissal (which results in the case being heard in an industrial tribunal (see: Volume 3, chapter 9) rather than an ordinary civil court) then you or your colleagues in personnel department should seek professional advice. 'Wrongful dismissal' in contrast may be claimed by any dismissed worker, regardless of length of service — a worker who has been with the firm for only a few days may be 'wrongfully' sacked. This occurs when the worker is dismissed with insufficient notice, and results in civil proceedings in a county court. The aggrieved party sues for damages equivalent to the actual loss incurred. There are major differences in procedure between county courts and industrial tribunals and whereas costs in the latter are intended to be minimal (and in normal circumstances are never awarded to the other side) costs in the county court can be huge.

If you dismiss someone unfairly your firm will have to pay compensation and/or reinstate the worker. But, quite apart from legal considerations, dismissals should on moral grounds always be demonstrably fair. Taking away a person's livelihood is an extremely serious matter which should never be undertaken frivolously or without following proper procedures, including the right of appeal. There is a minefield of legislation in this area. Mistakes can be costly, and the entire process is harrowing for all involved. Sound procedures are essential.

Self-check

What is the difference between:
— summary dismissal and constructive dismissal
— unfair dismissal and wrongful dismissal.

Answer
— summary dismissal is where no notice is given by the employer, the justification being the totally unacceptable behaviour of the employee. When an employee resigns because of unreasonable behaviour by the employer this is called constructive dismissal
— the term unfair dismissal can only be applied where the employee has worked continuously for an organisation for at least two years full time, or two years part time doing a minimum of 16 hours per week, or five years part time doing at least eight hours a week. Wrongful dismissal can be claimed by any dismissed worker, regardless of length of service.

The important point to remember is that the correct terminology must be used at all times. If you are unfamiliar with the terms used, you will find it helpful to keep your own dictionary of explanations.

The Employment Protection (Consolidation) Act 1978 lists four major reasons for which staff may be fairly dismissed: genuine redundancy (see Volume 3, chapter 9), gross misconduct, inadequate performance, or some other substantial reason. The term 'misconduct' has no legal definition, each case must be considered on its individual merits. Gross misconduct (theft, violence, etc) justifies summary dismissal in certain circumstances but the law insists that you 'act reasonably' at all times, and it is up to you to prove that misconduct vindicating dismissal actually occurred. You must be able to specify where and when the misconduct took place and how it affected the worker's job and/or workmates. Then you have to demonstrate that the worker's past record was taken into account and how exactly the organisation suffered on account of the event. Also, you need to show that the dismissed person was not selected unfairly from others who were equally guilty, that dismissal rather than some lesser action was required, that formal warnings were issued, proper investigations carried out and that a fair dismissal procedure was followed, including right of appeal.

Inadequate performance (incapability) means that the employee cannot satisfactorily complete his or her work, or does not have the qualifications for the job. Note that a sick employee may be 'fairly' dismissed on these grounds, although tribunals expect the employer to discuss the position with the worker concerned to ensure that the illness will in fact prevent effective performance and to seek less demanding work for the sick employee. Nevertheless, employers are entitled to dismiss any worker whose skill, aptitude, health or physical or mental qualities are not up to the demands of the job, but the employing firm must show that it acted reasonably at all times. Thus, you should have given that person written warnings of his or her inadequacies, offered the chance to improve (preferably with the offer of help and training) and have followed a proper procedure. If you promote somebody who turns out to be useless at the higher level of work, you should offer the opportunity to revert to a less arduous job before dismissing that employee. Always keep documentary evidence of an employee's incompetence and *do not* write glowing references for a worker immediately prior to dismissal, since such documents can subsequently be used as evidence against your allegations of inadequate performance.

Other reasons for fair dismissal include disruption of staff relations, 'organisational efficiency' (though the meaning of this must be established in each individual case) or a temporary job coming to an end — provided the impermanent nature of the work was fully explained to the worker when the employment started. You may also dismiss someone if the continuation of that person's employment would cause you to break a law (for instance, if one of your drivers lost his or her driving licence) and you can fairly dismiss any worker who goes on strike. However, *all* striking workers must be sacked and not just some of them, unless there are extenuating circumstances (such as certain strikers being convicted for violence on picket lines).

Tribunals will hold that some dismissals are automatically unfair and the victims of these sackings do not always have to satisfy the same eligibility criteria for being able to claim unfair dismissal in a tribunal. Three circumstances give rise to unquestionably unfair dismissal: sacking a pregnant woman simply because she is pregnant, dismissal for union membership or activity, or for refusing to join a union[1] or dismissal of workers when a business changes hands unless significant technical, economic or organisational changes warranting the dismissal of staff also occur at the same time.

Note finally that although you are entitled to expect your subordinates to cooperate with you and to obey all your reasonable, lawful and non-dangerous commands, all the orders you give must be covered by the worker's contract of employment. A worker is entitled to disobey you if an instruction is not essential to his or her work, as evidenced by contractual conditions of employment and even is it is, the dismissal is warranted only if the disobedience is wilful and important to the employee's work. Written warnings should have been issued and previous disobedience of similar instructions should not have been ignored. Dismissals for disobedience should not occur too long after the event or accusations of victimisation are likely. A worker is perfectly entitled to refuse to accept a change in the terms and conditions of his or her contract (pay, hours of work, shift systems, etc) provided the change is fundamental. Thus, for example, a requirement to change departments might not be deemed fundamental, whereas a change in the location of a worker's job from one part of the country to another probably would (unless this was explicitly provided for in the contract). Also, a worker may legitimately refuse to work overtime not agreed via a written or implied contact of employment.[2]

Self-check

List four reasons for summary dismissal and four reasons for which staff may be fairly dismissed.

Answer

Summary dismissal: theft, persistent drunkenness, violence, abusiveness to colleagues or customers, wilful disobedience, incompetence that threatens to damage the business.

Fair dismissal: redundancy, gross misconduct, inadequate performance, disruption of staff relations, end of a temporary contract, continuation would be illegal, taking strike action.

The employer must be able to prove that he or she has acted in a reasonable way, and where appropriate, given due warnings.

The disciplinary procedure

The purposes of a disciplinary procedure are to establish facts promptly and accurately (before memories begin to fade) and to ensure that accused individuals are fairly treated. Instant suspension pending a full investigation is vastly preferable to instant dismissal pending appeal, if only because of the legal implications of the latter course. Procedures should be written, easy to understand and made known to employees and their representatives. Without doubt, the most important guidelines on how procedures should be drafted are contained in the ACAS Code of Practice entitled *Disciplinary and other Procedures in Employment*, (HMSO, 1986). This was first issued pursuant to the Employment Protection Act 1975, s 6(1), (8) and came into effect in 1977. It has been updated since then, the last update occurring in 1986. Failure to observe the Code does not render the firm liable to legal proceedings, nor does it make a dismissal automatically unfair, but the Code is admissible in evidence before courts and industrial tribunals and if any of the Code's provisions appear to a tribunal to be relevant for deciding any question arising from the proceedings then it will be 'taken into account in determining that question' (EPA 1975, s 6(11)).

The Code recognises that the maintenance of discipline is a management responsibility, but emphasises the desirability of involving workers' representatives when drafting procedures.

Under the ACAS Code, employers should indicate the forms of conduct that are considered unacceptable, and in what circumstances. Rules should be particular rather than universal and justified in terms of the objective requirements of a job. Thus, for example, smoking may reasonably be prohibited in a food shop but not on an open air building site. The Code accepts the difficulty of specifying precise rules to cover all circumstances, but states that rules should not be so general as to be meaningless. It suggests that each employee be given a copy of the rules and have them explained orally as part of an induction programme. Employees should be informed of the consequences of breaking rules, particularly those rules which if broken may result in summary dismissal. Paragraph 10 of the Code recommends that procedures should be in writing, specify to whom they apply and what actions might be taken, be fast, and contain the provisions that:

- immediate superiors cannot dismiss without referring to senior management (the levels of management authorised to take various forms of disciplinary action should be clearly specified in the procedure)
- individuals be informed of complaints against them and be given the opportunity to state their case before decisions are reached
- the accused have the right to be accompanied by a trade union representative or by a fellow employee of his or her own choice
- employees should *not* be dismissed for a first offence (except for gross misconduct) and that disciplinary action should not be taken until after an investigation. If the worker is suspended during this period the suspension should be with pay, and the procedure should state how pay will be calculated
- full explanations be given for any penalties imposed, that right of appeal exist and the procedures for appeal be fully explained to the individual.

The Code distinguishes between informal oral warnings for minor infringements of rules, and formal written warnings

---

Activity

You should be familiar with the terms of the ACAS Code of Practice: Disciplinary and other Procedures in Employment. The main provisions have been outlined in the text.

Consider your organisation's procedures, in particular

— have the procedures been written down and made known to employees and their representatives
— are the rules of conduct fair and reasonable
— are the penalties for breaking rules clear and have they been made known to employees
— do they specify what actions can be taken and by whom
— are individuals given the right to access information and to state their case
— are individuals allowed to be accompanied by a union official or friend
— where necessary, are individuals suspended on pay while awaiting investigation
— are individuals given the right to appeal?

A negative response to any of these questions indicates an aspect of the dismissal procedure that may be in need of revision. While the Code of Practice is not legally binding, it is seen as evidence of good practice in an industrial tribunal hearing.

---

issued following serious offences. Formal warnings should set out the nature of the breach of discipline, the likely consequences of further offences, and should state that the warning constitutes stage one of the formal procedure. If misconduct is repeated, a second and final written warning should be issued containing an unambiguous statement that a further recurrence of the offence will lead to whatever action (suspension, dismissal, or some other sanction) has been determined. Assuming the errant worker's behaviour does not improve the next step is suspension or dismissal, accompanied by a written statement of reasons for the action taken and details of right of appeal. You are expected to act *reasonably* at all times, which means taking into account the worker's past record, any extenuating circumstances, and whether the worker was fully aware of the standards required and of the consequences of misbehaviour. Other factors to be considered (para 16) are:

- the employee's age, position, length of service and general performance
- whether domestic problems, etc make it appropriate to reduce the severity of the disciplinary action taken
- what action was taken in similar cases in the past.

Appeals procedures are dealt with in paras 23-27, which suggest that appeals be considered quickly, that time limits for lodging an appeal be immediately transmitted to the individual concerned and that appeals be heard by a higher level of authority than took the original disciplinary action. Wherever possible, the appeal should be considered by independent people who are not the immediate superiors of the manager who decided to dismiss the worker. The procedure should spell out the actions that may be taken by those hearing the appeal, and enable any new evidence to be made known to the employee. Existence of an appeals procedure demonstrates management's commitment to fair play. The 'convicted' employee is given the opportunity to explain why he or she believes the original decision was wrong and it shares the burden of taking unpleasant disciplinary decisions. (You are more likely to take proper disciplinary action against errant employees when you know they have the right of appeal). Independent arbitration might be an appropriate means of reaching a final decision, provided both parties agree.

Natural justice

Courts and tribunals expect all domestic hearings to adhere to the 'rules of natural justice'. These rules are not embodied in any statute, but have been established through legal custom and practice, case law and precedent over the years. Natural justice requires that:

- accusations be supported by evidence
- the accused be informed of the full details of a complaint
- any tribunal hearing the case must act in good faith, fairly and without bias
- the accused be allowed to state a case, to hear the evidence given against him or her and be able to cross-examine witnesses

> *Self-check*
>
> What is the sequence of actions recommended by the Code of Practice following a serious offence?
>
> *Answer*
> 1 — formal warning, stating that it is the first stage in the formal procedure, outlining the nature of the offence and the consequences of further offences
> 2 — if misconduct is repeated issue a second and final written warning, stating in clear terms the consequences of a further offence
> 3 — assuming that the offence occurs again, suspension or dismissal, depending on the nature of the offence and the action threatened in earlier warnings. A written statement is issued giving the reasons for the action taken and the appeal procedure.
>
> Failure to comply with any of the above may constitute grounds for claiming unfair or wrongful dismissal.

- the accused be allowed the right of representation (for instance by a union appointed lawyer), and have full access to all information and documents
- the tribunal should not include the other party to the dispute.

A breach of the rules of natural justice does not necessarily render a dismissal unfair, provided you acted reasonably and the outcome to the proceedings would have been the same had all the procedures been correct.

The ACAS Code (para 45) recommends that employers actively seek to pre-empt disciplinary problems by minimising the risk of poor performance and by 'creating conditions which allow employees to work satisfactorily'. In particular, probationary employees should be told what is expected of them, targets set should be 'realistic', and the consequences of failure to meet required standards should be fully explained during induction procedures. Regular performance appraisal is suggested (paras 46-47), so that when people do not come up to standard the cause is likely to be their own carelessness, negligence, idleness or misconduct rather than incompetence in the long run.

Disciplinary interviews

In practice, many disciplinary functions are undertaken via interviews conducted by departmental managers. These interviews are necessarily more formal than other types of interview because of their legal implications. You have to be able to demonstrate that a disciplinary interview was conducted reasonably and that even if there is some deficiency in your interview technique, the outcome would have been the same.

Do your homework before the interview. Identify the rule or convention violated, and ask yourself whether a breach actually occurred, whether the breach is serious enough to warrant further action and whether the real reason for taking action is breach of the rule and not some other reason? Check the accused person's record, looking particularly to see if similar conduct has previously been overlooked or condoned. Prepare a list of possible outcomes to the interview and the consequences of each. Confirm with your superiors that you possess the formal authority to impose appropriate sanctions and that senior management will back you up (subject of course to the worker's appeal).

Never conduct a disciplinary interview when you are angry, tired, depressed or otherwise emotionally upset. Allow a reasonable 'cooling off period' before discussions begin, though not too long — people quickly forget the details of events. Arrange for the interview to be conducted in private and without interruption. Preface your remarks with a precise specification of the allegations and, because it is a formal occasion with potentially damaging consequences for the accused person's career, outline the possible repercussions of the interview. Do not pretend that the interview is a 'friendly chat' when in fact its outcome will be recorded and perhaps used to justify disciplinary action. The ACAS Code (para 15) recommends that whenever action beyond an informal warning is likely, the employee *should be given a written statement* of the allegations *as well* as being told about them orally.

Next, outline the procedure that will be followed and ask whether the worker wishes to be represented by a trade union shop steward, by some other fellow employee, or by an outside person if the firm's disciplinary rules allow for this. If so, the meeting must be adjourned to arrange representation. In any event, the worker should always be given time to prepare his or her case, to request production of relevant documents, locate witnesses and study allegations in depth. Ask for an explanation of the worker's actions. Investigate facts. Find out exactly what happened and why. Where there is conflicting evidence and/or the accused denies having committed the offence you will have to reach a decision on what took place *before* deciding on disciplinary action. You should have a copy of both the firm's disciplinary rules and the employee's personal file beside you for quick reference during the interview. If the offence is admitted, ask whether there are any special circumstances to justify the errant behaviour.

Your final decision should be explained carefully to the worker and his or her representative, and confirmed in writing with full details of the procedure for appeal.

Self-check

Why is it advisable to follow a prescribed procedure when conducting a disciplinary interview?

Answer
It is essential that a disciplinary interview is conducted in a reasonable and fair way. You must be satisfied that there is a case to answer and have all the facts relating to the breach of rules, past record of the employee etc.

You must keep a record of the interview and any formal warnings must be confirmed in writing.

Today, it is common practice for both parties to the interview to be accompanied by a witness. The witnesses will not participate in the interview but confirm what was said.

Action short of dismissal

Action short of dismissal means any penalty imposed on the worker other than the sack. Examples are demotions, failure to promote certain employees, denial of pay increases, refusing requests for time off, loss of increments, allocation of unpleasant and/or low status duties and so on. These actions are lawful provided they do not discriminate unfairly with respect to race, sex or marital status, are not intended to penalise someone for joining or wanting to join a union, becoming involved in union activity, or for refusing to join or withdrawing from a union (Employment Act 1982, s 10(4)). Victims can seek redress not only from their employers, but also from individual employees (including union shop stewards) who pressurise employers into taking unfair action short of dismissal. Cases are heard in industrial tribunals, which decide how much compensation the employer *and* the people bringing the pressure on the employer should pay. Note, however, how useful an action short of dismissal (a demotion say) can be in offering an errant worker the chance to reform.

Disciplinary actions in well managed firms will be few and far between. They represent failure on the organisation's part: failure of recruitment, induction and appraisal systems, of communications systems, and of management's ability to motivate employees. The ACAS Code (para 16) suggests that precedents be followed when imposing sanctions (to ensure consistency of decisions and the avoidance of unfair discrimination) and that consideration be given to whether the written disciplinary procedure indicated the form of disciplinary action that would result from the misconduct. The Code considers formal oral warnings to be appropriate for minor offences — formal in the sense that they are recorded on the employee's personal file, with the employee being advised that the warning has been recorded. If the offence has occurred before, you should consider writing to the employee stating (as suggested by the ACAS Code, para 17) the precise nature of the offence, the likely consequences of a further repetition, what improvement is required and over what period.

Following a further repetition of the misbehaviour, you need to decide exactly what action to take. In reaching this decision, take account of para 50 of the Code which pleads for special consideration in the following situations:

● if the source of the disciplinary action is substandard work, then before imposing a sanction:
  — mention the inadequacy and remind the employee that he or she has a responsibility to achieve the required standard

---

Activity

In a well managed organisation, recourse to disciplinary procedures should be few and far between. Indeed, you may not have been directly involved in any procedures and therefore unable to draw on personal experience.

If you have been directly involved in a disciplinary case, what action was taken and why. Dismissal is the ultimate sanction but what other penalties does your organisation impose?

- — try to remedy deficiencies through enhanced communications, extra training, encouragement etc
- — give the employee adequate time for improvement, especially if he or she has recently been promoted and is having difficulty coping with higher level duties
- — ensure that the fault does actually lie with the employee and that adequate warnings have in fact been issued.

- In the case of illness, accident or advancing age, try to find alternative work for the employee (Code, paras 51-52). For a sick employee, seek to establish his or her precise medical condition. Allow a 'reasonable' time for recovery and, where possible, reorganise departmental workloads and/or engage temporary staff to cover the worker's absence. Ask the sick employee whether any residual incapacity is likely after returning to work. If so, look for suitable alternative positions where medical defects will not be important. Where there is doubt about the nature of a disability, ask for the employee's permission to consult his or her doctor and also to seek independent medical advice and inform the worker the instant that a medical condition seems likely to put his or her job at risk. Workers suffering allergies should, if possible, be found work away from the source of the allergy (para 35). The Code recommends that when employees become mentally rather than physically ill their relatives should be consulted to check on their progress.

Activity

Regular absenteeism and lateness can disrupt work routines and cannot be allowed to go unchecked.

How do you cope with an employee with a poor record of attendance and poor punctuality?

This is one of the commonest discipline problems you may have to deal with. You must have a standard procedure that you follow in all cases and you must be seen to follow it.

Compare your actions with those recommended by the Code of Practice outlined below.

Absenteeism

The Code has a separate section on absenteeism which, after incompetence, is perhaps the commonest source of disciplinary action. Regular absenteeism without justification, like latecoming, is a bad habit among some employees. It is a breach of contract in that the absent worker has reneged on the obligation to be at work during contractually agreed working hours. Occasional unwarranted absences do not normally justify dismissal (unless there are strict rotas, safety hazards or demonstrable interruptions in production due to absenteeism) and even if the absenteeism (or latecoming) is persistent, action can only be taken after formal written warnings (the ACAS Code recommends at least two) have been issued and full disciplinary procedures invoked. The first written warning might be a confirmation of a formal oral warning. It should state that on a certain date you warned the individual (a man, say) about his absences from work, that he provided no excuse for his behaviour and that you expect him to improve, otherwise you will have no choice but to invoke the disciplinary procedure. The next letter will remind the employee of the first, will point out that attendance has not improved and *specify* the dates the employee was unjustifiably absent from work. In closing the letter you should state that if he is again absent without good cause within (say) the next three months then a final warning may be issued and that any absenteeism after that might result in dismissal. A final written warning will refer to the previous warnings and again *specify* the dates of further absences. It should point out that previous warnings were ignored, that no satisfactory explanations have been offered (but that if any exist you should be informed immediately) and that he will be dismissed if he is absent without permission during the next three months. The next time he is absent he should be suspended pending a full disciplinary hearing as previously outlined.

Paragraph 38 of the ACAS Code recommends that absences be investigated promptly, that the worker be invited to explain his or her absences indicating any mitigating circumstances, that domestic circumstances be taken into account where relevant and that if following warnings the employee's attendance does not improve then his or her age, length of service, past performance, likelihood of reform, availability of alternative work where attendance is not so crucial and the effect of absences on the firm's overall operations should all be taken into account when deciding an appropriate course of action.

A sanction must be 'reasonable' in the context of the circumstances of the offence. Actions taken should be recorded on the worker's personal file, with full details of the offence and the reasons for your decision. However, the Code insists that, except in special circumstances (agreed between management and union), records of breaches of disciplinary rules should be discarded after some predetermined period of satisfactory conduct.

Other Codes of practice

The Race Relations Act 1976 ss 2, 4(2) make it unlawful to discriminate racially in the operation of disciplinary procedures, for example by victimising (ie treating less favourably) a person for having complained about racial discrimination or having given evidence about such a complaint. The Commission for Racial Equality's Code of Practice[3] recommends that, in applying disciplinary procedures consideration should be given to the possible effect on an employee's behaviour of the following:

- racial abuse or other racial provocation
- communication or comprehension difficulties
- difficulties in cultural background or behaviour.

In particular, required standards of behaviour should take account of the cultural and religious needs of certain ethnic minorities. For example, a Sikh should not be disciplined for having long hair and a beard or for refusing to abandon his turban to comply with company uniform requirements.[4]

The Sex Discrimination Act 1975, s 4(1)–(3) similarly renders illegal the disciplining of individuals for having complained or helped others complain about sex or marriage discrimination and it is illegal to dismiss someone on the grounds of sex or whether or not they are married. Section 32(a) of the Equal Opportunities Commission's Code of Practice (issued in 1985) recommends that care be taken to ensure that members of one sex are not disciplined or dismissed for 'performance or behaviour that would be overlooked in the other sex'.

Taking disciplinary action

If your employing organisation has fair and comprehensive formal disciplinary procedures, including right of appeal, and if you adhere to the advice of the relevant codes of practice you should not feel uneasy or embarrassed about taking reasonable disciplinary action. Your behaviour in these matters should be responsive rather than overbearing. Do not threaten, bully, intimidate or act in other high-handed ways. Where appropriate, seek advice and direction from the personnel department which, if it is any good, should be able to provide expert guidance on legal matters relating to employment, on precedents, custom and practice in other firms, details of workers' personal records and so on.

Base your disciplinary activities on established rules, not personal whims and always be consistent. Adopt a liberal approach. If you have a choice between imposing a rule that is not really necessary for the efficient functioning of the organisation, or turning a blind eye my advice is to select the latter course — there is little point in harassing people for no good reason. React to, rather than initiate, situations. Correct mistakes as inconspicuously as possible and try to improve rather than condemn an errant employee's behaviour. Treat all your subordinates equally, without malice or favour. Assume always that they are honest, hardworking, responsible people and express surprise whenever an incident contradicts this view. During a disciplinary interview, try to discuss *issues* rather than the personal characteristics of the individual. Direct your remarks to the alleged offence, not the personality of the offender. A problem here is that disciplinary matters have legal implications, so that your approach must be rather formal, if only to cover yourself in the event of an appeal. However, try as far as possible to avoid legalistic jargon and stick to the spirit rather than the letter of the rules. If the accused person 'blows up' and storms out of the organisation, make a second attempt after a reasonable cooling off period has elapsed to resolve the issue. Write a polite letter inviting that person to come back for an interview and if he or she does not reply write another. Loss of employment is an extremely serious matter, and you *might* have made a mistake. In your letter, point out the existence of procedures for appeal and that temporary suspension on full pay pending an investigation, as opposed to downright dismissal will not be possible unless he or she returns to work.

Note finally that the ultimate disciplinary measure, dismissal, makes impossible the reform of the offender. The best it can do is deter others from engaging in similar behaviour and indicate to everyone that management is not prepared to tolerate certain activities or low standards of work. Dismissal may be just retribution in some particular circumstances, but all the effort and expense that went into recruiting, training and developing the dismissed employee is wasted. A replacement must be found (who might turn out to be unsatisfactory) at considerable inconvenience and cost.

Summary

One of your tasks as a manager is to deal with 'people problems' within your department. Behaviour that you regard as undesirable or even dangerous cannot be allowed to go unchecked.

You have to choose between a gentle reprimand, an oral warning recorded on file and a disciplinary interview.

Care is needed as there may be legal considerations, but if you follow the procedure laid down by your organisation, you need have nothing to fear.

You must familiarise yourself with the formal procedures and if you have any questions, turn to your superior or the personnel officer for advice.

Notes

1 The book by Christopher Waud, *Guide to Employment Law*, Associated Magazines Ltd, London is a particularly useful quick reference guide on these matters. It is updated and reprinted each year.
2 The duty to obey has been strengthened by a recent case which established that it is reasonable for a manager to demand that workers inform on colleagues' misbehaviour. Suppose, for example, that a spate of thefts has occurred within your department. You cannot identify the culprit, but can prove that other workers know who is stealing from the firm. It seems that now you are legally entitled to insist that your subordinates name the thief, and may dismiss them *all* if they refuse.
3 HMSO, London, 1984.
4 A recent case seems to have established the principle that special considerations apply to constructive dismissals in race (or sex) harassment situations. Thus, if a subordinate (i) complains that he or she has been racially abused, (ii) insists that you discipline the offending worker, and (iii) you refuse or demonstrably fail to apply appropriate sanctions against the culprit, then the victim of the harassment can resign, claim constructive unfair dimissal, and will almost certainly win compensation.

10

Special Disciplinary Problems

Objectives

This chapter will help you to:

- identify individuals with problems related to alcohol and drug abuse, depression etc.
- handle such personal problems, when they affect performance at work.

It is none of your business how other people conduct their private lives, yet some problems experienced by colleagues and subordinates outside working hours — problems related to alcohol, drug abuse, depression and other emotional distress — will almost certainly affect their performance at work. Executive managers, especially supervisors, confront these situations directly. You cannot avoid becoming involved if members of your team cease to function effectively through personal difficulties; your own superiors will expect you to take positive action, while the people concerned may themselves ask for help. Note particularly that addictive habits are expensive, so that loss of income from employment is a devastating blow for the individual concerned and remember always that unfortunate personal circumstances can lead the most stable and stalwart employee to despair and reliance on addictive substances.

These are difficult and harrowing issues, but they will not go away. It is not in my view proper merely to warn and then dismiss an employee whose work suffers badly through this type of problem without first trying to help. There are of course numerous agencies, special clinics, professional counselling services and advisory bodies to assist people afflicted by these illnesses. Yet the simple fact is that victims rarely seek outside help unless compelled (or heavily encouraged) to do so. Instead, they look for informal help, relying on friends and colleagues, like yourself, who they already know and trust and with whom they feel confident. You are, like it or not, an important part of the afflicted person's life support system: a burdensome responsibility but one you cannot escape.

Activity

In your capacity as manager, have you had to deal with any of the personal problems outlined in the introduction? What action did you take?

You may feel that such problems may be contributory factors to unacceptable behaviour, and are covered within disciplinary and dismissal procedures covered in the previous chapter.

You may feel that it is none of your concern how people act in their private lives. Try to keep an open mind as you work through this chapter.

Alcohol abuse

In Britain, the consumption of alcohol has more than doubled since the mid 1960s. As a nation, Britain spends more on alcohol than on fuel and light, much more than on books, newspapers or any form of entertainment and nearly as much as on clothing and footwear.[1] Annual admissions to NHS psychiatric hospitals (ignoring private clinics) for treatment of alcoholism have increased twenty-five fold, and the number of people convicted for drunkenness has doubled during the last 20 years.[2]

Excessive drinkers generally have higher rates of absenteeism from work, are unpunctual, take more sick leave and are involved in more industrial accidents than non-drinkers. Their ability to concentrate and sustain effort is affected and, in the longer term, their physical health is damaged. Alcoholics are more than ten times more likely to contract cirrhosis of the liver than non-drinkers and are likely to suffer from inflammation of the pancreas, various ulcers, gastritis, and several types of blood and neurological disorders.[3] It is reasonable to expect that alcoholic employees are less productive than others and, at the managerial level, less competent to take important decisions. Yet drinking is often associated with certain aspects of managerial work — at informal consultations, before important meetings, to seal a negotiation, to discuss business with clients, suppliers, and with colleagues after work.

Alcoholism is a disease which requires proper treatment if it is not to become worse, yet those affected are not usually able to give up drinking independently: the more a person *needs* to stop drinking the less he or she is likely to be able to do so. If a member of your team abuses alcohol, your section's work is almost certain to suffer since the effects of alcohol persist during the (working) hours the victim is not drinking. His or her intellectual capacity declines, as does the ability to communicate with others and the accuracy of perceptions of other peoples' attitudes towards that employee. Alcoholics are typically unreliable, prone to irrational behaviour and frequently depressed.

Self-check

What do you understand by alcohol abuse?

Answer

There is no clear cut answer. Not all people who drink are guilty of alcohol abuse, but the potential is there. Perhaps alcohol abuse is measured by the degree to which the individual is dependent on alcohol, the frequency with which he or she drinks and the effect on his or her behaviour.

Most problem drinkers have jobs, but on average possess also five times the probability of being absent through sickness and three times the probability of experiencing an accident than other workers.[4] The danger is that since heavy drinkers are often personally likeable people and because of the positive image that social drinking enjoys problems such as frequent latecoming, missed meetings, uncompleted work etc are initially ignored, but when an employee's drinking reaches the point where he or she is unable to work efficiently, the worker is arbitrarily dismissed! You should try and prevent this happening. Apart from your losing a colleague, the firm also loses all the training and expertise embodied in the employee. Bear in mind that the circumstances which caused your colleague to begin drinking heavily might one day apply to you.

Indications that someone has a serious drink problem include regular late arrival at work (especially on Monday mornings) with a hangover, irritability, forgetfulness, inattention, lunchtime drinking followed by poor performance in the afternoon and personality changes. Alcohol is a short term stimulant but long term depressant. Immediately after a drinking session the individual may be sociable and alert, but not for long. Work efficiency declines and with it the worker's self-esteem. He or she will apologise repeatedly for letting you down, but the problem will worsen, until eventually the individual will not be able to undertake any routine duties without first having a drink.

There is little point *warning* alcoholic subordinates about the likely consequences of continuing drunkardness, since warnings simply upset them and cause them to feel even more wretched and inadequate than before and thus more likely to seek relief in drink. Equally however, you should not tolerate drunken behaviour, otherwise the afflicted person will get worse, placing intolerable burdens on working colleagues.

As drunkards deteriorate, their behaviour causes them to become unpopular with workmates, leading to social isolation, self-pity and hence further alcohol abuse. At first, you may be tempted to protect your colleague, believing that the problem is temporary and bound to improve. Indeed, you might expend a great deal of energy on covering up, finding excuses for his or her non-appearance at committees, explaining absences and so on but in the end you are bound to fail. Accept that your colleague is *ill* and look to a proper and established procedure for dealing with the problem.

One such policy is recommended jointly by the Health and Safety Executive, DHSS, and the Department of Employment.[4]

Self-check

In your opinion, what signs indicate that a member of your staff might have a drink problem?

Answer
The following list is not an exhaustive one and many of the signs may involve a change in the individual's behaviour and personality: frequent absences and poor punctuality both in the morning and after lunch; irritability with colleagues; decline in standard of work and general efficiency; anti-social behaviour; unreliability.

The major implications of these recommendations are as follows:

- the policy should be agreed jointly by management and workers' representatives, not arbitrarily imposed
- alcoholism should be regarded as a health rather than a disciplinary problem (although a disciplinary matter may have initiated the procedure). Personnel needing assistance should be assured appropriate aid and support
- individuals seeking help should not face the possibility of losing their jobs, nor should their terms and conditions of employment be altered
- either, the firm should offer treatment via its own medical services or, if it does not possess sufficient resources for this, refer the case to a specialist treatment unit.

Like all government backed Codes of Practice and policy recommendations, HSE guidelines do not carry the force of law, but when adjudicating cases courts and tribunals will ask whether they have been followed. Thus, although drunkenness on the job and/or diminished work performance due to the effects of drink do provide and always have provided grounds for 'fair' dismissal under the headings of 'misconduct' or 'incapability' (see chapter 9) tribunals, under the influence of HSE recommendations, increasingly lean towards interpreting alcohol abuse as a *sickness* rather than as a disciplinary offence. Chronic sickness leading to poor performance at work can itself lead to 'fair' dismissal, but tribunal decisions have established that definite procedures must be followed in this case:

- the position should be discussed with the worker to ascertain whether there is any chance of improvement
- proper medical advice must be obtained, and the worker given the chance to refute the medical opinions stated (perhaps by presenting evidence from another qualified medical practitioner)
- the employer must consider whether any other post is available or likely to become available where the worker's ill-health would not be a problem.

Note however that the above procedure need only be followed if the employee has a bad record for sickness *for which he or she is not responsible.* Thus, while tribunals have insisted that alcoholics, as 'sick' people, should be treated with patience and consideration, no tribunal would (I presume) ever decide that alcohol abuse was not the victim's own fault. Another factor militating against problem drinkers is that under the Health and Safety at Work, etc Act 1974, employers have a statutory duty to provide a *safe* working environment, as well as their being under a common law duty to take 'reasonable care' to ensure the health and safety of employees. Alcohol abuse impairs judgement, encourages slapdash approaches to safety and causes accidents. An employer who does not act against an excessively heavy drinking employee may be accused of breaching — by neglect — health and safety law.

A policy should apply equally to *all* grades of staff, not just management. It should be written and widely circulated specifying the help available and the procedure for obtaining (confidential) assistance. Conflicts inevitably arise between on the one hand the promoting of a policy for combatting alcohol abuse and on the other the provision of alcohol in the workplace (bars, clubs, licensed canteens) and the creation of environments conducive to heavy drinking (business lunches, receptions for outside visitors, office parties, retirement presentations, wine at staff meetings etc). My view is that there is little point in prohibiting alcohol from business canteens, social clubs, etc because drink is immediately available in local public houses, though I do feel that the serving of alcohol at informal staff meetings, leaving parties etc might project an inappropriate image of management's attitudes towards drink. If alcohol must be served, then plenty of soft drink alternatives should be freely available.

Firms which do not permit alcohol on the premises may need to adopt a policy towards lunchtime drinking elsewhere, especially if a diminution of efficiency caused by alcohol will greatly impair performance (as is the case with certain precision engineering skills). Technically, it is possible to impose contractual condition of employment that workers must not drink at lunchtime, so that breach of the condition provides grounds for disciplinary action up to and including fair dismissal. Note however that such a dismissal would, if challenged, be extremely difficult to justify in a court Unequivocal proof that the employee had been drinking would be needed; with witnesses, evidence that performance was impaired, evidence that proper formal warnings had been given etc and the firm would have to demonstrate that breach of its no-drinking rule was *fundamental* to the worker's repudiation of the contract of employment. A firm prepared to go through all this might be better off simply improving its 'dry' canteen arrangements (and prices) while reducing the total length of the working day by (say) half an hour through shortening the lunchbreak, thereby making it physically difficult for employees to go out for a drink.

Activity

Persistent drunkenness may be cited as the reason for the summary dismissal of an employee. However, the current trend is to treat alcohol abuse as a sickness and firms are encouraged to follow the Code of Practice drawn up by the Health and Safety Executive.

What is the attitude of your own organisation towards alcohol? Is alcohol available on the premises? Are staff encouraged to drink at meetings and functions? Does your organisation have a policy on coping with alcohol-related problems?

While it is not illegal to consume alcohol, drinking to excess is dangerous. In work situations, people may be encouraged to consume alcohol and to refuse is seen as anti-social.

Other issues requiring attention in an organisation's alcohol policy include decisions on whether employees who drive for the organisation will automatically be dismissed following conviction for drunken driving or whether they will be offered alternative work (the threat of automatic dismissal might be a powerful incentive against drinking), whether the extent of an individual's consumption of alcohol should be discussed during routine company medical examinations, and what should happen if evidence of excessive drinking emerges and who in the first instance shall be responsible for reporting alcohol abuse observed in employees (usually it is the departmental supervisor).

Role of the departmental manager

A heavy drinker might attempt independently to come off the bottle, possibly following a particularly unpleasant alcohol related incident, or might be compelled to do so as a condition of keeping a job. In the latter case the employee might be required to attend one of the numerous help agencies that exist to facilitate 'drying out' (details of these agencies may be found in the references quoted at the end of the chapter). Once an alcoholic accepts the need for treatment there begins a long and difficult process of recovery that is harrowing not only for the individual but also for his or her colleagues at work. Initially, your colleague may be depressed, confused, and express feelings of resentment, anxiety and guilt. All these emotions may be directed against you. Put up with this, since it is unlikely to last long. It results largely from disturbed sleep patterns and the immediate physical effects of withdrawal, particularly if loss of appetite causes your colleague not to eat. Talk to your colleague. Make yourself available for private discussions and try and get the individual involved with work. Much nervous energy generated during withdrawal can be profitably directed towards improved performance in a job. As your colleague dries out, he or she will adopt new perspectives on events and personal circumstances. Do not allow that person to take major long term decisions (eg resignation, applying for transfer, etc) during this traumatic period. If the worker offers to resign say no.

Accept that relapses are likely. It is probably best to determine in advance how many relapses you will tolerate (four perhaps) before dismissal. Relapses are most probable if your colleague becomes excessively tired, angry, or depressed. Steer your colleague away from work situations that might generate such emotions. When a relapse occurs, try not to appear annoyed — discuss its causes and consequences with the victim, with management and with your other colleagues, but do not cover up (doing so could help destroy that person). Recognise that further relapses are likely, and do not feel personally responsible if and when they take place. You must, of course, be prepared to rearrange your work routines to enable your afflicted colleague to have time off to attend his or her GP and/or an alcoholic's rehabilitation centre. Note finally that although, in the short run, your colleague may become quite dependent on you for help, advice, encouragement and general support; this will diminish as his or her alcohol dependence falls. You will *not*, in the longer term, be burdened with a mawkish, immature and helpless individual totally reliant on your direction. As the obsession with drink recedes, new lifestyle opportunities naturally emerge — new leisure interests, capacities for productive work, personal relationships and rewarding intellectual activities. You will not be personally contaminated through contact with a problem drinker.

Self-check

What is your role as manager towards a member of your staff who is suffering from alcohol abuse?

Answer
You may feel that this problem requires specialist help and you are right, but the individual will need support and encouragement in the workplace. The degree to which you are willing and able to help will depend on the extent to which you can empathise with the individual.

Theft

In principle, an employee who steals may be fairly dismissed on the grounds that such conduct causes irreversible damage to the firm. There is, however, much legal ambiguity in these respects. If the theft is serious and the case against the worker strong, then he or she may be dismissed under existing legislation *provided* the employer carries out a 'reasonable' investigation into the circumstances of the theft. An immediate investigation is essential because if the matter is reported to the police and the employee is consequently charged, the trial might not be scheduled for many months hence, and any interviews with witnesses conducted by the firm's representatives during the interim could be construed as interference with the course of justice. A conviction for theft not connected with the worker's employment might still be grounds for fair dismissal, as long as the firm can demonstrate that its public reputation would suffer or that trade or insurance terms would be adversely affected by the continuing employment of the convicted person.

'Theft' is defined in law as the dishonest appropriation of someone else's property with the intention of permanently depriving the other person of that property, but it is not 'dishonest' to appropriate property if the person taking it genuinely believes that the property belongs to him or her, or believes that the owner has given or *would give* consent to its removal. Thus great ambiguity can arise over whether something has been 'stolen' when, as is common in many firms, employees have free access to materials or equipment and frequently take work off the premises, including work taken home in the evenings or at weekends. Similarly, occasional 'borrowing' of small amounts from petty cash or a till is considered acceptable in many firms, with the proviso of course that the money is quickly repaid. Nevertheless, theft means taking *anything* that does not belong to the taker if he or she has no intention of giving it back. Thus, using the telephone at work for personal calls, keeping things that are found, even not returning excess change to a customer are all cases of 'theft'.

Self-check

What do you understand by the term theft?

Answer
The legal definition is the dishonest appropriation of someone else's property with the intention of permanently depriving that other person of that property.

Where the person genuinely believes that the property belongs to him/her, or that consent has or would be given, this may not be theft.

Strictly speaking, making private phone calls or putting private letters through the office post system may be construed to be theft.

Dealing with a thief

Suppose there is an outbreak of stealing within your department, and that you catch the person responsible (a young man say). I believe, on both moral and efficiency grounds (cost of recruiting a replacement, loss of skills and experience embodied in that man, waste of training expenditures etc) that you should not dismiss him for a first offence without offering a chance to reform. He must repay whatever he stole, but thereafter should be counselled to discover the causes of his errant behaviour and to encourage in him the desire to amend his ways.

Recreate the offence; ask him to describe, in detail, what he did the day before it occurred, how he felt on the morning of the day the offence was committed and his thoughts and actions after the event. This simulated action replay will help both of you understand the core motives underlying his behaviour and the patterns of interpersonal interaction associated with the theft. Try to identify a sequence of events that would have caused the incident *not* to have occurred. In what circumstances would the thief not have wanted to steal the goods? What was his state of mind at the moment of the theft, and what caused it to exist?

Why do people steal? There is no simple answer to this question. Indeed, it is a question that has perplexed philosophers, theologians, psychiatrists and the penal authorities for generations. Among the more common causes of theft by employees are the following:

- hatred of the employing institution. Desires to 'get one's one back' for perceived injustices (low pay, being passed over for promotion, poor relationships with colleagues and/or management etc) committed in the past
- shortage of money caused by circumstances not related to work, or through low wages inducing the employee to 'top up' his wages by stealing from the firm
- the 'Robin Hood Syndrome' — a desire to punish better off colleagues for being better off. Thieves often justify this notion by saying that most people are insured against theft, or that wealthier colleagues can afford to lose small amounts
- temptation, caused by poor security (unlocked offices, valuables left lying around) leading to 'opportunistic' theft
- excitement — the exhilaration of taking risks and not being caught.

To gain an understanding of your dishonest subordinate's particular motives, ask him to list the people he would *not* steal from. Would he steal from his parents, his wife and children, certain of his immediate workmates, yourself — and how does he explain differences in his willingness to steal? How far is he prepared to go? If he is prepared to steal a colleague's umbrella, would he steal the same colleague's wallet, or his or her car? Would he be prepared to enter a workmate's home and steal from there? Would he steal from workmates' families? Ask him if he would steal from his own close friends if he were absolutely certain of not being caught. Ask whether he would only steal only small amounts from friends, but large amounts from others. Answers to these questions may provide valuable insights into why your subordinate steals. It may be that he steals during moments of emotional distress — just after arguments with colleagues for example. Is his behaviour compulsive, or does he feel it can be controlled? This question and answer session, hopefully, will convince the young man that he has a problem and will encourage him to *want* to be cured. Counsel patiently. Do not bully, threaten, intimidate or harass. Adopt a professional emotionally detached approach.

Next, you should outline a programme for reform. Point out

the cost of his behaviour. Add up the value of the items you know he has stolen and deduct this amount from the value of (say) two years' loss of wages (emphasise the difficulties a thief, without work references, will experience in getting another job) less his estimated social security benefit. Then mention the shame, humiliation, loss of occupational status etc associated with being dismissed for theft. Tell your subordinate to list all the things he finds attractive about stealing (excitement, financial benefits etc) and all the reasons for *not* stealing (fear of discovery, a police record, loss of status in the eyes of other people and so on). Ask whether he still thinks that stealing is worthwhile. Many persistent thieves *would* like to change their behaviour and an interview along the suggested lines might offer the internal motivation they require.

Make the young man apologise to the people from whom he stole. This will at once punish him, force him to accept responsibility for what he has done, and partially assuage the (justifiable) anger of his victims. Offer him a second chance (you need your colleagues' permission for this, but people are usually prepared to give the first offender the opportunity to reform) and arrange to monitor his future work.

Activity

Some suggestions have been made to you on how to deal with a thief. What action do you or would you take when you catch someone stealing in your department?

Your actions may be governed by the policy of your organisation. You may view the actions proposed here as being too lenient. However, when it is a first offence, you should consider trying to identify why the individual stole and whether he or she is likely to repeat the offence.

Investigating theft

The usual procedure is to suspend a suspected thief (on full pay) pending a preliminary investigation. However, you should only do this if you are dealing with an apparently open and shut case. The fact that a person is suspended *implies* guilt and he or she will carry that label even if subsequently proven innocent. Nevertheless, suspension is better than summary dismissal because it avoids legal complications.

After the preliminary investigation, the employee should either return to work or be dismissed — it is not generally possible to suspend a worker *without* pay (say until a criminal prosecution has come to court) unless this provision is formally embodied in his or her contract of employment, since refusal to pay wages constitutes breach of the employment contract and is therefore tantamount to dismissal. Hence, a worker suspended without pay can claim unfair dismissal in an industrial tribunal and this case will be heard quite separately from and independent of the criminal proceedings. It could even occur that someone is found guilty in a criminal prosecution, but that a tribunal rules that the worker has been unfairly dismissed. For example, the 'theft' may have been trivial but the firm wished to 'make an example' of someone and in so doing acted, in the view of the tribunal, in an 'unreasonable' manner.

An employee suspected of theft cannot legally be searched without his or her consent unless the search is conducted by the police or agreement to submit to a search is incorporated into that person's contract of employment. In the latter case, refusal to be searched constitutes grounds for fair dismissal. The firm's own vehicles can be searched at will, but a vehicle owned by an employee cannot be searched without the employee's permission. You cannot arrest and detain an employee unless you have 'reasonable grounds' for suspecting that he or she has committed a *criminal* offence, otherwise the worker can sue your firm for wrongful arrest and imprisonment.

Unless you have been properly trained in these matters, do not attempt to extract a written statement from anyone who is not willing to provide this voluntarily. Statements are obviously useful as they can be presented in evidence in legal proceedings. Someone who admits a theft might therefore be invited to sign a document confirming verbal statements in order to clarify issues and prevent subsequent arguments about who said what, but a court will not accept as evidence any statement obtained:

by fear of prejudice or hope of advantage, exercised or held out by a person in authority, or by oppression.[8]

Thus, anyone bullied into making a statement can subsequently retract, and the statement will not be accepted by a court.

The accused party must convince the court that the statement was obtained improperly. Normally, a court will take the accused's word for this unless the police or reliable and truly independent witnesses were involved when the statement was taken. If during your initial interview with the suspected thief you start writing down what he or she says with a view to using these notes in a subsequent prosecution then you are obliged to tell the suspect of this intention and you should make a note of the point at which you issued the warning. All internal disciplinary procedures that do not result in criminal prosecutions must follow the rules of natural justice (see chapter 9).

Self-check

When investigating a case of theft in the workplace, what, under the law, are you not allowed to do?

Answer
It is essential that you proceed with care, since any infringement of the law or denial of individual rights, might prejudice any criminal prosecution brought.

You may not: suspend the individual without pay; search the suspect or his or her own property without permission unless it was written into the contract of employment; arrest or detain the individual without reasonable grounds; make a written record of what he or she says without permission; force a written confession.

Violence, abuse and threatening behaviour

Violence means hitting anybody, no matter how lightly, for any reason whatsoever. It is an offence for which employees may be fairly dismissed, but the test of 'reasonableness' must always be applied. Thus, for example, an employee (a man, say) might challenge a dismissal for fighting on the grounds that he merely defended himself against an unprovoked attack using the minimum force necessary. The dismissal would be 'fair' only if you could prove that this was not the case. Other matters that must be considered when assessing 'reasonableness' are whether the violence was serious (horseplay among employees is unlikely to justify dismissal) and the status of the employee (did for example the aggressor attack a supervisor, a senior manager, a subordinate, or a fellow worker of equivalent rank — a tribunal would probably consider it unfair to dismiss a lower ranking person for fighting with a supervisor who is not also dismissed). You need to collect all the facts relating to the incident, statements from witnesses and from the people involved (particularly in relation to provocation), the extent of retaliation and whether there was racial or sexual abuse.

Swearing at people and other forms of threatening behaviour short of physical violence might also justify dismissal, provided it is serious and persistent and you act 'reasonably' when deciding to dismiss. The dismissal itself will be for 'misconduct' which is a legally nebulous term. Thus, whether misconduct has actually occurred is more a question of fact than of law. Each set of circumstances must be considered separately, especially in relation to the following points:

- is this the first time the employee has engaged in violence and/ or abuse and threatening behaviour? If not; were previous incidents ignored and if so why
- is the offence (particularly if it only involves swearing at someone) substantial in relation to the employee's job? Can it really be said to have disrupted working relationships, staff harmony, and to represent in effect a repudiation by the employee of his or her contractual obligation to serve the employer and work properly
- were there any extenuating circumstances, such as ill-health, or the worker being under emotional stress at the time of the incident
- has the employee expressed remorse for the action?

Disciplinary action is justified only if the bad language used is so wilfully offensive that it may reasonably be assumed to distress the person to whom it is addressed. Thus a tribunal might rule that words used in the company of somebody occupying one occupational status (a female senior manager for example) are unacceptably disagreeable, whereas the same words used in other circumstances (if for instance one low ranking worker abuses another of the same rank) are words used 'as a matter of course' and therefore acceptable.

Violent acts committed outside working hours could justify dismissal but only if the incident can be proven to affect the reputation of the employing firm. For example, a man working with young children might be fairly dismissed if he is convicted for child molestation in circumstances entirely unconnected with work. Note the difficulty of justifying a dismissal for a non work related disturbance *without* a criminal conviction.

Self-check

Distinguish between violence and threatening behaviour.

Answer
Violence means any form of physical assault such as hitting, punching. Threatening behaviour falls short of actual physical violence, ie swearing, fist shaking. Both can constitute grounds for fair dismissal.

Dealing with acts of violence and abuse

Individuals with severe psychiatric disorders that cause violent behaviour rarely get jobs. As a manager, your most likely involvement with violent or abusive acts will therefore be concerned mainly with disturbances resulting from provocation or from bad interpersonal relationships which have deteriorated over a considerable period of time. The *demeanour* of one person may aggravate another. Perceptions that somebody is deliberately uncooperative, fractious, insolent or failing to show respect can lead to abusive confrontations.

Employees who are abusive or who commit a single violent act should not, in my view, be dismissed without being given the opportunity to reform. Violent or abusive people need to learn how to *control* their emotions and seek alternative ways of responding to situations they perceive as a threat. Assertiveness training (see Volume 3, chapter 5) can it seems be extremely useful here since, paradoxically, many violent people lack personal assertion skills.[9] They are not able to cope with stressful and distressing situations without becoming aggressive rather than dealing with troublesome people in assertive, forthright, but nevertheless polite and detached ways. A small financial outlay on sending such an employee on a short assertion training course may be a sound long term investment resulting in a better, more productive employee able to exert proper self-control.

Otherwise, the best way you can assist is by helping an abusive person explore and understand his or her own aggressive feelings. Three things are needed:

- development of that person's awareness of the *effects* on others of a violent or abusive act
- counselling to discover the situations and people that the aggressive person finds annoying (and why) and how that person perceives the attributes and characteristics of the individual that he or she has abused or attacked
- implementation of a programme, with clearly defined objectives, for exercising self-control.

At the counselling session, ask the person (a young woman, say) to list all the times she lost her temper during the previous two months and to describe what exactly caused the loss of temper on each occasion. Ask her to specify the worst thing she would be prepared to do to another person — how violent or abusive is she prepared to be? Would she for example hit someone with a bottle or with a knife? Are there any people she would *never* abuse or hit — a parent, children, a pregnant woman, a disabled person and *why* would she not attack such individuals? If she can restrain herself in those contexts why cannot she exercise control in others? What is the most destructive thing she has ever done to another person? Has she ever attacked someone in a manner that would justify the victim doing the same thing to her?

This conversation, hopefully, will tease out several aspects of the woman's aggressive nature that previously she was not aware of, and may induce some measure of remorse. Use this as the basis for a meeting between herself and the person she abused. Invite her to apologise to the injured party.

The conversation might also highlight future situations or people she should consciously avoid. Write out a list of these, and insert this on the first page of a daily 'aggression diary' that she promises to keep for the next month and which will record all losses of self-control, outbursts of temper and feelings of aggression. Each entry should include an attempt to explain how the situation occurred and why she felt upset. For example, was she defending a perceived right, her self-respect; did she feel harassed, exploited or physically threatened? You have to convince this woman that violent or abusive incidents do not 'just happen'; they result from identifiable and usually predictable, combinations of events.

Vandalism

Activity

What is vandalism? Is it a problem where you work or where you live?

Vandalism is violence against property and ranges from graffiti to the actual destruction of property. Studies have shown that there are several types of vandalism, each with its own characteristics.

Vandalism is violence against property rather than against people. Although seemingly motiveless, it usually results from deep felt resentments, anger, frustration and a feeling of not being able to control events. Wilful damage to premises is the most visible form of vandalism, though vandalistic acts can cover a wide range of activities, from outbreaks of graffiti, defaced posters, cigarette burns on carpets and furniture etc through to unmitigated criminal damage. The latter extreme means deliberately or recklessly destroying or damaging property which belongs to another person, or damaging or destroying one's own property in such a way as to endanger other people (eg racing a private car around the firm's car park damaging other vehicles in the process). Note however that it is permissible to damage other peoples' property in self-defence or if the person committing the damage genuinely believes the owner had given or would give permission. It is sometimes difficult to distinguish criminal damage from honest mistake.

An extensive and detailed study of vandalism conducted by the Home Office[10] concluded that most 'vandalism' is directed against communal parts of institutions (graffiti on walls, broken windows, etc) rather than personal property. Vandals perceive such communal parts as 'impersonal', and they are easier to attack without being caught. A useful taxonomy of vandalism is offered by S Cohen who distinguishes five types: acquisitive, tactical, vindictive, play and malicious.[11] Acquisitive vandalism is associated with theft — damage is done as a corollory to unlawful gain. Tactical vandalism is a means to an end; for instance, sabotaging a production line in order to have a rest from work. Vindictive vandalism involves destroying property as revenge for a personal grievance. Play vandalism is simply 'messing around' without malicious intent. Malicious vandalism results from feelings of failure, boredom, frustration and despair.

Vandalism, therefore, may indicate the absence of adequate grievance procedures, breakdowns in communications or the inability of employees to participate in decisions that fundamentally affect their working lives. Dealing with a vandal is akin in many respects to dealing with a thief and the techniques discussed earlier might be applied, though it is especially important in the case of vandalism to root out the *cause* of the behaviour, since the factors that motivate one person to commit a destructive act (resentment over recently imposed working conditions for example) might also affect other employees.

Drug abuse

Some people turn to drugs other than alcohol (or tobacco for that matter) to help them cope with the stresses of work or other social circumstances. Others use drugs because they are attracted to drug related lifestyles. Yet more are enticed by the states of euphoria that certain drugs provide. Persistent use of drugs, whether taken under medical prescription (as with tranquillisers and certain antidepressants) or illegally (use of heroin for example) may affect adversely the user's performance at work.

Activity

Have you received any instruction on how to detect whether an individual might be using drugs? If not, try to arrange some training.

Certainly in schools and colleges, staff are receiving some training to help with the early detection of drug abuse.

While drugs in the short term enable users to overcome anxiety, tension and perhaps even significant emotional distress, their protracted use causes dependence, eventually to the extent that users cannot survive a single working day without their use. All addictive drugs affect judgement, perception and the ability to concentrate. Tranquillisers cause doziness and lethargy; heroin, cocaine and other psychotic drugs have profound and lasting physical and mental effects.

Heroin (a narcotic derivative of opium) relieves anxiety, creating feelings of detachment from everyday worries and great personal well-being. Addiction is both physical and psychological. Physical addiction may not be severe — in Britain, heroin is typically distributed in powder form much diluted through mixture with other substances — but it is exceedingly dangerous nonetheless. Among the many harmful physical effects of persistent heroin use are frequent nausea and vomiting, severe loss of appetite leading to rapid weight loss, lack of energy and loss of interest in surroundings, dangers of blood and liver infections, the danger of AIDS caused by injection into the bloodstream using shared dirty needles, and a variety of illnesses associated with impurities in the substances with which heroin is mixed. Physical dependence is evidenced by unpleasant withdrawal symptoms when the drug is no longer available. These begin 8–24 hours after the last dose and are characterised by feelings of great anxiety, physical weakness, aches and pains similar to those experienced with a bad attack of 'flu', plus diarrhoea. More severe withdrawal symptoms include acute cramp, inability to sleep or eat and alternatively shivering and sweating. The worst phase is usually over in 24 hours, but in extreme cases it can last for over a week. Yet despite these horrors, ex-heroin users frequently return to the habit *after* their

their physical addiction has gone — users become *psychologically* addicted to the drug, missing the mental euphoria it creates. The drug acts as a sedative that blocks out mental anguish; it blunts the central nervous system and thus generates a false sense of emotional well-being. In consequence, ex-users crave for the relaxed peace of mind, exhilaration and freedom from worldly cares that heroin artificially provides.

Other hard drugs — cocaine, barbiturates, amphetamines, hallucinogens such as LSD, mescaline and many more — circulate (increasingly) in Britain today; with devastating effects, but heroin at the moment is the cheapest and most common, especially among young people (at least half of all UK heroin users are between 15 and 25 years old[5]) and the number of users is constantly expanding.[6] How should you behave towards a fellow employee who is hooked on hard drugs?

Self-check

What are the signs that an individual might be using drugs?

Answer
The signs may differ, depending on the drugs being used, but these may be taken as a general guideline:
— lack of concentration and poor judgement
— weight loss and frequent attacks of nausea, diarrhoea
— variations in personality
— perpetual 'flu' symptoms
— no interest in personal appearance
— unreliability.

The drug user at work

Drug problems at work are sometimes compared to alcohol abuse. The analogy is inappropriate. In the first place, whereas the sale and consumption of alcohol is entirely legal, the possession of narcotic drugs is a criminal offence. Drug users, therefore, will not normally discuss their habit with non-users. Moreover, outsiders (such as yourself) are frequently reluctant to become involved with a drug user because of the legal implications. Secondly, lay people typically feel they lack the knowledge of drug related addictions to be able to do anything of practical value to help. Nearly everyone experiences alcohol, but few people have experienced non-prescribed illegal drugs, thus whereas many managers feel confident and at ease when discussing alcohol, they experience great discomfort when discussing drugs. Supervisors might honestly believe they can influence a heavy drinker into coming off alcohol, but despair at the prospect of helping someone abandon hard drugs. Consequently, employees who would be helped if they were alcoholics, in accordance with a procedure similar to that previously outlined, are summarily dismissed for job inadequacy caused by drugs. This is a pity, because much can and needs to be done to help drug addicted employees. Drug abuse in Britain is growing alarmingly and as drug usage expands, manifestations of drug abuse will be increasingly evident at work.

Drug abuse is a difficult and contentious issue and I need to state quite clearly where I stand. Whereas I *would* discuss a colleague's alcohol problem with others, I would not reveal to anyone that someone is using drugs. Apart from the legal implications of drug abuse, society overall does not yet accept that drug addiction is as much an *illness* as a misdemeanor; drug abusers are thus harassed much more than heavy drinkers. You will not be able to help unless the confidentiality of the conversations you have with the afflicted person is guaranteed. The fact that someone is seriously abusing hard drugs will soon become apparent: loss of interest in personal appearance, weight loss, frequent absences, slow and halting speech, drowsiness and inability to concentrate and a collection of symptoms very similar to those experienced with a heavy cold — coughing, reddened eyes, running nose, and so on. Behaviour in general will change.

Conventional disciplinary measures are essentially useless. Drug addicts rarely cease to be addicts for fear of suspension or the sack, but drug abusers do often want to be rid of their habit (usually because of a crisis — an overdose, being arrested by the police, acute lack of money etc). You will encounter a colleague's drug abuse either through a single dramatic incident that clearly indicates he or she has a drug problem affecting performance at work or you will notice signs of drug abuse. In the former case, counselling should occur immediately and by compulsion. In the latter, you will have to raise the subject yourself. Do this frankly and as quickly as possible. Faced with this situation, here is how I personally would proceed:

- I would advise the person to break the habit — even if he or she is an 'occasional' user with only a light addiction — no matter how distressing the experience. Heroin in particular takes everything from the user, yet offers little of lasting value in return. It temporarily suppresses the natural emotional defence mechanisms (anxiety, depression etc) but at a fearful price in the longer run. Without the drug — which itself has severely debilitating and dangerous physical effects — the addict becomes ill and experiences great mental anguish and the physical effects are felt intensely because deprivation increases the body's sensitivity to pain. Likely responses from an occasional user are that narcotic drugs are less physically damaging than tobacco or alcohol (which in aggregate terms is true) and that although hard drugs are illegal, no-one has the moral right to prevent others from regulating the states of their own minds. I would reply with two points. Firstly, that I am concerned *only* with performance at work (the rest is none of my business) and I cannot allow his or her work to continue to decline (as it surely must) for the sake of other members of the team. Secondly, that heroin and other narcotics are *vastly* more addictive than other drugs, including tobacco and alcohol. Occasional light use is *extremely* likely to degenerate to more serious addiction and if the employee had not been adversely affected by the drug we would not be having the conversation!
- I would point out the frequently ignored fact that most people who give up drugs do so of their own accord, and without medical supervision.[7] Gradual cutting down *is* possible, given some self-control, for light users. While I would, of course, strongly advise my colleague to see a doctor or otherwise seek specialist help (lists of contacts are contained in the references at the end of the chapter) I must recognise and accept that many drug users are not willing to go this far, since to do so requires them to admit openly their dependence on the drug. In the way of encouragement to seek medical help, I would emphasise that GPs and doctors at drug dependency clinics

may be able to offer a short term substitute drug, and generally help alleviate the symptoms of withdrawal.

Thereafter, the victim must seek independently to change his or her lifestyle (as must the dried out alcoholic). Without a *personal* commitment, no-one else can help. The individual must avoid contact with other drug users, responsibilities have to be faced, fundamental causes of emotional distress confronted. These longer term adjustments are not, and cannot be, any of my concern. All I can do is offer sympathy and support during the immediate transition.

Summary

This chapter has dealt with some of the most serious problems facing modern society. The resulting behaviour in the workplace is often unacceptable and grounds for dismissal. You as a front line manager have to cope with these personal problems when they are brought into the workplace.

The modern philosophy is to treat those who suffer from alcohol and drug abuse, violent outbursts and who steal and vandalise property, as sick people who need help rather than punishment.

Organisations cannot close their eyes to these problems and must ensure that their management are given adequate training and advice to cope with them.

Now is the time to take a close look at your own organisation and examine the attitudes and policies towards these special disciplinary problems. Do they meet the criteria outlined in the text? Are there members of your staff, who show signs of suffering from any of the problems covered? If so, what can you do to help?

Notes

1 Tether, P, and Robinson, D, *Preventing Alcohol Problems: A Guide to Local Action*, Tavistock Publications, London, 1986.
2 Up to date figures are contained in the annual reports of the national alcohol abuse charity, *ACCEPT*.
3 For details see, Eastman, C, *Drink and Drinking Problems*, Longman, 1984.

4 Statistics are collected by the DHSS and the Health and Safety Executive, see for example *The Problem Drinker at Work*, prepared by the HSE and published by the Department of Employment, HMSO, London, 1981.

5 Quoted in Field, T, *Escaping the Dragon*, Unwin, London, 1985.

6 It is impossible to state accurately the number of users, since figures are available only for 'registered' addicts whereas the number of users is perhaps fifteen or twenty times as great. One way of estimating the number of users is to assume that (say) 90 per cent of all illicit drugs are seized by the authorities. On the basis of current levels of seizure this assumption leads to an estimate of there being enough heroin (let alone other drugs) entering Britain to supply about 400,000 regular users. For details of these calculations and further references see Manning, M, *The Drugs Menace*, Columbus Books, Bromley, 1985. The Home Office estimates that heroin use is rising by about 40 per cent per year.

7 See Duncan, R, and Tippell, S, *How to Stop: a do it yourself guide to opiate withdrawal*, Institute for the Study of Drug Dependence (ISDD), London, 1985. See also, *Heroin and Other Opiates*, also published by ISDD.

8 This quote is taken from a procedure known as 'Judges' Rules' which courts expect to have been followed by anyone taking statements from suspected thieves.

9 For details see McGuire, J, and Priestley, P, *Offending Behaviour*, Batsford, London, 1985.

10 Clarke, R V G, (ed) *Tackling Vandalism*, Home Office Research Study number 47, HMSO, 1978.

11 Cohen, S, 'Property destruction: motives and meanings' in Ward, C, *Vandalism*, Architectural Press, 1973.

Appendix
Theories of Motivation

Objectives

The objective of this appendix on theories of motivation is to help you to gain insight into why people work based on the findings of experts.

You do not have to accept all the theories put forward but the information may help you to understand people.

Academics have for many years investigated the question of why some people work harder than others and how management can induce employees to work harder, faster and more efficiently. Motivation may be formally defined as the causal drives, needs and aspirations which determine behaviour; it can arise within the person or from outside influences, including inducements offered by the firm. Theories of motivation centre on how individuals seek to satisfy their needs, the most basic of which are physiological: food, drink, sleep and shelter. Thereafter most people experience needs for affection and contact with others; they like to feel wanted by and useful to the community in which they live and work. Higher level needs include demands for social status and personal development.

Employment satisfies many needs — wages pay for food, clothing etc and jobs bring people into contact with fellow employees. Working environments and company personnel policies can help individuals fulfil their needs, or may be sources of worker dissatisfaction. For instance, a fundamental need is for security; people seek assurances that basic requirements will always be met no matter what the circumstances. A job supplies security through tenure arrangements, sick pay and pension schemes, redundancy payments and so on. Similarly, needs for status, self-esteem and personal enhancement might be satisfied through promotion systems, participation in decision making, training and the provision of fringe benefits. Some employees are satisfied merely to exercise a particular skill, others actively seek increasing authority and responsibility, thriving on competitive authority which might take them to senior levels in their organisations.

According to F W Taylor, the founder of the 'scientific' school of management thought, workers are motivated primarily by the prospect of high wages. Thus, management should organise work as efficiently as possible in order to enable workers to earn high wages. This meant stringent application of the division of labour, work measurement and method study. Taylor did not recognise the existence of conflicts of interest between workers and their employers, believing that provided employees were offered high material rewards they would support whatever working conditions were imposed. Reactions against Taylor's approach generated a number of alternative approaches to motivation theory. The major contributions are briefly outlined below.

The work of A H Maslow[1]

Maslow suggested that individuals are motivated by five levels of need. When the first level has been satisfied the individual will attempt to satisfy second level needs, then move on to the third, fourth and finally fifth levels. The five categories of need; in the order in which (according to Maslow) a person will seek to satisfy them are as follows.

Physiological

These must be satisfied for a person to survive. They include food, shelter, clothing, heat and light. Income from employment allows people to satisfy such basic needs.

Security

Once physiological needs have been met the individual will, Maslow argues, seek security of tenure at home and work, and protection against reduced living standards. Examples of attempts to achieve security are purchases of life, house and medical insurance and collective action through trade unions.

Social

Most people desire affection; they want to 'belong' to a community and to *feel* wanted. Hence, social groups, religious, cultural, sporting and recreational organisations naturally emerge. At work, people create activity groups, trade unions and formal and informal communication systems.

Esteem

Esteem needs include needs for recognition, authority and influence over others. Also relevant are the desire to acquire possessions and internal needs for self-respect which can be met through occupancy of highly ranked jobs and the provision of status symbols (large expensive company cars, wall-to-wall carpeting etc).

Self-actualisation

The highest level of need in the Maslow hierarchy involves creative activity and the search for personal fulfilment. Having satisfied all other needs the individual will want to accomplish everything he or she is capable of achieving, to develop individual skills, talents and aptitudes. Few people ever reach this final stage.

Maslow offers a convenient taxonomy of human needs, and he is much quoted in management studies literature. There are, however, a number of problems associated with the approach:

- some needs might not exist in certain people. What is considered important by one person could be regarded as trivial by someone else. Social environments influence individual perceptions; much depends on the traditions, cultures and life styles of the societies in which people live

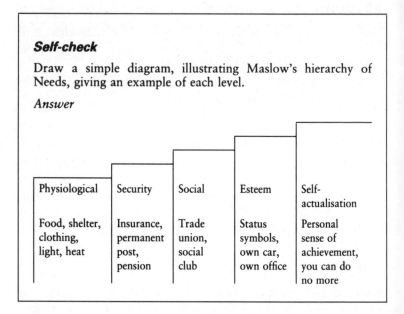

Self-check

Draw a simple diagram, illustrating Maslow's hierarchy of Needs, giving an example of each level.

Answer

Physiological	Security	Social	Esteem	Self-actualisation
Food, shelter, clothing, light, heat	Insurance, permanent post, pension	Trade union, social club	Status symbols, own car, own office	Personal sense of achievement, you can do no more

- assuming that all the needs suggested by Maslow are in fact present, they might not be ranked in the order outlined. Needs can exist simultaneously and horizontally as well as vertically and sequentially
- Maslow had little to say about sources of needs. In fact, many basic 'needs' are learned responses with cultural rather than physiological origins. Behaviour can be conditioned; wants may be created. Equally, current perceived needs can be suppressed by social pressures
- the theory states that individuals will seek to attain higher level needs only when lower needs have been satisfied. Many people, however, are acutely conscious of 'higher' needs even though their fundamental physiological needs have not been fully met. In a consumer society, the poor may yearn for status symbols even though they are unable to satisfy their immediate requirements.

The work of F Herzberg[2]

The importance of financial reward relative to other motivating factors was investigated by F Herzberg. According to Herzberg, two separate sets of factors influence human behaviour — on the one hand people want to avoid pain and obtain the basic necessities of life, while on the other they need to develop their personal capacities and potentials. Herzberg asked professionally qualified employees (engineers and accountants) what events at work had increased or reduced their satisfaction. It seemed that the things which provided satisfaction were quite different to the things which caused dissatisfaction. Factors generating dissatisfaction were: inadequate pay, bad personal relations with colleagues, poor supervision, unpleasant physical working conditions and the absence of fringe benefits. These were called 'hygiene' or 'maintenance' factors (from the analogy that hygiene does not improve health, but does prevent illness) — they do not increase a worker's job satisfaction, but their deficiency creates dissatisfaction. Note that hygiene factors relate to the conditions of work rather than to the work itself; thus, an improvement in a hygiene factor will not be noticed for very long. For example, a worker who feels cold may complain and as a result the firm's heating it turned up, but the worker quickly becomes acclimatised to the higher temperature and forgets how cold it was in the first instance. Improvements present dissatisfaction, but do not increase satisfaction in the long run. The factors responsible for creating satisfaction ('motivating' factors in Herzberg' language) were:

- sense of achievement from completing work
- recognition from others within the organisation
- responsibility assumed
- varied work, involving an assortment of interesting tasks
- prospects for promotion.

Motivators encouraged better quality work, hygiene factors did not: a worker might resign because a hygiene element was inadequate, yet would not work harder simply because the factor was satisfactory. Likewise, the absence of suitable motivators would not cause employees to resign, but an increase in the strengths of motivating factors would significantly improve effort and performance.

Herzberg was concerned with the attitudes towards work of qualified professional and managerial staff and not with shop floor workers who might be much more concerned with

---

Activity

Compare Herzberg's hygiene and motivating factors. To what extent do you agree with his contention that money does not act as a motivator?

It is true that money, in particular pay differentials, is at the heart of many industrial disputes. The level of pay is seen by many as a measure of the importance, status attached to the job. Teachers, nurses in comparing their pay with that of some manual workers, feel undervalued.

There is evidence from experts such as Goldthorpe, which would seem to contradict Herzberg. Perhaps one should bear in mind that while Herzberg interviewed professional/managerial staff, Goldthorpe questioned production line workers.

---

prospects for immediate financial reward. Managers themselves respond to different factors in different ways. Perhaps the most controversial of all Herzberg's conclusions was that pay and fringe benefits were hygiene and not maintenance factors. Bearing in mind Herzberg's research methodology) questionnaires and interviews with managerial staff) it is reasonable to suspect that many employees stated that money was not an important motivator whereas it actually was. Nevertheless, it would be wrong to overestimate the influence of the financial element. The value of Herzberg's work lies in his pointing out the importance of job satisfaction in employee motivation, though it must be said that relegation of pay to the role of hygiene factor is probably an oversimplification. Indeed, strong contrary evidence was discovered by a team of sociologists headed by John Goldthorpe[3] who conducted an extensive survey of industrial attitudes and behaviour among *manual* workers employed in three large manufacturing firms in Luton during the (prosperous) early 1960s. Two hundred and twenty-nine male operatives (and their wives) were interviewed in depth, with the investigators concluding that:

- these workers adopted 'instrumental' approaches to their jobs, seeing work as little more than a means of achieving a higher standard of living

- the workers did not expect to obtain job satisfaction; they were motivated primarily by the prospect of higher wages.

Interestingly, moreover, the interviewees still regarded themselves as 'working class' despite their enjoying relatively affluent lifestyles. Their lives at work lacked variety, autonomy and challenge, and the work itself was often undertaken in quite unpleasant physical conditions. Yet the men earned good wages which enabled them to offer their families standards and styles of living never previously experienced by manual workers. It followed that money was a great motivator to these employees.

The work of V H Vroom[4]

Vroom's expectancy theory states that an individual's behaviour is affected by:

- what the person wants to happen
- that person's estimate of the probabilities of various events occurring, including the desired outcome
- the strength of the person' belief that a certain outcome will satisfy his or her needs.

Predictions of what will happen in the future are usually based on what has happened in the past. Thus, situations not previously experienced (for example, new working practices, job changes, environmental alterations) give rise to uncertainty and may in consequence reduce employees' motivation. This is because the individuals concerned have no precedents upon which to base their assessments of the probable consequences of new situations. Hence, management should make clear to employees what precisely it expects from any alterations in policy or working practices that management might impose. Employees should be able to see a connection between effort and reward and the rewards offered should satisfy workers's needs. Vroom would argue that a complicated, unintelligible bonus scheme is unlikely to increase effort because participants cannot distinguish clear relationships between harder work and higher wages, even if higher wages are offered as part of the scheme. Similarly, experience of particular jobs gives workers precise knowledge of how output is connected to their activities.

In this case expectancies are easily formed; workers know that the quantity and quality of production depends on how they perform their work. This implies that innate satisfaction derived from working hard and actually seeing the results — planned, predicted and brought about by the worker involved is a primary motivator. Of course, motivation alone is not sufficient to guarantee successful outcomes; ability is also required. Vroom suggested that levels of competence affected the relationship between performance and motivation. If a person's ability is low, then even a large increase in motivation will not cause performance to improve by very much. Equally, a poorly motivated employee of exceptional ability will not perform significantly better. Therefore, it is just as important to train and develop employees to improve their competence as it is to motivate them through offers of reward.

The work of Porter and Lawler[5]

Porter and Lawler attempt to explain the relationship between effort and performance. There are, they suggest, two factors that determine the effort a person puts into a job, firstly, the extent to which the rewards from an activity are likely to satisfy his or her needs for security, esteem, independence and personal self-development and, secondly, the individual's expectation that effort will lead to such rewards. Accordingly, the higher the person's perception of the value of a reward and the higher the probability that the reward depends on the exertion of effort then the greater the effort the individual will devote to an activity. The efficiency of a person's effort depends, the authors argue, on his or her ability (skills, intelligence, etc) and on that person's interpretation of his or her role in the organisation.

Another influential writer in the motivation field is Douglas McGregor, whose work is dealt with elsewhere. All motivation theories, however, suffer the disadvantage that they are difficult to apply in practice. They have *implications*, but rarely offer practical prescriptions for motivating employees. Herzberg's theory, for example, suggests that job enlargment will enhance motivation; but applies only to professionally qualified managerial staff — manual workers may (or may not) be motivated by entirely different factors!

Notes

1 Maslow, A H, *Motivation and Personality*, Harper, New York, 1954.
2 Herzberg, F, *Work and the Nature of Man*, WPC, 1966.
3 Goldthorpe, J H, Lockwood D, Beckhhofer F and Platt J, *The Affluent Worker: Industrial Attitudes and Behaviour*, Cambridge University Press, Cambridge, 1968.
4 Vroom, V H, *Work and Motivation*, Wiley, New York, 1964.
5 Porter, L W and Lawler, E E, *Managerial Attitudes and Performance*, Irwin-Dorsey, Homewood, Illinois, 1968.

Index

Other titles in the Effective Supervisory Management Series

Managing Activities and Resources

Personal Effectiveness